They Used to Call Me Snow White... But I Drifted

Also by Gina Barreca

Babes in Boyland:
A Personal History of Co-Education in the Ivy League

Make Mine a Double:
Why Women Like Us Like to Drink (Or Not)

Gina Barreca

They Used to Call Me Snow White . . . But I Drifted

• • • • • • • • • • • • • • • • • •

Women's Strategic Use of Humor

With a New Introduction by the Author

University Press of New England
Hanover and London

University Press of New England
www.upne.com
This edition © 2013 University Press of New England
Manufactured in the United States of America

First published in 1991 by Viking Penguin,
a division of Penguin Books USA Inc.

Library of Congress Cataloging-in-Publication data
are available upon request.

ISBN 978-1-61168-445-2 (pbk.: alk. paper)
ISBN 978-1-61168-446-9 (ebook)

5 4 3 2

In memory of
my father, Hugo, and my mother, Antonine

Contents

• • • • • • • • • • • • • • • • • •

Acknowledgments

....

Sometimes the demands of a linear argument are even worse than others: there is no way to order these acknowledgments so that everybody comes out in the right place. Everybody, to be honest, deserves to be first on the list of thanks. The comedians and comic writers who generously offered their time for interviews deserve to come first: Nicole Hollander, Cynthia Heimel, Joy Behar, Susie Essman, Lara Kightlinger, among others. Their counterparts in the business and professional world should also be first: Mary Davis, Natalie Becker, Pamela West, Lynette Lager, among many others. The women who have prepared patterns for feminist criticism in general and about humor in particular are clearly the ones who should be mentioned before anyone else: Nancy Walker, Judith Wilt, Judy Little, Sandra Gilbert, Susan Gubar, Mary Daly, Jane Marcus, Rachel Brownstein, Nina Auerbach, Mary Ann Caws—with special thanks to Margaret Higonnet—and the dozens of other critics and teachers whose ideas have permanently changed the color of our thinking the way a drop of ink spreads through water. Thanks, too, to everyone in *Last Laughs,* to my students who have been relentlessly honest and riotously entertaining, and to my colleagues at the University of Connecticut.

There is no doubt that I must thank Fay Weldon before thanking another soul, since I would have lacked the courage to write this book but for her encouragement, affection, and inspiration; she was central to its creation. So was Rose Quiello, whose indefatigable research and constant support helped me through good and bad days alike, and whose laughter (and occasional lack thereof) shaped the book in its early days. Although men have perhaps grown too accustomed to leading the list to be permitted to continue doing so, a number of men should be mentioned at the very beginning: Michael Meyer, always full of surprises (*sic*), whose annoyingly accurate remarks scribbled in the margins of the book made life harder and the book better; John Glavin, who listened and directed with his inimitable flair for the dramatic and the good; as well as Lee Jacobus and Scott Bradfield, whose attention and good advice sustained me through some trying times. Before I mention them, however, I should thank Sue Watkins for her thorough and enormously useful reading of the manuscript.

But first of all I must mention my female friends, those women who have offered their stories, support, and love with equal generosity: Bonnie Januszewski, who was at the slumber party all those years ago and who has remained an excellent conspirator ever since; Pam Katz, whose wit and imagination make her one of the world's best companions; and Nancy Lager, who laughs more than she lets the world know. There are other friends to thank as well, including Joe Cuomo, Brenda Gross, J. J. Martindale, Tim Taylor, and Robert Zweig. Indeed, the women who have supported the book throughout the process of publication must be thanked immediately: Carole DeSanti, whose early support of the project turned it from a project into a book; Diane Cleaver, who helped guide the manuscript to a good home; Nan Graham, who dealt swiftly and wonderfully with the text; Kathryn Harrison, who was a great help; and Gillian Silverman, who answered all my questions with patience and accuracy.

Nevertheless, it is certain that those people who have put up with me the longest deserve both my initial and my continuing gratitude: my father, Hugo, merits first place for his patience and love, alongside my brother, Hugo, for his wit and impatient understanding, and my sister-in-law, Wendy Schlemm, for her delight at a well-told story. Before any of them, however, I wish I could thank my mother, Antonine, who, although she died far too young, left for me the gift of a wicked sensibility coupled with an unembarrassed enjoyment of the absurdities of life. It is an honor to dedicate this book to the memory of my mother. And it is a treat to dedicate it to that of my father, who lived long enough to enjoy making fun of the fact that the original version of *Snow White* was, for twenty weeks or so, a national best seller in Canada. "Sure it's a hit in Canada. It has 'snow' in the title, Gina." There has never been a tougher or better audience than my family.

Snow White Grows Up

· · · · · · · · · · · · · · · · · · · ·

Twenty-Two Years of Women's Laughter—Now What?

What's changed about the creation and reception of women's comedy since *They Used To Call Me Snow White . . . But I Drifted* hit the shelves in 1991?

Depending on your age, background, and politics, either everything has changed—or not very much at all. Over the past twenty years, women's autonomy and visibility have increased. And if we agree with Elizabeth Janeway that power can be defined as the ability not to have to please, surely the wider availability, visibility, and diversity of women's humor over the past two decades is a felicitous marker of women's advancement.

Two decades ago it would have been tough to imagine that a soft-spoken lesbian comic would become not only one of the most admired daytime talk show hosts of her time but also the "face" of Cover Girl cosmetics.

Twenty years ago, supermodel Christie Brinkley, a bombshell known for her smile but not for her quick wit, was the "face" of Cover Girl. Now the Emmy Award–winning Ellen DeGeneres (who once performed in a leotard with a fake swan across her body and told the 2009 graduation class at Tulane, "Life is like one big Mardi Gras, but instead of showing your boobs, show people your brain; if they like what they see you'll have more beads than you know what to do with") is the person telling us how to keep our lipstick from feathering. DeGeneres, who celebrated her marriage to Portia de Rossi in 2008, argued that there should be a Barbie with a "buzz cut" and shortly after Hurricane Katrina hosted the Emmy Awards, where she began by pointing out: "This is the second time I've hosted the Emmys after a national tragedy [she had hosted them in 2001, as well], and I just want to say that I'm honored, because it's times like this that we really, really need laughter. And be sure to look for me next month when I host the North Korean People's Choice Awards."

As I write, Cover Girl has paired DeGeneres with a woman who is this generation's version of Lucille Ball—one of the great comic television stars, and a beauty who's able to make herself heard as well as seen: Sophia Vergara.

(Interestingly, it can be argued that Sofia Vergara is really a hybrid version of Lucille Ball and Desi Arnaz. As we recall from *I Love Lucy*, Ball was an almost unparalleled physical comic, while her husband, Arnaz, played the pronunciation-tied, hot-blooded, passionate foreigner. It was Arnaz who was taunted for not knowing American customs, for having an accent, for being exotic; now Vergara has, in her role on *Modern Family*, assumed that position.)

And who would have imagined that the African American lesbian comic Wanda Sykes would become both the speaker for the White House Correspondents' Association dinner and the spokesperson for Gain detergent? Sykes, after all, addresses difficult political, sexual, and class issues without hesitation and in a way that a woman might not have been able to manage with such widespread success back in the '80s. In Sykes's 2010 HBO Special "Ima Be Me," the film, television, and stand-up star wonders, "Isn't it funny how the only time your race or gender is questioned is when you're not a white man?" Sykes questions whether it's really "reverse racism" that white men fear, since "reverse racism" would be more clearly defined as what happens when a "racist is nice to somebody else." She argues, instead, that what straight white men fear is that any other group that gets power is going to do to them what they did to that group. What these guys are afraid of, Sykes declares, "isn't reverse racism." She pauses. "It's karma."

There are men who argue, as we'll see, that women have no sense of humor. Of course, there are some parts of the country where "creationism" is taught alongside the theory of evolution. When asked in 2009 whether comedy is now "easier for women," Joan Rivers answered, "Comedy is still a man's game. . . . You have to take such command of the stage. . . . You have to be very, very confident and strong." The stigma attached to women's comedy is perhaps best illustrated by the Irish comic Mary Bourke's joke about her father's attempt to obscure her real profession by "telling the neighbors I'm a crackhead whore."

The year *Snow White* was first published, *Thelma and Louise* hit the big screen and Anita Hill hit the Clarence Thomas Supreme Court hearings. It was the year that Comedy Central began broadcasting in its current format and the Soviet Union ceased to exist in its familiar format. In 1991 the Cold War ended and the Gulf War began. *Designing Women, Roseanne, Seinfeld, The Simpsons,* and *Married . . . with Children* were television hits, and books by Erma Bombeck were national bestsellers.

It seemed as if we were growing up and changing our mind about the way women lived. By 1991 virginity seemed as anachronistic as a rubber girdle. Instead of revering the hymen as a manifest symbol of spiritual worth, we thought of it the same way we think about baby fat: something you'd lose once you grew up. We wore T-shirts that announced, "I lost my virginity, but I still have the box it came in." Given these changes, we thought life would be better for women, and men—yes, we thought it would improve for men, too—when women were seen as being productive rather than merely reproductive members of society.

After Thelma and Louise blew up the truck, we were hopeful. We imagined that the saw edge of patriarchy would have been worn down, its teeth filed flat; we thought that so-called traditional values would go the way of, say, travel by mule, given that they had proved to be outdated, soul-destroying, and really uncomfortable over the long haul.

Even at that moment, however, some humorists were warning that the apparent advancement of women was not going to happen without a backlash. Cynthia Heimel suggested as much in *If You Can't Live Without Me, Why Aren't You Dead Yet?* when she wrote in 1991, "So don't think for a second I'm trying to wheedle and cajole men into thinking of women as peers and pals, or asking women to come back baby, feminism never forgets." Heimel argued, "If I were a man, a man as successful as I am, they'd be lining up. I'd go to cocktail parties and snap my fingers: 'you! Take me home and cook me dinner! Then maybe if I'm in the mood we'll have sex!' And they would." And yet it wasn't working that way for most women, according to Heimel: "Get a job, your husband hates you," wrote Heimel. "Get a good job, your husband leaves you. Get a stupendous job, your husband leaves you for a teenager."

But we remained optimistic. After all, comedy had traditionally been a bunch of boys with balloons made out of condoms until, in the 1980s, there suddenly appeared on the scene a bunch of girls with pins, a sense of humor, and their own reliable birth control—Heimel among them. Women who were changing the way comedy was being played on America's stages and pages made the popping noises we heard. The best humor has always collapsed the distinctions and walls between groups; sanctimonious and self-righteous individuals are revealed as two-dimensional cardboard cutouts that can be not only mocked but also virtually dismantled by any smart comic. An increasing number of these new smart comics were female.

Twenty years ago most of us didn't anticipate the resurgence of the New Right and the power behind America's growing social conservatism. Let's start with the basics and the very idea of feminism itself; if you'd told me twenty years ago that women would be arguing over who was a "real feminist," my response would have been to point and giggle. In 2008 the fiercely conservative Republican vice-presidential nominee Sarah Palin called herself a feminist; this was from a woman who believed a woman's right to choose was neither a right nor a choice. Palin belonged to an organization called Feminists for Life, so her decision to claim the word is a curious moment in history of the f-word. Was it a good thing that Palin identified herself this way?

As far as I'm concerned, Palin identifying herself as a feminist was the gender equivalent of "shanda for the goyim," a nearly untranslatable Yiddish phrase describing an individual who, merely by being associated with a group, causes that group disgrace.

Why did Palin have to become the poster child for a kind of weirdly nonprogressive women's movement, when I already have trouble with the next generation of young women rejecting the word? I have female students who trip over themselves to avoid using the term "feminist": "I'm getting a doctoral fellowship from NASA after I complete my NEA grant, but it's the work I did for girls in Tanzania that makes me proud. But gosh! No, I'm not a feminist. I like bracelets and hope to get married one day." They fear that feminism is about wearing your hair in braids and yelling slogans blaming men for stuff. (There are six women in Berkeley still doing this. They're fabulous and I'm grateful to them for getting the whole thing going, by the way.) But as I argued in *Snow White*, I like to think that feminism is the belief that women are human beings with the full privileges of adult citizens.

I assume now, as I assumed back in 1991, that everybody I meet—men and women alike—is a feminist. I give people the benefit of the doubt. You're using cutlery to eat? You walk upright, without knuckles dragging on the ground? You don't wear T-shirts saying "Men: no shirt, no service; Women: no shirt, free drinks!" You don't think women are just a man's way of making more men? Hooray! You're a feminist.

In other words, my version of feminism is sort of like a hip nun's vision of Catholicism—affirming to all and not guided by rulebooks or doctrinal declarations. Yet I couldn't have imagined that so-called virginity pledge programs supported by the likes of Palin (programs named True Love Waits and Silver Ring Thing) would become part of a drive to have "abstinence only" teachings replace sex education in schools both private and public. I didn't think there would emerge, as if from the woodwork and floorboards, politicians who would argue—in all seriousness—that women's bodies can spontaneously block conception after "legitimate rape," that some women "rape easy," and that "even when life begins in that horrible situation of rape, that it is something God intended to happen." I thought that kind of ignorant misogyny would have been the subject of comic's punch lines rather than politicians' political platforms.

Little did we think, either, when Madonna first wore torn-up lace fishnet tights and sang "Like a Virgin" that in thirty years megastores would be selling lines of clothes to actual little girls making them look like actual little hookers. Celia Rivenbark is not the only columnist to have discussed this trend, but she might be the only one to have titled a best-selling humor book after it: *Stop Dressing Your Six-Year-Old Like a Skank: And Other Words of Delicate Southern Wisdom* was published in 2007.

Sure, it was inevitable that what once passed for invention and freedom would be co-opted and exploited by the established economic and power structure, but somehow we didn't think it was going to happen to us. We didn't think that telling girls they shouldn't feel any shame about their bodies or sexual urges would mean that our daughters (or granddaughters) would be participating in blow job parties at age twelve. (No less a sage than Joan Rivers defines the new category of adolescent that has emerged since 1991—the "'tween"—as "just a teen that hasn't given a blow job yet.")

So, yes, the passing decades have been complicated. Some theorists have argued that we're now in a "Post-Postfeminist" stage of our culture. In trying to define the differences between the "Classic Feminism" of the '60s, the Postfeminism of the '80s, and the Post-Postfeminism of the New Millennials, the best I could do was come up with examples: the Classic Feminist embraced her anger; a Postfeminist embraced anybody she found attractive; a Post-Postfeminist embraces her Bowflex. A Classic Feminist's theme song was "I Am Woman, Hear Me Roar" by Helen Reddy; a Postfeminist theme song was "Where Have All the Cowboys Gone?" by Paula Cole; a Post-Postfeminist theme song is "I'm Fucking Matt Damon" by Sarah Silverman.

For the record, Clarence Thomas made it to the Supreme Court, where he is known for record-breaking periods of silence. Since his appointment, two justices not exactly known for their reticence have joined him. Sonia Sotomayor, who seems never to appear in a photograph without her signature smiling face, unapologetically declared her hope that a "wise Latina woman with the richness of her experiences would more often than not reach a better conclusion than a white male who hasn't lived that life" when she was interviewed about her appointment to the highest court in the land.

And Elena Kagan, in 2010, proved what I've been saying all along: give us women an education and a chance at the microphone, and we'll prove we are funnier than most men. During the hearings that confirmed her appointment to the Supreme Court, Kagan got the last laugh at the expense of South Carolina's Republican senator Lindsey Graham during a moment that can serve as a template for women's smart answers. When Graham, rather lackadaisically, intoned, "Christmas Day. Where were you on Christmas Day?" I'll admit that I held my breath.

Kagan began what sounded like an elaborate, roundabout, and detailed response concerning the finer points of law in conjunction with a question about the 2009 Christmas Day bomber (a.k.a. the Underwear Bomber).

Kagan, remember, was being examined precisely on those finer points of law, but Graham interrupted Kagan and drawled, "I just asked where you were on Christmas." That's when the world heard Kagan's laugh—it was a real laugh, not some tinkling-bell girly self-deprecating simulation of laugh. It was a serious Bea-Arthur-ish "You got me" guffaw.

And then the soon-to-be fourth female member of the Supreme Court did something remarkable: she refused to let this gentleman's funny remark stand at her expense. She was going to win because she would get the last laugh. And win she did. Kagan shifted the ground. She answered, matter-of-factly, "Like all Jews, I was probably at a Chinese restaurant."

It's great when somebody can answer a question while addressing the invidious issues beneath it: Why is the Senator from South Carolina asking where she was on a Christian holiday, anyway? Some of us thought Kagan should have asked Graham where he was on Purim.

What she did, of course, was better. Kagan's comeback is right up there with one of my other favorite smart-talking-women-in-Washington stories, concerning Liz Carpenter (chapter 3). Kagan guffawed and smiled, but she did not giggle. For that, I am grateful. Many things have not changed, but that one has.

Sometime during the last twenty years we have witnessed the death of the giggle in North American females over age twelve. When was the last time you heard a smart, competent, and sober woman go, "tee-hee-hee?" on purpose and without at least a touch of irony? The "tee-hee-hee" was a sound associated with the Good Girl, the one who was afraid to laugh out loud and make her real feelings obvious. She sort of wanted to laugh, or was afraid not to laugh, but couldn't commit either way; the giggle is, in effect, the equivalent of a wince or a fake smile that never reaches the eyes. The giggle was an excuse for laughter—a feint and an act of infantilization, twinning the sexy with the childish.

If the giggle is gone, the women's movement has indeed made some progress.

Over the past twenty years, a very different courtroom setting has also captured the imagination of the American public, and humor is a big part of the reason. I'd like to invoke the character of Judge Judith Sheindlin. When the *Judge Judy* program started in 1996, few in the industry gave the former Koch-appointed New York City Family Court judge much of a shot at lasting fame. But in the sixteen years (and counting) of her show's tenure, Sheindlin has surpassed in the ratings the final two seasons of *The Oprah Winfrey Show*. Sheindlin is syndicated worldwide and draws an average of eight million viewers per episode, in large part because of her quick wit and fierce refusal to project anything but power behind the bench.

"If you live to be a hundred, you will never be as smart as me. On your *best* day, you're not as smart as I am on my *worst* day," quips Sheindlin, who is given to other declarations such as "The sexes are not equal. They only start out equal, and then something happens along the way. . . . You think it's sports? Contact sports, maybe, to the head." I have a clipping from Judge Judy on my office door by way of warning to my students, in much the same way as some of my colleagues have "Omnes relinquite spes, o vos intrantes" on theirs. Mine says: "Judge Judy: 'You're not intimidated by me, are you?' Defendant: 'No, ma'am.' Judge Judy: 'That's your first mistake.'" Sheindlin, too, opposes the giggle. She is whatever the opposing force to the giggler happens to be in the universe. Perhaps that force is simply a woman with a gavel.

We've seen other landmark changes as well.

Authentically edgy comedy wants to shake things up. Like sex, the best comedy is improvised, performed before midnight, and not witnessed by drunks (or at least not witnessed only by drunks). That's one of the reasons so many of the newer voices in comedy emerge from various "outsider" groups that perform not only in clubs but for colleges or organizations and at political rallies. Some will be part of two distinct cultures and eager to comment on both (such as Shazia Mirza, a self-described moderate and devout Muslim, who regards the "whole point" of her stand-up comedy as being "to help reduce Islamophobia"), and some will be like Tig (whose bio explains her take on life: "During hot Mississippi summer days, her artistic and free-spirited mother would feed them all three meals at once, then down their diapered bodies into highchairs to cut back on cooking and cleaning, leaving more time for her to paint donkeys on the outside of their house"). Issues of class are inevitably mixed with issues of sex, gender, and race, and pretty much any performer who isn't a straight white educated middle-class male will reserve scant tenderness for the powers that be. Lisa Lampanelli, who is not exactly known for tenderness, is also not shy about her feminine identity or sexual appetites ("I grew up in Connecticut. The Connecticut license plate should say, "Connecticut: You won't find your clitoris here!"). Despite the fact that she is a favorite of comics such as Don Rickles and Howard Stern who are not necessarily associated with the f-word as we've been using it in this discussion, Lampanelli's raw and raucous examination of women's lives deserves attention; she's one of the comics who questions directly what the f-word means in everyday life.

Lampanelli is a sort of "shock jock" when it comes to women's bodies. Her perspective on childbirth, for example, is one we rarely hear: "The blood! Oh, the blood. The vagina looks like it owed the Gambinos money and didn't pay up," and "Feminists and people without health care try to go au naturel and don't even go to the hospital. They have a midwife—also known as a 'maid with special training'—and attempt to give birth at home. These people always end up at the hospital anyway when the baby is coming out sideways and the stoned midwife is on the phone with her boyfriend back in Holland. Birthing at home? No, thanks. I'll have mine in a public place under the influence of drugs—just like the conception." Lampanelli began her stand-up career around the time *Snow White* was first published.

That same year, *Saturday Night Live* featured Julia Sweeney, Victoria Jackson, and Jan Hooks; their male counterparts included Mike Myers, Chris Rock, Al Franken, and Adam Sandler. Many of the men from that season went on to become famous, rich, and influential in entertainment—but not in entertainment alone. Myers became the star of the Shrek franchise, as well as the lead in the Austin Powers series of box office hits; Rock's one-man shows regularly sell out concert venues worldwide, and the actor is a recognizable voice in hugely successful animated films and a best-selling author; Franken, who also emerged as a best-selling author and broadcaster, was elected to the Senate; and Sandler is a an international star, producer, and screenwriter.

And women from that same season? Are they in comparable positions of fame and influence? Well, Jan Hooks appeared as a guest star in a 2010 episode of NBC's *30 Rock*. Although only nine years Jane Krajkowski's senior, she was cast as Verna, the mother of Krajkowski's character Jenna. Julia Sweeney has chronicled for NPR and Public Radio International her battle with lymphoma, the adoption of her daughter Mulan, and her fervent atheism. And Victoria Jackson, the one with the big bow in her blond hair, moved to Florida, where she has become a face for the conservatives' Tea Party, partnering with a right-wing media group for a "webshow" where, according to her official Web site, her Christian and "conservative revolution" fans can discover "what's it like to be a Baptist virgin hanging out at the Playboy mansion."

Maybe Hooks, Sweeney, and Jackson faced what Rachel Dratch, a later graduate of *Saturday Night Live,* did once she left the program. Dratch said "pretty much the only parts" she had been offered since being off *SNL* were "Lesbians. Secretaries. Sometimes secretaries who are lesbians. Usually much older than I am in real life. Usually about 100–200 pounds more than I am in real life." In Dratch's 2012 memoir *Girl Walks into a Bar . . .*, she sums it up as follows: she was asked to audition or offered "solely the parts that I like to refer to as 'The Unfuckables'" or, to be more precise, "Amy Poehler's mutant lesbian mother."

30 Rock's Tina Fey, a colleague of Dratch's not only from *SNL* but from their earlier days at Second City in the mid-'90s, makes a similar point in her best-selling book *Bossypants:* "I've known older men in comedy who can barely feed and clean themselves, and they still work. The women, though, they're all 'crazy.' I have a suspicion—and hear me out, 'cause this is a rough one—I have a suspicion that the definition of 'crazy' in show business is a woman who keeps talking even after no one wants to fuck her anymore. The only person I can think of that has escaped the 'crazy' moniker is Betty White, which, obviously, is because people still want to have sex with her." All great humorists run toward pain and injustice—and then they trip over them. Some take a pratfall, some a subtle stumble; some do an apoplectic St. Vitus' dance, and some a soft-shoe. But none of them—and this is the important part—end up on their knees.

And that, in art, is why we can see that some things have changed, while others have not: Chelsea Handler picked up where Cynthia Heimel left off; *Designing Women* gave way to *Sex and the City,* which has now turned into *Girls; Golden Girls* morphed into *Hot in Cleveland; Married . . . with Children* became *Modern Family.* Nora Ephron hated her neck but everybody loved her; Joan Rivers still hates everybody, and some return the favor; Wendy Wasserstein's legacy still searches for the next great American woman comic playwright; and Phyllis Diller kept her edge until her nineties, as Betty White continues to do, thereby proving that life only gets funnier with age.

Women who are a combination of Imogene Coca, Elaine May, Carol Burnett, Marlo Thomas, Gilda Radner, and Lily Tomlin have come together like wickedly clever improv fairy godmothers and fashioned a world where Tina Fey, Amy Poehler, and Kristen Wiig flourish. Susie Essman, Joy Behar, and Lizz Winstead have grown from the fledging stand-up comics I could interview personally in small, smoky venues to hosts, stars, and producers with layers of assistants, like Bubble Wrap, protecting them from too much knocking on the dressing room door by pesky, if admiring, academics. Rita Rudner now has the longest-running, most successful one-person comedy show in the history of Las Vegas. Bette Midler continues to star in films and shows, and to win awards for her performances, having left her own long-running show at Caesars Palace to return to New York and L.A. Carol Leifer, Elayne Boosler, and Margaret Cho have attained international fame and have influenced a new generation of performers, male and female, who grew up enthralled by their work.

It can be argued that Roseanne Barr and the ubiquitous Whoopi Goldberg—one of the few individuals ever to win the Oscar, Tony, Emmy, and Grammy Awards—practically raised the younger generation of comics, so pervasive and entrenched was their influence. Named one of *TV Guide*'s "50 Greatest TV Shows of All Time," *Roseanne* was the first show to focus on a family where both parents worked outside the home at blue-collar jobs; it was the anti–Donna Reed, showing a mix of muddled emotions and tough times even as it made America laugh. From 1989 to 1992, *Roseanne* was the most-watched television show in the country, and it kept a position in the top five for six of its nine seasons. We should remember that these were the years when Rush Limbaugh was in his ascendancy, saying things like "Feminism was established so that unattractive women could have easier access to the mainstream of society"; and that Roseanne's weight and—in those early years—untouched features were not the focus of self-deprecating humor was a political triumph.

In many ways, so was the show's working-class foundation. When Roseanne says, "What's the worst that can happen? So the tornado picks up our house and slams it down in a better neighborhood," she's defying both class and gender expectations by refusing to offer the audience evidence of either shame or anxiety. Another class-crossing character who found her way into '90s pop culture was Fran Drescher's *The Nanny*. As in *Roseanne*, class in *The Nanny* is not defined merely by economics. Instead, culture—including manners, consumption, and gender roles—is the primary distinguishing mark between the haves and the have-nots. It's all about where you put the accent, and not just what your accent sounds like (despite the inescapable nature of Drescher's own Queens borough lilt).

The character of Murphy Brown, played by Candice Bergen, didn't cross class boundaries but crossed enough political ones to become the subject of a "family values" debate in the 1992 presidential campaign. Vice President Dan Quayle slammed Murphy Brown (as if she were a real person and not a character on a sitcom, as many critics pointed out) for being a single parent; this prompted the Brown character to comment, "Several people do not want me to have the baby," and then list those she regarded as being at the head of the conservative "family values" movement: "Pat Robertson. Phyllis Schlafly. Half of Utah." Bergen won an Emmy for that season and, during her acceptance speech, thanked Dan Quayle.

As the new century approached, Roseanne, Murphy, and Fran gave way to the sexualized and moneyed urban glitter of HBO's *Sex and the City*; actually, *Murphy Brown*, *The Nanny*, and *Sex and the City* occupied one year simultaneously (1998). Styles of women's humor were changing as swiftly as women's hair and shoe styles.

How much do the inheritors of these earlier shows owe to their predecessors? After all, Tina Fey's character in *30 Rock* is given to staying up all night to watch *Designing Women* marathons.

In the 2007 Season 2 of *30 Rock* called "Rosemary's Baby," Tina Fey's character Liz Lemon meets Rosemary Howard, played by Carrie Fisher. Rosemary is introduced as "the first female writer for *Laugh-In*," who also did "all the political stuff for Donny and Marie." Liz waits in line to be introduced to Rosemary at a book signing. Asking Rosemary to sign her book, Liz explains breathlessly, "I don't want to sound like a weirdo fan, but I'm obsessed with everything you've ever done. . . . You are my heroine. And by 'heroine' I mean I lady hero; I don't want to inject you and listen to jazz."

In what turns out to be a disastrous move, Liz hires the unemployed Rosemary to work on TGS, where Rosemary offends and annoys the rest of the staff. She drinks wine from a thermos all day ("It's heart-healthy!") and when she's fired, Liz insists they have to fire her as well. Her boss, Jack, has no problem complying. Liz and Rosemary go back to Rosemary's apartment (in a neighborhood known as Little Chechnya), which is cluttered with Emmys and various other awards, to begin their own feminist project. It turns out that Rosemary's brilliant idea is to write movie where "women in their fifties go on spring break and get laid by a bunch of grateful eighteen-year-olds!" Horrified, Liz is silent, as Rosemary shows how far she is from reality by saying with gusto, "I predict opening weekend: a million dollars!"

Realizing that "her heroine" is not the idealized version of powerful, creative womanhood Liz had imagined ("I went to her apartment; I don't think she has a toilet; I saw my future"), Liz desperately fiddles with the locks to escape from the apartment, as Rosemary cries out, "You wouldn't have a job if it wasn't for me. I broke barriers for you. . . . I sat around while my junk went bad. . . . I didn't have any kid. You are my kid. You're my kid that never calls!" Liz gets her job back and asks her boss to help her understand how to "do that thing that rich people do," where she can make money from her money, so that she can send Rosemary four hundred dollars a month forever.

In a great line from the show that anticipates what Fey and Dratch will later argue in their respective books, Fey tells Jack, "Rosemary says that women become obsolete in this business when there's no one left that wants to look at them naked." Jack, played by Alec Baldwin, responds without hesitation, "If you make enough money, you can pay people to look at you naked." As Fay Weldon says at the end of *Life and Loves of a She-Devil,* "It is not a matter of male or female, after all; it never was: merely of power." And what is money, if not power?

By the second season of its six-year run, one of the characters in *Sex and the City* could consciously address the increasing materialism and narcissism associated with the lives of successful women by blurting, "All we talk about anymore is Big, or balls, or small dicks. How does it happen that four such smart women have nothing to talk about but boyfriends? It's like seventh grade with bank accounts!" While criticisms of *Sex and the City*—too glib, too glitzy, too shallow—abound, it has to be noted that Candace Bushnell's column for the *New York Observer,* on which the show and movies were based, was witty and sharp—as well as being less circumscribed by traditional marriage plots or, at the very least, less bound by their inevitable conclusions than the television or film adaptations.

In Bushnell's book, the heroine, Carrie Bradshaw, does not marry "Big" but rather, according to Bushnell, lives her life "happily single." It's interesting to note that however shocking the characters seemed on television, the text version of them was even more decidedly and deliberately iconoclastic.

Bridget Jones is, of course, Carrie Bradshaw's equally famous British counterpart. Like Bushnell's, Helen Fielding's characters first materialized in newsprint in the mid-'90s. Appearing as a column in the *Independent* of London, "Bridget Jones's Diary" offered a representation of thirty-something single women that was both an extension of Jane Austen ("It is a truth universally acknowledged that when one part of your life starts going okay, another falls spectacularly to pieces") and a contemporary manifesto about life as an "unmarried" in ways that it's fairly safe to say Austen would not have anticipated: "Oh GOD. Why can't married people understand that [asking how a single woman's love life is going] is no longer a polite question to ask? We wouldn't rush up to THEM and roar, 'How's your marriage going? Still having sex?' Everyone knows that dating in your thirties is not the happy-go-lucky free-for-it-all it was when you were twenty-two and that the honest answer is more likely to be, 'Actually, last night my married lover appeared wearing suspenders and a darling little Angora crop-top, told me he was gay/a sex addict/a narcotic addict/a commitment phobic and beat me up with a dildo,' than, 'Super, thanks.'"

Unlike Bushnell, however, Fielding's 2006 update on her characters has her heroine giving birth to a son, to whom she now devotes all her time. Although she, too, remains unmarried, her two suitors remain in her life and her child becomes the object of all her attention. She is, we are told, "too busy" to continue writing in her diary.

While the television work of the late-night talk show star Chelsea Handler has not translated into a successful narrative series (yet), she seems like the most obvious successor to Bushnell and Fielding—with more comic bite. Handler is awake to the absurdities of a world attempting to legislate sex, affection, and family ties, and she questions the standards and categories of accepted behavior.

By no means anybody's keeper—not even that of the inmate with whom she was briefly incarcerated for a DUI in California, as she describes in her *New York Times* bestseller *Are You There, Vodka? It's Me, Chelsea,* Handler offers her experiences not as a casebook on what to avoid but instead as a chronicle of a part of her life—a confession, perhaps, but one proffered without the need for absolution.

In her first book, *My Horizontal Life: A Collection of One-Night Stands,* for example, Handler illustrates the difference between women's lives as they appear in film and as they are when actually lived: "At some point during almost every romantic comedy, the female lead suddenly trips and falls, stumbling helplessly over something ridiculous like a leaf, and then some Matthew McConaughey type either whips around the corner just in the nick of time to save her or is clumsily pulled down along with her. That event predictably leads to the magical moment of their first kiss. Please. I fall ALL the time. You know who comes and gets me? The bouncer."

Like Chelsea Handler, Sarah Silverman embodies the shattering of every rule. She appears in complete control over any situation and as far beyond anyone else's control as a falling star or a wild animal. Drop-dead gorgeous, apparently brilliant, and filthily funny, she's a puzzle society must solve. Silverman relies on the outsider's recognition of society's deeply entrenched moral hypocrisy. Her deviance has increasingly become the essence of her self-definition, and rape jokes a staple of her routine. "I was raped by a doctor," declares Silverman and smiles sweetly before adding, "So bittersweet for a Jewish girl." But she saves the killer line for last: "I need more rape jokes," she explains, unblinkingly making a direct appeal to the audience. "Who's going to complain about rape jokes? Rape victims?" She pauses. "They barely even report rape."

In delivering that line, Silverman didn't join them; she beat them. By confronting the authentically taboo subject—not that rape happens, but that rape victims are still too afraid, ashamed, or appalled to admit they've been criminally assaulted—she's using humor to slice, dice, and present for examination one of the culture's most deeply buried dirty secrets. Silverman, building on a long tradition in women's humor, gives the microphone to the prey, thereby challenging the predator. The funny woman wields humor in such a way as to remove one gag (through her refusal of silence), even as she makes another—a joke. Thus, she simultaneously resists shutting down and shutting up.

Having passed her fortieth birthday, Silverman is no longer an ingenue. Mindy Kaling (best known for her episodes on *The*

Office and her 2011 book *Is Everyone Hanging Out Without Me?*), working in what she calls a "post–Sarah Silverman world," ensures that the complications, delights, and frustrations of the life of a woman humor writer in the second decade of the twenty-first century are unflinchingly examined.

Young women in particular don't understand—and perhaps it's impossible for us to ever communicate this perception to those under thirty-five—that almost every woman at some point in her life has been an ingenue or could have been. This is a young woman who, perhaps even without knowing it, manipulates her youthful attractions to her advantage, receiving attention because she is adorable and yet believing that the attention she receives is given to her because she is brilliant, witty, clever, sensitive, or "one of the boys." No woman is one of the boys. That's one of the hardest things to learn, and you don't learn it until you give up the idea that you have sprung Athena-like from your father's head with no help from your mother.

It's interesting to realize how commonplace it is for smart women to think they are their fathers' daughters and how little credit they give to the influence of their mothers or other women in their lives. Only by acknowledging the significance of the adult female in their own lives can women get on with the process of growing up and accepting, with gratitude and generosity to themselves and others, their lives as women. (Unless, of course, the only adult women in their lives have been ones like Rosemary Howard in *30 Rock,* in which case it's acceptable simply to send a monthly allowance.)

Kaling talks about the "post-Silverman" world because she was not expecting to face certain challenges; after all, she grew up during a time when the basis of equity for women wasn't questioned and when outrageous behavior was a "given": "I was freaked out," she writes in *Is Everyone Hanging Out Without Me?* "Sexual harassment was a real thing. You can't just joke about rape at work. We had endured a lengthy sexual harassment seminar on how fireable this behavior was. Sarah Silverman could make jokes about rape because, the fact of the matter was, she was much funnier and cuter than us. This was the problem of living in a post–Sarah Silverman world: lots of young women holding the scepter of inappropriateness did not know how to wield it."

Which does not mean that women are the only ones dealing with jokes about rape. In 2012 it was still possible for the popular performer Daniel Tosh, when heckled by a woman in the audience, to ask a comedy club audience, "Wouldn't it be funny if that girl got raped by like, five guys right now . . . like right now?" Tosh received a lot of criticism, unsurprisingly, for his response—but he also received a lot of support. Fellow comics like Doug Stanhope tweeted, "You're hilarious. If you ever apologize to a heckler again I will rape you." Other male comics offered what passed for explanation: Kumail Nanjiani tweeted, "Two things about the Tosh thing. 1. It was said in the moment and not a pre written thing. 2. If you think he's pro rape you're an idiot."

On *The Daily Show,* Louis C. K. explained his take on the incident, saying that the effect of Tosh's remark was to ignite "a fight between comedians and feminists, [who] are natural enemies. Because stereotypically speaking, feminists can't take a joke" and "comedians can't take criticism." As Louis C. K. continued his discussion with Jon Stewart, however, he performed a sort of neat rhetorical somersault, suggesting to many viewers that this very pronouncement was itself ironic. The argument over the meaning behind C. K.'s commentary occupied bloggers and writers for weeks and, for some, overshadowed the shrill, unnuanced, and unsophisticated quickie from Tosh. The final result of the brouhaha was that for the 2013 season, Comedy Central renewed *Tosh.0*—not surprising, given that it's the channel's highest-rated series. Yet Tosh felt the need to offer an apology, if only to assuage the anxiety of his marketing team. Given the edgy nature of his humor, it might be the most significant cultural marker of the entire exchange. Tosh tweeted to his followers: "All the out of context misquotes aside, I'd like to sincerely apologize."

Maybe the biggest difference in the twenty years since *Snow White* was published is that a male comic feels a need to apologize, whereas a female comic feels she doesn't. Tina Fey explains in *Bossypants:* "Amy Poehler was new to *SNL* and we were all crowded into the seventeenth-floor writers' room, waiting for the Wednesday read-through to start . . . and she did something vulgar as a joke. I can't remember what it was exactly, except it was dirty and loud and 'unladylike.' Jimmy Fallon, who was arguably the star of the show at the time, turned to her and in a faux-squeamish voice said: 'Stop that! It's not cute! I don't like it.' Amy dropped what she was doing, went black in the eyes for a second, and wheeled around on him. 'I don't fucking care if you like it.' Jimmy was visibly startled. Amy went right back to enjoying her ridiculous bit. With that exchange, a cosmic shift took place. Amy made it clear that she wasn't there to be cute. She wasn't there to play wives and girlfriends in the boys' scenes. She was there to do what she wanted to do and she did not fucking care if you like it." A woman making humor and creating comedy is a woman who is not going to apologize for wanting to be in control.

Fey continues, "I think of this whenever someone says to me, 'Jerry Lewis says women aren't funny,' or 'Christopher Hitchens says women aren't funny,' or 'Rick Fenderman says women aren't funny.' . . . 'Do you have anything to say to that?'" Because of Poehler, Fey has an answer. "Yes. We don't fucking care if you like it."

Fey is referring, of course, to Christopher Hitchens's 2007 article in *Vanity Fair,* where he wrote in all seriousness, "Why are women, who have the whole male world at their mercy, not funny? Please do not pretend not to know what I am talking about."

Hitchens argued in his widely quoted piece, "Women, bless their tender hearts, would prefer that life be fair, and even sweet, rather than the sordid mess it actually is." Hitchens had no problem suggesting that "precisely because humor is a sign of intelligence . . . it could be that in some way men do not want women to be funny. They want them as an audience, not as rivals."

After Hitchens's death in 2011, Adam Carolla, former host of *The Man Show,* assumed the women-have-no-sense-of-humor mantle. Carolla told the *New York Post* that television producers "make you hire a certain number of chicks, and they're always the least funny on the writing staff. The reason why you know more funny dudes than funny chicks is that dudes are funnier than chicks." To illustrate his point, Carolla made it personal: "If my daughter has a mediocre sense of humor, I'm just gonna tell her, 'Be a staff writer for a sitcom. Because they'll have to hire you, they can't really fire you, and you don't have to produce that much. It'll be awesome.'"

Comedy teaches us that anybody smart is restless, just as it teaches us that anybody with a real mind is very nearly always out of it. And you could argue that, in the parlance of vaudeville, everybody's trying to get into the act. Sister Simone Campbell is the executive director of NETWORK, an organization, consisting of socially liberal nuns who were deemed "radical feminists" by the Vatican in 2012. She took her case not to the church but to the comedy shows. When asked by Stephen Colbert on *The Colbert Report* whether she considered herself a radical, Sister Campbell answered that members of the NETWORK are "oriented towards the needs of women and responding to their needs; if that's radical, I guess we are." Colbert's adamant reply? "Yes, yes! That's radical feminism!" Samantha Bee, a regular "correspondent" on *The Daily Show* (for which Lizz Winstead was a longtime producer), also interviewed Sister Campbell: "When you're advocating for poor people, you're not also telling them gay marriage and abortion are wrong?" asked Bee, in her best feigned-earnest-serious voice. She continued, "Have you ever helped any poor married gay couples?"

Campbell: "I helped a gay couple, yes." Bee tsked-tsked: "And you couldn't take two minutes out of your day to shame them?"

For former *SNL* cast member Kristen Wiig, who, with her co-writer Annie Mumolo, was the force behind 2011's block-buster *Bridesmaids,* shame is precisely that which needs to be co-opted. *Bridesmaids,* a movie that grossed $24.6 million its opening weekend, gathers together a lot of so-called women's issues: it deals with friendship, family, the intricacies of romance, and getting really drunk on a plane.

But—and it's a big butt and yes, I mean that—it still has to include scenes where someone takes a crap in the middle of the highway. The fact that it's a female character wearing a wedding gown doesn't make it any less of a "guy" scene. I do believe that producer Judd Apatow wrote that section of the film. Rumor has it he wrote the crapping scene because the guys that had been dragged to see the girly movie needed to have at least one part that they would find funny, too. The gross-out humor in *Bridesmaids* received a lot of attention because of its What-thing-here-is-not-like-the-rest? aspect. It didn't seem to fit with the rest of the movie's humor.

Humor, after all, is not some kind of artificial flavoring that you insert or inject. You wouldn't write something, for example, and say, "I'll go back and put in the intelligence later," or "I'll go back and put in the creativity later." The same applies to humor. It's not an accessory or a whipped topping.

Humor has become a topic for examination in the way that previously undiscovered body parts come into focus in the medical community. Suddenly everyone realizes that we should be spending more time looking at our spleens, for example. And it becomes almost impossible to get through the day without wondering whether your spleen is up to snuff. How does it compare to the spleens of others? Is it a great spleen or just a good spleen? You start posting pictures of it and wondering if it measures up. Humor has become a sort of corkboard where everybody is putting up his or her own bits and pieces. Probably the biggest difference, of course, is that there really is such a corkboard—the Internet is the county bulletin board, and everybody's jokes get posted there, so we're also exposed to a lot more humor on a regular basis. This doesn't necessarily make individuals funnier, but I think it does raise everybody's awareness of humor. But let's say everything does have to go down to 140 characters; this doesn't allow for the nuanced exploration of lot of topics, does it? (Although Fran Lebowitz seemed to anticipate Twitter; most of her best lines from *Social Studies* could fit nicely into a Tweet). If we all go back to relying entirely on one-liners, it would be a loss, especially for women's humor. Women's humor, as we know, isn't all about punch lines; it is about telling stories.

Yes, I see women's humor as having made great inroads into new territory since I first wrote *Snow White*, but I nevertheless have some worries. For one thing, I worry about young women believing that they have to imitate men in order to be considered funny. YouTube hasn't made this any easier either, since the whole YouTube phenomenon has made the Internet into a forum where humor is being treated as if it's been vetted, when all it's been is downloaded.

The result is that if some guy decides to fill his mouth with ginger ale, baking soda, and kitty litter "just to see what happens" and places it on YouTube, he might well be considered a new comedy star. He could get his own series. He could become famous as "the Exploding Kitty Litter Guy." And there will be some girl who will think she'll be the female equivalent of the kitty litter guy. It won't be pretty.

I worry that women's humor will continue to incline toward the imitative—but I worry less than I did twenty-two years ago.

Excessive, playful, blasphemous, indulgent, insurgent, and fiercely courageous, great humorists have one crucial thing in common: they know that humor is the shortest line between two people. They set about connecting the wires, so that the rest of us can hear the noise inside their heads. To them, nothing is sacred. Nothing scares them. The only thing they have to fear is the grim, tight-lipped, earnest specter of humorlessness itself.

What's our role in this spectacle? We laugh while we watch their antics, and we change—because they make us think. We stare, enthralled, during which time they pull the comfortable rug out from under us. It's their job.

The culture has changed in a way that has given us women more freedom to discuss our bodies, our emotions, our desires, and our ambitions with less shame than we've had in previous generations, but self-deprecating humor is still at the heart of much girls' humor. I would say that most women have learned to rely on it less; but in the same way that girls' voices continue to go up at the end of their sentences when in fact they are making declarative statements, so do self-disparaging comments come easily to young women who fear that without appearing vulnerable, they have no chance of appearing attractive. Humor continues to serve a crucial function in women's lives: it helps them realize they're not crazy and they're not alone. Liza Donnelly, a staff cartoonist for the *New Yorker,* the author of *When Do They Serve the Wine? The Folly, Flexibility, and Fun of Being a Woman,* and the editor of *Sex and Sensibility: Ten Women Examine the Lunacy of Modern Love . . . in 200 Cartoons* sums it up as follows: "Humor is lunacy contained. Cartoonists easily create lunacy: It is their nature to push the envelope. If the situation itself is lunatic, we just reflect that, with embellishments. By seeing the foolishness, humorists show us ourselves by making us laugh. If we are laughing, and once the happy tears clear, the truth can be spotted."

In other words, knowing that you're not the only one experiencing something takes the misery out of commiseration: to laugh at something is to drain the fear out of it. That's at least one reason suffering and humor, when shared, are both validated and validating. They serve a purpose, which is to abolish or mitigate a sense of alienation.

To recognize that women, far from being mere symbols or archetypes, are full-fledged human beings with individual identities is still to be both risky and seditious, which is one of the reasons women's humor is fun. Humorists in every generation, always at the head of the class, willfully and wickedly push, prod, and pinch their audiences into thought, emotion, and laughter. Women comics and humorists have the wit and courage to say what most of us are too cowardly or anxious to admit, and articulate awareness of the situation around us that no one else voices. While they're at it, the best of them help us find our own humor in the everyday; they help us remember to laugh at what we didn't see the first time. By questioning, mocking, and demystifying the world, funny women illustrate that humor is our culture's third rail: electrified, powerful, and dangerous.

They Used to
Call Me
Snow White...
But I Drifted

1

Getting It

• • • • • • • • • • • • • • • • • • •

Strategies for Recognizing and Using Gender Differences in Humor

Seeing the Differences
• • • • • • • • • • • • • • • •

I grew up watching *The Dating Game* and *The Newlywed Game* and soon became aware of the differences between the way men and women deal with humor (I called them boys and girls then, but the theory still holds). On *The Dating Game,* answers could be sort of dirty; on *The Newlywed Game,* answers could be really dirty, because the couples were already married. The idea was to make people in the live audience laugh; they shrieked with laughter when the contestants got something wrong: "What does your spouse miss most about his bachelor days?" Her answer: "Playing baseball." His answer: "Playing the field." When the honeymooners on *The Newlywed Game* agreed and gave the same answer, nothing was funny. If he also said baseball, nobody laughed. Agreement was cute, sweet, nice, but cute, sweet, and nice never kept company with funny. The losers kept the show going, but they never won the Amana range. The badly matched couples were the stars because they were the ones everybody tuned in to watch, but they went home empty-handed. The imperfect couple couldn't be rewarded even if they were terrifically entertaining. They didn't fit. They never would be the proud owners of an apricot-colored lounge suite.

But there was something wrong with this picture, even to my pre-liberation—early-junior-high-school mind. Why was the perfect couple so dull and yet so privileged? Why were the funny, nasty, arm-punching pairs sent home with only garden hoses and blenders? Something was out of place; the boat was in the tree, or the duck was flying upside down. I stared at the television and tried to figure it out.

On *The Dating Game,* my girlfriends and I always picked the boys who were funny. All the contestants were pretty cute. Even the bad choices on *The Dating Game* looked good to us, because they were all over seventeen and probably could drive. But the boys we really liked, the boys we went for, were the boys who had a sense of humor. The boys who could make us laugh. Making us laugh was the boy's job.

The job of the show's bachelorette was to ask questions that sounded innocent enough but could be answered by lines stiff with innuendo. The audience was given permission to understand the double meaning (clean/dirty) and laugh in appreciation of the guy's worldliness and wit, but the female contestant could not, under any circumstances, show that she understood the underlying meaning. If she laughed, she was doomed, because her laughter would give away a terrible secret about her: that she *got the joke.* That she knew what he was talking about. If she asked "If we were on a date and the car's tire went flat, what would you do?" and he answered "I'm always prepared. I'd just get out my pump and do what I could . . . ," she had to provide the requisite glassy stare. No way could she react except by waiting until the audience finished laughing. She couldn't return his volley by saying something like "Why get out your pump right away? How about finding out what kind of pressure is needed?" If the question had been asked on *The Newlywed Game,* and the wife had answered that he should get out his pump, that would have been okay. The married lady was allowed to make such remarks, although she still had to maintain some sort of decorum. She couldn't, for example, really smile when she made the remark, even if her husband was grinning from ear to ear. But she would have at least been allowed to say it. The bachelorette could not betray any understanding of the sexual innuendo. She had to be the Barbie doll, the virgin sacrifice, and the potentially perfect wife all at once. She wasn't allowed to make a dirty joke; she wasn't allowed to react to the man's joke, nor even allowed to be offended at the overtly sexual nature of his reply. It was in his script to make the dirty joke, and it was in her script only to smile. The girl couldn't laugh, because Good Girls just didn't "get it"— "it" being, almost inevitably, the not-so-hidden sexual meaning in male humor.

Good Girls Don't Get It

Where I grew up, the rules of *The Dating Game* applied to real life. Good Girls didn't get it, or much of anything else. Not only didn't Good Girls have premarital sex (which is what everybody really cared about), there was a long list of binary oppositions mapping the territory of the Good Girl and the Bad. One group had to exist in order for the other to be defined. Good Girls wore miniskirts but not hot pants. Good Girls wore patterned tights but not fishnets. Good Girls wore bras and were embarrassed if the tops showed above the blouse line. Or if any trace of nipple could be detected through the fabric (the female equivalent of the male fear of a sudden erection on the way to the front of the class). Bad Girls bounced. Even after Good Girls stopped wearing bras (after the late sixties had established that even Good Girls could have some mild politics), they usually wore some Laura Ashley–type printed undershirt, and their breasts just stayed put, out of general good behavior. Good Girls kept their knees together.

The image of the Good Girl was a product developed in a conspiracy among parents, the media, and advertising, with support from the church, educational and economic institutions, and the government in general. Good Girls didn't make trouble for anybody. They did what they were told, whether that was keeping their rooms clean, watching TV while they baby-sat on Saturday nights, or buying all the current Cover Girl merchandise. They never questioned why women weren't allowed to be priests or rabbis, always handed in homework on time, and did not support such revolutionary causes as equal rights for minorities or women. Good Girls were taught to believe that everything would continue to be just fine, and that someone else was out there taking care of things. Good Girls did not draw attention to themselves or their ideas. They looked around to see what the other people in the audience were doing before they let themselves smile or cry, because, after a certain point, they had learned not to trust their instincts. Laugh tracks were invented so that the audience would have a guide to the appropriate response. And Good Girls, we were told, laughed with their mouths shut, if they laughed at all.

Significantly, Good Girls didn't keep raising their hands in class even if they always knew the answer. That was showing off, and Good Girls didn't show off. It was showing off if you said you wanted to go to college, or go to a "good" college, or go to medical school after college. "Ambitious" was still not a very nice thing to call a lady until these past few years, until we learned to see that we needed to acknowledge our ambitions if we were going to succeed in our professions. Or that we needed ambition to have professions at all. Saying a woman was ambitious was like saying she was selfish, crass, or bad tempered. Not very feminine. Not the attributes of someone well behaved or well brought up.

We have had to learn to embrace the idea of ourselves as striving for our goals, as aiming for success, as willing to set our sights for the very top. We have learned to love the thought of our own ambition. And we are learning to love our own laughter, to see that our sense of humor makes sense and can help us make sense of the world around us. Which means re-learning to trust our instincts and to stop checking whether the guy sitting next to us is laughing before we laugh. If it's funny, we should let ourselves laugh, loud and clear. Mary Davis, a vice president of Time-Warner, Inc., and director of Magazine Manufacturing and Distribution, argues, "It is as important for a woman to speak up during a meeting to make a pertinent funny remark as it is for her to speak up to make any important point. It shows that her mind is working fast and well, and that she's willing to take the risk of being funny because she has confidence that she'll get the desired response. The ability to joke, a confident sense of humor, is as much a leadership quality in women as it is in men."

C'mon and Smile, Sweetie

Humor means more than being able to laugh at a man's joke. We always knew that we had to smile at his stories, giggle at his jokes. Nobody said we should giggle at his jokes only if we found them funny; we had to giggle at his jokes even when we thought they were dull, insulting, or dumb. We were expected to look into his eyes and laugh invitingly, even if the story wasn't amusing. We are still supposed to "fake a passion that's bound to turn men on," meaning that we're supposed to read our part of the script correctly. We are supposed to give the desired response instead of expressing whatever response is actually our own. That piece of advice is from a recent issue of *Cosmopolitan*, by the way, and refers to showing enthusiasm for sports even when you don't have any. The idea that women should be interested in what bores them—or laugh at what they do not find funny—still holds sway.

When we were growing up, a lot of girls tried not to laugh at what they themselves found funny, at least not around boys.

In a book typical of its era and values, *Teen Scene—1001 Groovy Hints and Tips* (published in 1972), the advisers sum it all up: "You may be a quick wit with your girl friends, but cool it when he's around." If you were a Good Girl, you giggled and tittered (although you had to be crazy to use that word), smirked and smiled. How you smiled! Smiling was allowed, encouraged, even demanded. The general sentiment was "Laugh at his jokes, but do it naturally. Nobody likes the donkey's hee-haw some girls are saddled with." Laughing out loud was out of the question.

One observant viewer of early sixties movies, the comedy writer Anne Beatts, notes that Annette Funicello, the original fun-date Good Girl, never laughed. The boys would joke around, and Annette would give a little, almost maternally indulgent "boys will be boys" smile, or she'd stamp her foot impatiently, with just a trace of pleasure, in protest of the joke that was not quite nice enough to suit her fastidious tastes. Annette never cracked a joke: "She didn't even laugh; she just put her hands on her hips and got mad at Ricky or Tommy or Eddie or whoever was carrying her surfboard, so that they could tell her how cute she was when she was mad." The slightly corrupt "vocational school" girls did joke with the boys, however, and came to a bad end. Their ability to joke was seen as evidence of both their sexual awareness and their lack of femininity, although how these two can be paired without canceling each other out raises some complex issues. The girls with scary hairdos, black leather jackets, heavy eye makeup, and spiked heels (or low, pointed leather boots) chewed gum and laughed with their heads thrown back.

But Good or Bad, women have been labeled as "unfunny," as less likely to laugh than their male counterparts. It's been an unspoken but unwavering assumption that women and men have different reactions to humor, as well as different ways of using it. The noted psychologist Rose Laub Coser argues, "In this culture women are expected to be passive and receptive, rather than active and initiating. A woman who has a good sense of humor is one who laughs (but not too loudly!) when a man makes a witticism or tells a good joke. . . . The man provides; the woman receives." Beatts makes much the same point in her article "Why More Women Aren't Funny": "If you say that a girl has a sense of humor it typically means only that she gets the joke, not that she makes any jokes of her own. A boy with a sense of humor, on the other hand, is supposed to supply all the entertainment." And boys, Beatts observes, learn to count on this pattern: "If you were a boy, having a sense of humor meant pouring salt on the head of the girl who sat in front of you so it would look as though she has dandruff. If you were a girl, having a sense of humor meant laughing when someone poured salt on your head." The boys made their jokes and we smiled, encouragingly if the prank was directed at somebody else, weakly if we were the object of all the kidding.

Can't You Take a Joke?

One of the worst things that could be said about a girl was that she couldn't take a joke. This was almost as bad as getting the joke. There you were, stuck between being afraid to show that you got it and being embarrassed to say that you didn't want to take it. You were supposed to avoid the jokes that had to do with sex, but to be a good sport about the ones that had to do with abuse or insults. Beatts suggests that the cliché "women have no sense of humor" was started by a girl who just couldn't put up with the salt poured on her head one more time.

This relationship to joking put girls in a position similar to the sexual dilemma that proposed we be attractive but unavailable, caught between being cheap and being prudish. We were taught not to trust our own instincts but instead to submit to the established script, laughing along with the laugh track.

Good Girls Can and Do Laugh
with Their Mouths Open
· ·

Even the Goodest Girls have a Bad Girl inside who not only gets it but who gives it and, maybe worst of all, isn't going to take it from anybody. We are brought up to believe that the Good Girl/Bad Girl split is natural, right, unchanging, and definitive. Like the myth that women have no sense of humor, the idea that we can't be sweet and wicked at the same time just isn't true. Good Girls can and do laugh with their mouths open.

Despite all the pressure not to, we found ways to laugh. Some of us were better than others at keeping it under cover and acceptable. We laughed, for example, at slumber parties, where we'd pool our scant sexual knowledge and scream hysterically into pillows about what we'd heard. At one such party, I remember, was a friend who had managed to steal a condom from her older brother's underwear drawer. We examined the evidence, trying to figure out what the male sexual organ was really like—textbooks never supplied details. The condom didn't help much, even when it was unraveled. Surely it was as misleading as the panty hose that comes scrunched up in the L'Eggs package; how could you tell what they looked like when somebody put them *on*? Being a scientific group—or so we thought—we decided that the one way to find out size and shape was to fill the condom with water. I was elected to carry out the task. When I returned to the basement where we were all piled into sleeping bags, I was carrying something nearly a foot long and about three inches around. My friend Annemarie started to weep softly in one corner, and the rest of us tried to imagine what happened to one's internal organs. Surely your liver had to move around to accommodate this thing? But even though we were ill informed, insecure, and utterly horrified, we were together. So, together, we laughed out loud, for hours, until our hostess's father yelled from upstairs, telling us to be quiet.

Can Men Get It?
· · · · · · · · · · · · ·

It's important to keep in mind that the focus of this discussion is the way men and women react in general. Of course, there are men confident enough, generous enough, and smart enough to laugh at our jokes when they understand or find them funny, and who, even when they don't get it, allow us our own laughter undisturbed. But let us remember that there are also men who find it a physical impossibility to read more than three sentences about women without retreating, as the author Joanna Russ has catalogued them in *How to Suppress Women's Writing,* to their personalized version of the following "rational" and "status-enhancing" remarks: "Hm! How can you prove that?" "Not all women." "I think we have to examine your assumptions."

You can tell some men that they're insensitive and immune to the subtleties and textures of the finest aspects of existence, and they'll nod sheepishly in agreement. You can tell some of them that the appropriation of power, based on force and ill will, has resulted in a culture of thievery, baseness, and ignorance and they'll protest but feel compelled to agree. Tell them that men create art only because they cannot have children, tell them that paternity is a legal fiction—but just don't tell them that you know a joke that they won't get. They'll kill you. They simply don't believe that you could laugh at something they won't appreciate. Tell them there are gender differences in humor, and they'll block your way to the door until you've told them, like Scheherazade, every story you've ever heard so that they can show you how much, how very equally, they laugh.

Many men get uneasy when they're not included in something. Professor Emily Toth of Pennsylvania State University tells a story illustrating this point concerning her book *The Curse: A Cultural History of Menstruation.* She and her collaborators did the talk-show circuit to promote the book. During one such program the host was angry that she'd written an "anti-male book." "Why don't you give equal time to men?" he demanded. Give equal time to men in a book on menstruation? "In fact," Professor Toth writes, "we did have a chapter on male men-struators—but his objection was really to the bold idea that one sex could be relegated to being a special interest or sideshow." Of course, women have until very recently occupied just such a "sideshow" position. Men want to know that they're not missing the good part, that the material isn't being cut or changed before they get a chance to see it. They can then decide they don't like it, that it's boring or insignificant, but they want to be in the position to decide. If you say that a woman has a sense of humor that's different from a man's, a man might well interpret "different" as meaning "inferior." If you disagree, you might make him nervous and defensive, which will mean, of course, that he won't be able to laugh at anything naturally at that moment, no matter how funny he might have found it under other circumstances. At this point, it's likely that he'll tell you that he finds whatever joke you tell him funny even if he says it through clenched teeth. Or he'll tell you that the reason you think your sense of humor is different is because, in his judgment, it's nonexistent. You might then be subject to endless stories about all the humorless women he's ever met until you either walk out of the room on him or kiss him to keep him quiet. In the case of a man who doesn't think women are funny, the first option is far healthier.

Of course, some women come to laughter unmediated by all the mythology the rest of us have prepurchased like a package deal. Some women, brave and fortunate souls that they are, have always known that having a sense of humor is important and wonderful. These women will be shocked at the timid nature of the rest of us, who have to learn to laugh, or relearn to enjoy and use humor. But they will no doubt be able to help us in our endeavors, charting the course. We all need support in our struggle to rediscover ourselves in order to laugh out loud.

Discovering Our Sense of Humor
· ·

For most women, humor occupies a different space emotionally and socially than it does for men. For most women, humor is something we aren't sure how to use, because we've been told it's something we haven't got. In vast numbers of Victorian novels, the heroine has to cope, usually to the horror of those around her, with the idea of her own intelligence, because her society has no place for a smart woman. She has to figure out what on earth to do with this gift, which is properly considered masculine. Jane Eyre had to live by using her mind. So did the majority of the heroines in George Eliot's (Mary Ann Evans's) novels, with Maggie Tulliver from *The Mill on the Floss* and Dorothea from *Middlemarch* being the primary examples. Catherine from Emily Brontë's *Wuthering Heights* plays roughly alongside Heathcliff and possesses great intelligence as well as great passion. If the heroines of Victorian novels were separated from their less interesting counterparts by their pronounced intelligence, then the heroines of contemporary novels are distinguished by their sense of humor. Modern heroines, ranging from those created by Colette and Virginia Woolf to ones created by Erica Jong and Margaret Drabble, claim the witty remark as their signature. It is her sense of humor that allows one of Colette's characters to describe a seven-year liaison as being rather like "following a husband to the colonies; when you come back no one recognizes you and you've forgotten how to wear your clothes" and to say "My true friends have always given me that supreme proof of devotion, a spontaneous aversion for the man I loved." Woolf's heroines are equally witty. When a young woman has just been kissed by an aging Member of Parliament whom she finds interesting but not necessarily attractive, her older friend muses about "this confusion between politics and kissing politicians." Indeed, a sense of humor is now standard issue for the modern heroine, replacing even beauty as the essential ingredient for some writers. Margaret

Drabble's trio of heroines from *The Radiant Way* is described as worthy of the reader's attention: "... they were not beautiful, they were not rich. But they were young, and they had considerable wit."

Women do not often laugh at the genuine misfortune of others—women are, according to the psychoanalyst Natalie Becker, less likely than men to laugh at a situation where someone is hurt or embarrassed. Women are more likely to attempt to console than laugh at anyone who can be considered a victim. This is perhaps one of the reasons certain forms of slapstick comedy appeal far less to women than to men: when the Three Stooges poke one another in the eye, women tend to wince or sigh more than laugh. When the guys in the *Porky* movies trash the nerd's room or dress up the fat kid in women's clothes, women tend not to find these scenes wonderfully comic. The men who have laughed, then, in turn, feel embarrassed at their own reaction. They cover this embarrassment by blaming the women around them for not joining in and thus making them feel bad about enjoying themselves at another's expense. "What's the matter with you?" the embarrassed laugher might ask. "Don't you know a joke when you see one?" Then he'll blame the non-laugher for making him uncomfortable, although he probably won't be able to explain why. By not finding someone else's pain funny, a woman will probably remind him of the female figures of authority from his childhood, the mother or the elementary school teacher who tried to teach him that it wasn't nice to laugh at other people even while his buddies out on the playground were teaching him exactly the opposite. The whole thing gets pretty complicated psychologically, but we see it played out so often we hardly notice anymore.

Even "masculine" comedy recognizes this dynamic. Ralph Kramden in the TV program *The Honeymooners* laughs at Norton's black eye until he sees Alice's serious face. He sheepishly wipes the smile off his face and, with Alice, begins to help his friend rather than laugh at him. Think of all the looks given by women in TV situation comedies that squelch the smiles of the men: in *I Love Lucy*, when Ricky is laughing at something Fred says and then turns to Lucy, his face falls when he sees her disapproval. The same thing will happen when Lucy gives him a dirty look for flirting with a chorus girl: he's smiling until he sees her face. It's as if flirting and laughing are the two things men aren't allowed to do in front of their wives or mothers—the Good Girl figures in their lives—and can be done only around Bad Girls.

"The Humane Humor Rule"

The critic Emily Toth wrote in her article "Female Wits" that women use what she calls "the humane humor rule." The humane humor rule declares that we should not make fun of what people cannot change, such as social handicaps (such as a stutter) or physical appearance. Toth notes that women rarely use the typical scapegoat figures in their humor. "Rather," she asserts, "women humorists attack—or subvert—the deliberate choices people make: hypocrisies, affectations, mindless following of social expectations." In contrast, women's comedy takes as its material the powerful rather than the pitiful.

Women are more likely than men to make fun of those in high and seemingly invulnerable positions. Consider some recent television programs: women are more likely to be irreverent toward their bosses than men are. The bosses in *Roseanne* and *Murphy Brown* are barely treated as human beings. Rather than presenting laughter at the insecure office boy who always drops his papers, a "woman's show" will turn its humorous lens on the upper-level figures and ridicule their incompetence. In *Designing Women* the heroines challenge the most repressive institutions, such as nonunionized workplaces, the National Rifle Association, and the judicial system, by ridiculing the absurd mind-sets and rules that keep such institutions strong. When Suzanne gets out a shotgun to protect her prize pig from possible pig-nappers, the show turns its humor on the fact that she was permitted to have a gun in her house according to laws that allow anybody to own and so potentially misuse firearms. Interestingly, *Designing Women* was originally canceled, and revived by the network only when the outcry from the show's mostly female viewing audience was so insistent that CBS decided not to risk offending it. Again, television reflects the reality of female humor. Most women agree that to make fun of someone in a powerless position is not only unkind, it is too easy— like shooting fish in a barrel. Not much sport there.

So women look at those in power, or at those institutions we were taught to revere, and laugh. In this way women's comedy is more "dangerous" than men's, because it challenges authority by refusing to take it seriously. When Lily Tomlin's character Trudy in *The Search for Signs of Intelligent Life in the Universe* claims "I refuse to be intimidated by reality anymore" because "After all, what is reality anyway? Nothin' but a collective hunch," she is calling into question the fundamental questions of existence. When Elayne Boosler talks about the right-to-lifers' attitudes, she is challenging the entire conservative movement: "You ever notice that the same people who are against abortion are for capital punishment? Typical fisherman's attitude, throw 'em back when they're small and kill 'em when they're bigger." By refusing to accept the sanctimonious tone of the right-to-lifers, she strips away the authority of their position. (The audience's response to that line was remarkable: the applause continued for several minutes.) She went on to illuminate the conservatives' approach to sex education: "Reagan was against sex education in the schools because he thought there was a connection between promiscuity and sex education—that kids did it because they learned about it. No way. I had four years of algebra and I never do math. These guys say they're against abortion because birth is a miracle. Popcorn is a miracle, too, if you don't know how it's done." Such comedy is risky. It is confrontational and boundary breaking, since you walk away feeling angry even as you laugh. This sort of comedy does not do away with women's feelings of powerlessness—instead it underscores the political nature of a woman's role. It should make us even more determined to change those aspects of our situation that confine us. It is comedy that inspires as well as entertains.

The Secret Code of Irony

Certainly most of us would not choose to take the risks that professional comedians must face. But it also takes courage and self-confidence to risk using humor in an everyday situation. Women are sometimes afraid to make jokes or tell amusing stories around men for fear that men will not find them funny. Oscar Wilde wrote, "Nothing spoils a romance so much as a sense of humor in the woman—or the want of it in a man." A woman's ability to use humor, especially if she can couple it with an ability to think quickly, can have a daunting effect on men. Perhaps it is fortunate, therefore, that occasionally a woman's wit is too quick or too "different" to be understood by a man. Countess Catherine Sedley (1657–1717), who was the mistress of King James II, tried to figure out why she so appealed to the king and could say only that "It cannot be my wit, for he has not enough to know I have any." If men cannot understand your humor, then they cannot dislike you for using it. If it is disguised in such a way that it acts as a sort of secret code that other women can understand but so that it remains hidden from men, then you don't have to risk being thought unfeminine or labeled a Bad Girl.

It is probably fair to say that, in 1970, when the girls on *The Dating Game* gave their straight-faced replies, they were more wary than daring. But even those answers carried with them an air of possibility—you had to watch carefully to judge the nuance and texture of the line. Perhaps the questions themselves, often scripted by the studio, were nevertheless delivered with a hint of complicity in their possible dangers. Learning to sound like a Good Girl, while half-concealing the text of the Bad Girl, has been the subject of a great deal of women's humor.

In other words, if you present yourself as being so completely naive that nothing you say can be interpreted as having sexual or aggressive connotations, then you can give any covert message you choose to the proper audience. When Marilyn Monroe told Tony Curtis "I always get the fuzzy end of the lollypop" in *Some Like It Hot,* she played the innocent even though she played the sexually alluring woman—the listener hears the remark, sees the sexual side, then understands that he daren't risk seeing only the sexual side—he doesn't want to offend her. Women use this kind of "innocence" to mask, in mixed social situations, their risky comments. You make a remark but leave it to your audience to decide how to read it.

While in *Some Like It Hot* Monroe played the genuine sexually experienced but naive young woman, she played a more complex version of the supposedly dumb blonde in another film, *Gentlemen Prefer Blondes.* In 1925 Anita Loos's best-seller *Gentlemen Prefer Blondes* was hailed by such luminaries as Edith Wharton, who thought the book was a great American novel, and James Joyce, who, even with failing eyesight, read it straight through from sheer delight. Loos created a character so emblematic of the "dumb blonde" who in fact outsmarts everyone around her, that Lorelei has appeared in a number of stage and screen versions independent of Loos's scripts (although Loos wrote the first screenplay, the other versions were spin-offs). Lorelei is the mistress of innuendo, as well as being the mistress of several important businessmen, including Gus Eismen, affectionately known as The Button King. Lorelei makes no specific mention of "affairs" in her diary, but instead talks about how men "want to educate" her. She begins the book by describing how one gentleman, a senator "from Washington d.c." (*sic*), said "A girl with brains ought to do something else with them besides think," and that she seems "to be thinking practically all the time."

Loos created the character of Lorelei in response to a male friend's passion for pretty, uneducated, greedy young women. Lorelei's diary acts as a not-so-gentle satire on this literary gentleman's preference for rather unliterary ladies. But, as Muriel Spark noted twenty years later in *The Girls of Slender Means*, "Literary men, when they like women at all, do not want literary women. What they want is girls."

Even without Lorelei's kind of shrewdness and, it should be noted, without her financial acumen, many women disguise their wit under a mask of social acceptability. You have to decipher the code to understand the real message underneath. In this respect, Loos was a particularly valuable asset to the early motion picture industry. She was renowned for her ability to couch subversive, slyly comic messages within acceptable discourse. One producer, Sam Marx, wrote that Loos could be "counted on to supply the delicate double entendre, the telling innuendo," lines that would have no trouble getting by the censors despite the fact that the hidden message could easily be understood by the audience.

For example, you can use irony undetected by its subject but apparent to the correct audience. Girls are taught to do this very early on, blinking darkly fringed round eyes at the most boring man in the room and telling him that he is fascinating, which he believes without the shadow of a doubt (having been told this by his relatives since birth), while her girlfriend stands behind the guy laughing silently but thoroughly at how completely, because of his arrogance, he is taken in by false flattery. Often such women are characterized by men as both sweet and devoid of a sense of humor. Men read the woman's funny, ironic, and sometimes even sarcastic text as straight ("Oh, you're so strong. Can you really crush that beer can?") and are delighted to meet a woman who can finally "appreciate" them. I was once in a car with a few friends, including one not unlike a contemporary Lorelei. When the nice enough but perhaps overly earnest man at the wheel finally maneuvered into a parking space after a good four or five minutes, she purred, "Oh, you park so well." You could see his face light up. He bought the flattery wholesale, and considered her an excellent judge of both character and vehicular dexterity. Her joke was interesting in its twofold effect: it made everyone happy. We shared with her the irony behind her flattery, but the driver felt only pleased. I was later to hear him describe her as one of the few "really sweet women" left in the world. In her novel *To the North*, the British writer Elizabeth Bowen has described a similar relationship by explaining that what one woman's lover saw as "divine humorlessness was, in reality, a profound sense of irony."

Risking Humor

Women who want to preserve a carefully constructed facade of femininity even as they explore the intricate contradictions and absurdities of that facade might find themselves involved in this sort of double-voiced dialogue. They are aware of the humorous nature of some moments, but they cannot make that humor public. They hesitate to share, especially with a man, their awareness of the possible comic aspects of a situation. And, it must be emphasized, this is occasionally the only acceptable reaction. If you really want to laugh at a ridiculous remark your boss makes during a big meeting, you still aren't allowed to— so you do have to plug in the glassy stare and smile until you can excuse yourself and go to the bathroom and laugh there. There are certainly times when Good Girl training comes in handy. But when you find yourself repressing your laughter more often than you let it out, or when you repress it by habit instead of on occasion, then a reevaluation of the situation is called for. When you find yourself being afraid to make jokes, then you've got to see whether you're just acting appropriately or whether you're afraid to take any risks. All humor involves taking a risk, and as we all know from other lessons, without risk there is no possibility for improvement or success.

Especially when initiated by a woman, humor *is* risky. Even women professional performers have to prepare themselves to face the risk. In a recent *Ms.* report, "The New Stand-Up Comics," Julia Klein writes that these women know that "Comedy is itself an aggressive act; making someone laugh means exerting control, even power. But a woman cannot come off as over-aggressive or she will lose. . . ." What will she lose? She'll lose the approval of her audience. She'll make people nervous, and nervous people don't laugh.

What else could she lose? Masculine approval? Perhaps even something more specific? A male friend suggested to me that the real reason many men are worried by funny women isn't even the most obvious one: it's not, he explained, that men are afraid that women will laugh at them. It's not even that men are afraid that women will laugh at them during sex or guffaw at the size of their sexual apparatus. Rather, it's that a man can't *really* laugh and maintain an erection at the same time. A woman who can make a man laugh when he doesn't want to is as dangerous as a Medusa. All that energy loses its focus and starts to move around again, playfully. It is perhaps difficult to prove scientifically that men cannot truly laugh at a joke told by a woman (they can laugh at their own jokes, it seems, and this doesn't bother them too much) and maintain an erection, but an informal survey of both men and women indicates that it's so. (No doubt there will be men reading this last passage who are lying next to their lovers, saying "Go on, tell me your best jokes. Go ahead, I'll show you. . . .")

And it is risky to initiate humor not only because men might not like it. It is risky to admit to one's self that a situation might be funny or absurd, because to do that means taking into account the idea of change. When you see the humor in a situation, it implies that you can also then imagine how the situation could be altered. Once you can imagine altering a situation that is not to your liking, you confront your own desire for change. That, in turn, makes it increasingly more difficult to put up with what you don't like or to accept as a given what you are in the process of questioning. The cartoonist Roz Chast, whose work delights readers of *The New Yorker* and *Mother Jones*, has placed as the opening page of her collection *The Four Elements* the following scene: A class of kids sitting two by two is obviously taking a math test, the kids' stuff spread out over the desks, wadded-up pieces of paper next to compasses, all the familiar materials. Everyone has his or her head down and is working away, except for one kid, who's looking up and thinking "Why should I care if I pass this exam or not?" The title of the cartoon is "The End of Innocence," and the moment of recognition that Chast depicts is emblematic of the one that humor affords us. We see, suddenly, that the emperor is wearing no clothes, and we laugh.

Once we realize that what we've been told is an unalterable truth ("Women like to stay home and look after the family. It's what comes naturally" or "All any woman really needs is a good man" or "Women are too emotionally erratic to occupy executive positions") is actually manufactured and perpetuated by someone who will benefit by our believing it, then we can escape its confines. The stand-up comic Susie Essman tells a story about a man in her life who kept explaining that he had a great sense of humor. "I believed him," says Essman, "for *years,* even though I never thought he was funny. But he argued that he was this remarkably witty man, and he sounded so sure of it that I could hardly bring myself to disagree. I didn't think of it as his opinion; I thought of it as the truth." It's like realizing that the old statistics claiming cigarettes don't harm anyone's health were paid for by the tobacco industry—once you realize that the person giving you supposedly objective information has a vested interest in winning you over to his opinion, the idea that the information is unbiased becomes so ridiculous that it's funny. You come to understand that very little of what passes for authoritative and objective truth is neither. You begin to laugh at what you were told just wasn't funny—it *is* funny, because it isn't what it makes itself out to be. The great big monster turns out to be a hand puppet, and a little green hand puppet trying to act like a great big monster is pretty funny. Even kind of cute, as long as you keep it in perspective.

Clearing Space

The screenwriter Pamela West claims that women use humor to "clear space" for themselves within an unhappy situation. "Since we're all too scared even to appear scared, hysterical, complaining or whining—all those things women have been accused of being whenever we don't smile politely—we have to come up with another way to make ourselves heard. If you make a joke out of your misery, then you'll be tolerated. They won't shut you off as quickly." West described her time working with a particularly difficult producer. She needed his continued approval—he was a big name in the business and this was a particularly important project—but she could not convince him to make time to listen to her. "I tried everything," West explained. "I wrote lengthy memos with sub-headings so that he could get the main ideas without having to read the details, but I included every detail just in case. I had his personal assistant schedule meetings before breakfast, at midnight. Nothing worked. I realized that he was beginning to think of me as a complainer, as a whiner and a drag. Finally, I caught on. This guy was so overworked and stressed out, I could only make him listen to me if I made it easy on him. I could make it easy on him by keeping it light—still keeping it on target, focused on what I saw as my needs—but without any hint of a complaint because I'd make it amusing. I'd exaggerate, play but keep my points at the center. He would smile instead of flinch when I caught his eye—he stopped feeling guilty when he saw me and this helped more than any earnest pleading ever did." West shrugged her shoulders and summed it up by saying "When you make men feel guilty, they hate you." Making them laugh at their own inability or refusal to help might change that pattern.

Diffusing Pain Through Humor

Women use comedy to narrate their experience and so diffuse the pain. How many times have you woken up your best friend by telephoning in the middle of the night to relate the most horrible story about being abandoned at a party, about being set up on the world's worst blind date, about being fired, about being embarrassed, and have begun the conversation with tears of anger or depression and ended with tears of laughter? Your friend will try to retrieve your sense of perspective by introducing humor. Your boyfriend left you? Your friend knew right from the start that you should have chosen somebody higher up the food chain. Your old boyfriend just called to say you should get together again and he has two tickets to Hawaii? Tell him to sell both tickets and use the money to see a doctor, because he's obviously a very sick man to think you'd consider such a thing.

Our disappointments can be transformed through our ability to tell the story to someone else. Traditional forms of therapy work on the same principle—tell somebody your troubles, and it'll help solve them. The world tells us that it's all wrong to complain, but that we can secure permission to complain as long as we don't seem self-pitying and narcissistic. In other words, we get permission to talk about ourselves if we present our pain in such a way that it will not disturb others. "If men complain about their lives," says one woman, who reads scripts for a major motion picture company, "often it can be called tragedy. But when women complain, they're not being universal, they're being neurotic women. Probably they want a baby or they're menopausal. With men it appears as a crisis of existential conflicts. With women it appears hormonal. That's how it works."

In other words, when women complain about their lives, they'd better make it comedic if they want an audience. Women's stuff isn't seen as being about people—it's seen as being about women. "Universal" examples include the "universal" struggle: man against nature, man's flight from himself, man's search for truth. Joanna Russ writes in her article "What Can a Heroine Do? or Why Women Can't Write" about the ways in which, when the sex of the protagonists is changed, the plots no longer work, thus proving that the so-called universal plot depends heavily on the sex of the main character. In the supposedly universal plots we've all read in "great" literature (that is, literature by men), changing the sex of the main character changes the paradigm so completely it becomes comic. Russ's examples include the following: "1. Two strong women battle for supremacy in the early West. 2. A young girl in Minnesota finds her womanhood by killing a bear. 3. A phosphorescently doomed poetess sponges off her husband and drinks herself to death, thus alienating the community of Philistines and businesswomen who would have continued to give her lecture dates. 4. A young man who unwisely puts his success in business before his personal fulfillment loses his masculinity and ends up as a neurotic, lonely eunuch." Russ illustrates that the sex of the character in a story is never a neutral matter—it always has an implication. In regard to humor and joking, we can see that jokes with women as the main characters are typically seen as being applicable only to women, whereas jokes with men as the main characters (except for those jokes depending solely on sexual apparatus) are seen as applying to "everyone."

The Self-deprecating Joke

The self-deprecating joke is considered to be the most "traditional" form of women's humor. This is what comediennes in the fifties and early sixties relied on for their standard fare. It's what Phyllis Diller used to do when she said that the best birth control for her was to leave the lights on. Diller sees comedy "as a hostile act" and thought it best for a woman to keep the object of her hostility herself, in order not to make men nervous or to threaten the audience. When Joan Rivers says that the moment she saw liver spots on her hands she thought her nipples had moved, she's using self-deprecating humor. When Jean Kerr writes that she bought an expensive brown dress only to realize that it makes her look like a large bran muffin, she's relying on self-deprecation. Or when Erma Bombeck points out that "one-size-fits-all" is an incomplete sentence, the implication is that the garment doesn't fit her, and her humor is directed against herself. In domestic humor it has traditionally been okay for a woman to make fun of her home, her children, and her husband, because she was seen as responsible for them. Therefore, if Bombeck says "In general my children refused to eat anything that hadn't danced on TV," we see this as a sort of extended self-deprecation, because we see children as an extension of their mother. If they're that way, it means that she's responsible. To kid her kids is to kid herself.

Nancy Walker, a professor of English whose book *A Very Serious Thing: Women's Humor and American Culture* explores the history and impact of women's humor in America, discusses the way self-deprecating humor seems to support the stereotypes of women's incompetence while still managing, on several levels, to offer a challenge to those stereotypes. "Self-deprecation," Walker writes, "is ingratiating rather than aggressive." She goes on to explain that to make fun of one's self—or one's group—"allows the speaker or writer to participate in the process without alienating the members of the majority." It renders the joke "harmless," because it can be seen to be shared. In other words, it's okay to be funny if you're a woman as long as the only thing you're laughing at is yourself—or other women. Thus we return to Diller's assertion that a lot of women's comedy is humor directed against the self. According to the psychologist Paul McGhee, who has researched gender differences in humor appreciation, "When male comics did make self-deprecating remarks about their own sex, it tended to be done in an impersonal way, rather than being at their own expense. Female comics must have made the judgment that the chances for success are maximized by engaging in self-directed put-downs rather than by directing put-downs at others."

The unnerving message transmitted by these self-deprecating jokes is that it's okay to be hostile as long as you make yourself into the object of the hostility. Blacks tell black jokes, Jews tell Jewish jokes, gays tell gay jokes, women tell jokes about women—and this way, according to Freud, we get to make fun of ourselves before, and better than, anyone else. We beat the others to the punch line and render ourselves the victim. This makes people in positions of power comfortable. If we tell these jokes about ourselves, we'll make the straight, white, patriarchal man our pal, because he finds these jokes funny too. He knows at this point that he's probably not allowed to tell any of these jokes himself, at least not in mixed company, but he still enjoys hearing them. If a joke, especially a joke laced with aggression, is directed at the power structure in front of a member of the power structure, however, the results can be dangerous. If you tell a joke about the Bush administration ("Did you know that Mickey Mouse wears a Dan Quayle watch?") to a die-hard Republican, be careful. He really won't think it's funny, and he might turn nasty in response. When these guys turn nasty, it's like the invasion of Grenada: swift, silent, nasty, and infused with a sense of moral victory.

In a landmark study of the social functions of humor in the workplace, the psychologist Rose Laub Coser notes that jokes are told most frequently by those occupying a superior position in the hierarchy. She found that these jokes were directed downward, made at the expense of those lower in status than the joker. The victims of these jokes did not respond by directing their own wit back at those who had just kidded them, but they instead turned it either on those below them or, interestingly, at themselves. In other words, if you're high up in the status structure, you tend to make jokes at the expense of those below you. If you're low in the status structure, you are as likely to make jokes at your own expense as to make jokes at the expense of others. It's as if, having been singled out as a target for humor by others perceived as above you, you absorb their perspective and see yourself as a target for humor—even your own humor. When you make self-deprecating jokes, you are solidifying your own lowly position in the power structure by seeming to agree that you deserve to be the victim or target of such humor.

Women have to be careful of even the supposedly harmless self-deprecating jokes when in the workplace. Women's humor often misfires in the office, because self-deprecating comments are taken literally instead of ironically. Helen, who worked as a legal assistant in a large Wall Street firm, would use self-deprecating humor to call attention to herself. She got attention all right, but not the kind she wanted. Helen waited for people to contradict her when she used her favorite line, "Gosh, I'm such a dumb blonde!" But she said it so often that people started to believe it, although nothing about her work suggested that she was anything but capable, efficient, and talented. She'd go into long and funny stories about her trouble keeping facts straight ("If I ever learn the alphabet I don't know what I'll do with all my extra time" or "It's such a shame that my foot size is larger than my IQ") even as she kept track of a sophisticated system of confidential information. When her boss started to refer to her as "the dumb blonde," Helen finally realized that her humor had backfired.

Humor as Control

But occasionally humor directed at ourselves allows us to have some measure of control over a situation. The brilliant Gilda

Radner once explained that she learned to make fun of herself because "If somebody does something mean to you, you laugh at yourself first before anyone else gets a chance to, so then they can't get to you." Radner said that she "was the kind of person who, if I woke up with a pimple on my nose, would say 'Hey! I have a pimple on my nose!' before anyone else noticed." Radner summed it up when she explained that she had such a fear of looking like a fool that she decided to "play" the fool. That way she maintained a level of control. But that "control" can lead to the habitual self-deprecation so characteristic of the comedy of the fifties and early sixties.

It also can lead to a perpetual mask of clowning, a figure who falls somewhere outside the Good Girl/Bad Girl split by desexing herself, who can be counted on "not to show envy, not to flirt competitively," and not to wonder why she isn't considered sexually attractive. The clown gets attention by realizing, like Margaret Atwood's heroine in *Lady Oracle,* that "if you're going to be made to look ridiculous and there's no way out of it, you may as well pretend you meant to." Atwood's character Joan learns early that, despite being an astonishingly overweight, disheartened seven-year-old, she can get a certain kind of positive attention by making people laugh even though she did not set about to do so intentionally. Joan, for example, is supposed to be a butterfly in the dance class recital, but the costume, beloved as it is, turns out to look worse than she imagined: "In the short pink skirt, with my waist, arms and legs exposed, I was grotesque. . . . I must have looked obscene, senile almost, indecent; it must have been like watching a decaying stripper." She is told by the teacher that she must play the part of a mothball, whose role is to scatter her pretty, pink classmates. Joan is miserable inside her white suit (originally a teddy-bear outfit, revamped by a sign reading MOTHBALL so that "they'll all understand, dear, what you're supposed to be") but goes through this "humiliation disguised as privilege." Left in the center of the stage, however, she realizes that the audience is "not only laughing, but applauding vigorously." She enjoys this individual attention but "wasn't sure it was the kind I liked. Besides," she wonders, tellingly, "who would think to marry a mothball?"

She's Got a Terrific Sense of Humor

We might worry if we heard ourselves described first and foremost as a woman with a terrific sense of humor, for the same reason Joan isn't sure she likes being center stage: Can they laugh at you and love you at the same time? Can they laugh at you and desire you? Respect you? The description "She's got a terrific sense of humor" is often used as the cliché that sums up the blind date no boy wants to have—"She's got a terrific sense of humor" has become a kind of shorthand for "physically unattractive." We have come to believe that, as Joan Rivers once said, "There was never a funny woman who was a beautiful little girl." It seems unlikely, however, that this was ever true, especially when we think of the wonderful lines from the likes of eighteenth-century courtesans to Mae West and beyond.

Erma Bombeck comments on the way a "sense of humor got to be a joke . . . then it got to be a stigma." She explains that personality or a sense of humor never attracted boys, but that if "a girl was stacked she could get a date to take her to have her teeth cleaned." The label she-has-a-terrific-sense-of-humor meant that they were "trying to palm you off with a girl who breathed through her mouth and had a nice tooth." This is perhaps one of the factors contributing to our distrust of being labeled women with a sense of humor. If we have a sense of humor, the myth goes, aren't we making up for a lack of some other more acceptable or desirable quality? Don't you cultivate a sense of humor only when you're left dateless on a Friday night and need to cultivate something—anything—useful?

If the first thing someone says about a woman is that she has a sense of humor, too often the stereotyped image that comes to mind is a vulgarly dressed, big-mouthed, shrill-voiced, bingo-playing redhead who will slap her hands down on the table every time she laughs at her own bad jokes. We think of the leopard-print-hatted character played by Andrea Martin whose nasal voice whines through one clichéd punch line after another. We think of a female version of Buddy Hackett or Don Rickles— not a nice thought. We don't think of the "real" funny women we know, meaning most of the women we know. Once again, it's a situation similar to the one that existed in the sixties and seventies, when the idea of a businesswoman or career girl called up visions of big-footed, bushy-haired, fedora-wearing women who mostly resembled the prison matrons depicted in B movies. Now when we think of women in business, we think of *ourselves* and it doesn't seem odd at all. The same switch needs to occur with labeling someone as "a woman with a sense of humor." It should mean a typical rather than an atypical woman, and it should conjure up a picture of a confident, poised, successful woman wearing the perfect pair of red shoes.

Unhealthy Uses of Humor

One of the ways humor can work against us is when we use it falsely, when we use it to mask rather than to change our emotions. When humor comes out of a true lack of self-confidence, rather than being drawn from a solid basis of belief in one's self, the results can be hurtful. The woman who believes that *only* by placing her experience in a comic frame will she be acceptable has learned to use humor in a manner that will ultimately frustrate her, because she probably will not be taken seriously even when she needs to be. Fanny Brice, the vaudeville performer whose life was the model for the film *Funny Girl,* explained one of the risks of being funny *all* the time: "Being a funny person does an awful lot of things to you. You feel that you musn't get serious with people. They don't expect it from you, and they don't want to see it. You're not entitled to be serious, you're a clown, and they only want you to make them laugh."

There's a woman I worked with several years ago whom I'll call Carol. Carol was in love, but it was the foot-in-the-mouth-head-over-heels-punch-in-the-stomach kind of obsessional love that leads to some bad ends. Not typically a clowning girl, Carol became obsessed with a man who could deal with her *only* if she was entertaining and amusing him. He never made time for her when she expressed any depression or need. She worked at being funny as other women work at making quilts—looking for scraps and putting them together with enormous attention to detail.

Giving Away the Best Lines

Carol, in fact, would often do what a number of other women have told me they've done: attribute their own funny lines to other people. It's the opposite of plagiarism. Instead of taking other people's material and pretending it's your own, you take your own and pretend you got it from somebody else. "I didn't want to seem like I had an answer to everything. I suppose I didn't want to seem like I was working as hard as I was at keeping the thing together," says Carol, three years after the breakup of her relationship. "So I'd tell him a story about a neighbor, a school friend, anybody besides me. He'd get nervous if I spoke too much about myself." Carol realized, after months of frenzied smiling, that the relationship couldn't work if she had to be the jester the whole time. "I started to realize that I had to learn to speak straight, too. I knew it was over when I started to lose my sense of humor. He'd laugh and I just couldn't supply the next line. I was tired of putting my own troubles on hold and words into other people's mouths."

Carol's lover was waiting for Carol to devalue her own worth through her humor, a bad sign. He liked it when she joked about herself, and even introduced her to his friends as someone who could, in the British phrase, "take the piss out of herself," meaning to turn her humor on herself. He would repeat what she said about herself ("When I try on a flowered dress, I don't look like a country girl, I look like an ottoman"), laughing, but of course it sounded different coming from him. He used her humor against her, and she complied by refusing to confront the real problems of the relationship. She relied on her humor not to empower her but to avoid taking control. She learned to disparage herself without keeping a firm grip on her sense of self-esteem.

The greatest female comics have always complained about their lives, and the new performers still do. But from the late sixties through the eighties, things have changed. Carol Leifer's complaint about her ex-husband ("It was a mixed marriage," she confides. "I'm human, he was Klingon") is very different from the tedious repetition of wrongs so familiar to us all—it also differs in an important way from the traditional self-deprecating humor. Leifer's comment does not, it is important to notice, locate her disappointment in something she lacks. She's disappointed, but not in *herself*.

She Who Laughs, Lasts

Often women's humor deals with those subjects traditionally reserved for tragedy: life and death, love and hate, connection and abandonment. A woman's comic novel, for example, can end with the heroine leaving her children, divorcing her husband, and even burning down the house. So end books such as Fay Weldon's *Life and Loves of a She-Devil* and Margaret Atwood's *Lady Oracle*. We laugh and applaud when the modern heroine lights the match, whether that match is literal or metaphoric, seeing it as the only possible path of action. Cynthia Heimel, whose best-sellers *Sex Tips for Girls* and *But Enough About You* contain some of the most incisive comedy available, suggests that "Just below the surface of consciousness, there lurks . . . a subterranean giggle. Nurture it, give it its space, and it will be fruitful and multiply and cheer your days and warm your nights." She advises that, when we are confronted by a situation that can be seen as either terrible or funny, we should see that "It's all funny if you let it be. Even death, the biggest joker of them all." Surely this applies to Gilda Radner's account of her battle with cancer, *It's Always Something*. Radner confronts her own illness and the prospect of her death with the humor that characterized her life.

Cynthia Heimel titles one chapter in *But Enough About You* "In the Abyss." She begins this chapter by quoting Florence Henderson's character from *The Loveboat*—"I don't know whether to kill myself or go bowling." If you can see, in the most obscured curve of your peripheral vision, the way the situation could be funny, you might just be able to save yourself. In Fay Weldon's novel *Female Friends*, the long-suffering Chloe has been taught by her mother only to understand and forgive everyone, without exception. It is the only lesson she learned as a child and the only way she operates in her adult life. She must understand and forgive her mother's helplessness, her friend's betrayals, and her husband's affair with the rather hairy au pair girl. She cannot free herself from the tedious and perpetual tragedy of her life or escape her dependence upon her unloving husband. At least, not until a moment when he is particularly petulant and she sees him clearly as a child spoiled beyond control: "Is she laughing at him?" the narrator asks. "She is. Her victory is complete." Chloe's ability to laugh at her husband, and at herself for having tolerated him for so long, leads to her ability to change her life. Chloe recognizes the funny nature of her situation, and so she is able to view her situation with emotional distance and, therefore, with clarity.

I should emphasize that the two experiences are simultaneous. It is not that Weldon's character has a flash of perspective and then decides to laugh. Her laughter and the brilliant flare of recognition feed each other in a delightful conflagration. Chloe sees that the man she had once endowed with enormous significance and power is really pretty feeble. Hers is the simple form of laughter that proceeds out of a misperception of scale, when something that seemed enormous and frightening turns out to be tiny and harmless.

There is laughter in the relief that occurs when you realize you've misinterpreted what someone's said. You can make a joke out of a misunderstanding as long as the misunderstanding works in your favor. I remember once being enormously disappointed when a man I thought was dating me exclusively seemed to indicate that during the one vacation he had all year he was going to see another woman. "I want to see Virginia," he told me. Immediately my defensive/jealous/paranoid self took over and I got busy telling him that, although it had been fun, I was not about to stay involved when he obviously couldn't be faithful, when there had been another woman whose name I hadn't even heard before now. . . . I couldn't bring myself to be anything but incredibly angry. If you'd told me I'd ever laugh again I would have smacked you. This poor guy had started looking progressively more puzzled and unhappy until he realized what I was going on about, and then he interrupted and explained that he meant the *state* of Virginia. We burst out laughing, both of us relieved to avoid a fight. (Later he did visit another woman, but her name was Tammy.) So laughter occurs when you regain your sense of perspective, when you defuse a situation the way you'd defuse a bomb. In *Female Friends*, it's Chloe's understanding that her husband, Oliver, is an emotional hand puppet rather than a monster that makes her laugh and allows her finally to respond to Oliver's cry of "You can't leave me" with the triumphant line "I can, I can and I will."

Gender and the Joke
. . . .

It should be noted that many women stand-up comics reflect back to us our own experiences by depending on these tragic situations for their material. Since much of the material done by professional women comics is still very reminiscent of women's everyday conversation, it is a small leap to move from their script to our own. When Rita Rudner tells us "My boyfriend and I broke up. He wanted to get married . . . and I didn't want him to," the surprise of the punch line dislocates us for a moment—it is not what we were expecting to hear—and then shocks us into awareness. It is interesting to imagine how differently that joke would operate if the genders were switched, if a male comic said "My girlfriend and I broke up. She wanted to get married, and I didn't want her to." The joke changes when the pronoun does. When told by a woman, the joke operates one way, is "framed" by one set of cultural expectations. We hear the joke's premise: she and her boyfriend broke up. Then we hear that he wanted to get married and we think (despite my most militant feminism, I still think this, mea culpa) that it's odd that they should break up if he wants to get married, because women are the ones expected to want to get married. Then we hear that he's marrying another woman and we read the incongruity another way—the joke doesn't break the frame by saying that the woman doesn't want to get married (which would be a real step forward), but rather, it breaks the frame of sexual exclusivity. It isn't marriage she's against, it's somebody else's marriage to her boyfriend that doesn't sound so great.

In a way it's our own feminism that's surprised. We might feel a pique of our interest when we hear she turns down a proposal, only to be shocked to hear that she never got one. At least not a marriage proposal. If a man told the joke, we would be so surprised to hear that his girlfriend expected to have both a lover and a husband that the joke would seem untenable and would lose its impact. The premise is less likely, less recognizable, and so less funny. The humor that is most appreciated is humor that works from a likely premise, an instantly recognizable scenario.

Certain jokes about women, when they are told by women, have a completely different impact than when they are delivered by the traditional male comic. Carol Leifer does a routine about how she wants to have children—"so that I can be called Mama by someone other than strange men on the street." She goes on to explain that she hasn't had any children yet: "At least none that I *know* of. . . ." This turn on the traditional masculine brag that implies a man has slept with so many women he's bound to have an illegitimate child somewhere becomes wonderfully absurd when said by a woman, who (no matter how many men *she's* slept with) could not have a child without knowing it.

A great deal of traditional humor has depended on a surprise switch of masculine and feminine roles. We've all seen shows like *Bosom Buddies,* where guys put on falsies and pretend to be women. As the cartoonist Nicole Hollander has noted, one of the things men find funny is other men dressed as women but with their hairy legs showing. We still have programs like *She's the Sheriff,* which depend on the woman cop being a cute blonde in a tight uniform. (Is that a pistol in her pocket or is she just happy to see us?) The humor of these shows depends on the cliché that women cannot be put into positions of authority without being adorably inept. They can dress up like the boss, but what they really need is a good man around to pick up the pieces. That such a program can be popular in the late 1980s, after we've seen such shows as *Cagney and Lacey* and *Hill Street Blues,* with their admirable women officers, shows how long it takes stereotypes to disappear. A few clichéd ideas about women have changed enough, however, so that a program called *She's the Lawyer* or *She's the Editor* would not in itself raise a laugh.

There are jokes that we associate completely with the sex of the teller. According to Dr. Bernice Sandler, director of the Project on the Status and Education of Women at the Association of American Colleges, who has been collecting gender-based jokes for years, there are no father-in-law jokes. "Have you ever heard of a father-in-law joke? Never. I've offered audiences around the country a reward if they could come up with a viable father-in-law joke. So far nobody's collected." Consider all the other jokes that depend on gender. Has anybody ever asked you "Who was that gentleman I saw you with last night?" so that you can answer "That was no gentleman, that was my husband"?

The Challenge of Humor

Minna Antrim, a turn-of-the-century writer, claimed that "Man forgives woman anything save the wit to outwit him." A woman who jokes with a man may find herself faced by a man who sees her wit as a challenge. That challenge can be very positive. When the anchorwoman Connie Chung was asked a fairly insensitive question by a new co-worker about the relationship between her position as an Asian-American woman and her rapid rise in the field, her response was both pointed and humorous: "I pointed to the senior vice president and announced, 'Bill likes the way I do his shirts.'" Chung's reply is the sort of response we all wish we had at the tip of our tongues. Delivered with the right touch, she could both instruct her questioner (Her answer implies: "That was a pretty racist statement") and show that the question was not even worth dealing with seriously. Anybody who can come up with such a quick and perfect response hardly needs to justify her position.

At times we make jokes of our own in rooms of our own, among only those people we know will share our view of the world. But we can see from the way the material supplied by fiction writers, screenwriters, and stand-up comics has changed that we might have to hide our laughter less these days than we did twenty years ago, laughing in the living room (or the boardroom) instead of confining ourselves to the kitchen. Spending your life as an adult woman listening to other people make jokes is the equivalent of spending your childhood watching other kids play. Having a sense of humor means making a joke, not just listening to ones made by other people. Valuing your sense of humor means telling a story, having a sense of delight that is really your own. It means trusting that someone else will share your laughter. As in so many other areas of life, women have come to see themselves as the observers of performances given by men. But being an audience member is not enough, however much we enjoy seeing other people's pleasure. Having a sense of humor is like playing—you've got to do it, be part of it, to enjoy it fully. And the enjoyment is there for the taking, even though very little attention has been given to the tradition of women's humor.

I've written this book keeping in mind the kinds of women I know: for the high school girl who needs to know that she can make a joke in class and still get a date; for the college student who needs reassurance that she doesn't have to laugh at the sexist humor of the professor or the fraternity jock, because she's confident that she can distinguish what's funny from what isn't; for the woman at the corporate health club who would like to have at her fingertips the confidence that her witticisms are welcome and impressive; for the mother who will see that the comedy in her daily life is part of a long-standing tradition and that she is in excellent company; for the corporate executive who delineates the perimeters of acceptable humor in the workplace; for all the women who have laughed themselves silly leaning on bathroom and kitchen sinks who are eager to integrate the pleasure of their humor into the other, more public, areas of their lives.

Of course, it will surprise very few women to hear that women have a sense of humor, and probably will no longer come as a shock to most men. But to see the way wit functions is to see a map of our culture: to focus on things we've seen but not necessarily processed or analyzed, explaining what we've sensed but not yet bothered to define. We have finally arrived at a point where both Good Girls and Bad Girls can laugh out loud.

2

Do Good Girls Laugh with Their Mouths Open?

• • • • • • • • • • • • • • • • • • • •

Why Making a Joke Is Like Making a Pass

Cathy adores a minuet, the Ballet Russe and crêpes suzette,
But Patty loves to rock and roll, a hot dog makes her lose
* control.*
What a wild duet!

But they're cousins,
Identical cousins,
And you'll find
They laugh alike, they walk alike,
At times they even talk alike.
You can lose your mind
When cousins are two of a kind.

The Identical-Cousin Syndrome
• •

It's a wonder we didn't lose our minds, given the outrageous premise of a TV program that promised identical cousins. What isn't surprising is that the producers made sure the song prefaced every episode of *The Patty Duke Show*, since it explained the relationship between the two girls. Cathy, brought up in England and "abroad," had a posh accent and fancy tastes (for crêpes suzette), in contrast to Patty, who chewed gum incessantly and could be counted on to mess up at least once during every program. The primary recognizable difference between the two was that Cathy wore her hair in a pageboy, the curl turned under. Patty had hers in a flip, like the one sported by Marilyn Quayle. This hair device worked well for a number of reasons, not the least of which was that when one cousin faced the camera, we saw only the back of the other's head, coiffure intact. In addition, Cathy typically looked out from underneath her eyelashes and tilted her head while listening to someone else speak, whereas Patty looked straight up and snapped her gum while she spoke. Cathy was the great listener, a hallmark characteristic of the Good Girl. Patty was the fast talker who often had to ask people to repeat what they'd said because she wasn't listening carefully, a sure sign of the Bad Girl. Cathy listened to classical music, and Patty's father would sigh and say "I hope some of Cathy's good taste rubs off on Patty!" because Patty enjoyed loud and raucous rock music by the likes of Chad and Jeremy and Bobby Vinton. Patty would occasionally have to lock Cathy in the closet so that she could pretend to be her (all true), and Cathy's response was to sigh and say "I shouldn't let her do this to me, but I will because I know how easy it is to get carried away." It is interesting to note that the Bad Girl locks up the Good Girl in this plot. In their landmark book *The Madwoman in the Attic*, Professors Sandra Gilbert and Susan Gubar discuss in some detail the literary convention that forces the good heroine to keep the bad woman locked away, much as Rochester's first wife is kept under lock and key in *Jane Eyre*. Gilbert and Gubar argue that the angry madwoman is the flip side of the gentle, docile heroine, and that both of these aspects of female identity come into play for the author, and for women generally. If Cathy from *The Patty Duke Show* knew anything about getting carried away, she knew it because of her identical cousin's experiences, not her own. She was the Good Girl through acquiescence, through passivity. Being a Good Girl requires inaction. Being Bad, like Patty, depends on action, doing something—almost on doing *anything,* since passivity was the single most important requirement for being Good. Thus the two characters from *The Patty Duke Show* illustrate perfectly the split between the Good and Bad Girl.

Patty Duke, already a well-established actress (she won an Oscar for her portrayal of Helen Keller in the film *The Miracle Worker*), played both roles. So there was a double weirdness in operation—one actress played two girls, who would then play each other, pretending to be one girl. *The Patty Duke Show* was certainly a favorite among my girlfriends, and not only because most of us, like Patty, had "only seen the sights a girl could see from Brooklyn Heights." We were essentially neither good nor bad, but a mixture of both. We were certainly more like Patty than Cathy. But we tried to behave like Cathy, because we knew that she was the more feminine and so the more desirable. If we acted out versions of the show in somebody's garage, there was always a fight over who would be Cathy. Getting stuck playing Patty was almost as bad as having to play one of the boys (nobody wanted to do that), and this in itself is interesting in retrospect. So why did we like the program in the first place? What keeps us watching the reruns?

I think the program's popularity was based on what could be called the Identical-Cousin Syndrome. The Identical-Cousin Syndrome (ICS) is the explicit working out of the Good Girl/ Bad Girl split discussed in the first chapter. The Good Girl/Bad Girl split presupposes that any one woman cannot be both sweet and wicked, nice and bitchy, generous and selfish. We know that traditional heroes, for example, can be both brave and cowardly, mean and melting—a hero is hardly a hero without a measure of vulnerability. Mel Gibson plays characters wronged by fate, and we long to reassure him that the world still holds pleasure. Dennis Quaid looks like a little kid with a silly grin, and we want to muss his hair. Michael Douglas looks like a dumb jock who can be redeemed. David Bowie looks as if he's just come off heavy medication, but that doesn't stop him from being attractive. The masculine hero has within him a feminine, vulnerable side. But women are not allowed to have a tough, masculine side; women are not, as Professor Sarah Blacher Cohen has written, permitted to have chutzpah, even metaphorically. Women are supposed to be all woman, or, what's even worse, the "total woman." The Good Girl/Bad Girl split is the division of woman into two parts that seem never to meet: madonna and whore, angel and seductress. Heroines, unlike heroes, are not allowed to show any emotional cleavage.

The Patty Duke Show, of course, was the embodiment of the Identical-Cousin Syndrome. Cathy was the perfectly Good Girl, even better than Annette Funicello, because she spoke with an English accent and often wore little white gloves. Patty, after all, didn't behave that badly (put it this way: she came home late, but she never got pregnant), but she was as close as mid-sixties television could get to the Bad Girl. She was loud, uncouth, and, most important, she expressed her emotions openly. She would not only laugh out loud, she would even laugh at her own jokes. She would yell if angry, be bad if irritated. If her boyfriend said something stupid, as often as not she'd whack him on the forearm. Patty and Richard were destined to be the losing couple on *The Newlywed Game.*

Patty wouldn't put up with very much abuse, and she protested against what she considered to be injustice—although in those days "injustice" was limited to a plain but sweet girlfriend not being invited to a party or to a dumb but sweet girlfriend getting a bad grade. Patty would devise a scheme to right the wrong and would follow her own enthusiastic but misguided initiative. Then she would fail. She would fail because she would get carried away—Patty's strong emotions or ideas would trip her up. Cathy, the eternal moderate, the Melanie (from *Gone With the Wind*) of the program, would be called in like some member of Miss Manners's cavalry to rescue her cousin. Cathy would turn her pageboy into a flip, put a slightly guttural twang into her voice, and "become" Patty. She could then attend the benefit fund-raiser for the Brooklyn Botanic Garden and know which fork to use (Patty, presumably, would use the forks to tease her hair). Cathy could be counted on to speak to the vice principal calmly, whereas Patty would roll her eyes or crack an inappropriate joke. Cathy could be counted on not to laugh at the wrong moments. She never lost control, not over a hot dog, not over anything.

Good Girl / Bad Girl Prototypes

An earlier cinematic prototype for the Good Girl/Bad Girl division is Scarlett O'Hara and her rival (and sister-in-law), Melanie Wilkes. Scarlett is, as Rhett Butler puts it, "no lady," but as a direct consequence, she does have the best lines in the film. This is in spite of her protest "If I wasn't a lady, what wouldn't I say. . . ." Scarlett, for example, taps her feet to dance music even as she wears mourning for her first husband. Scarlett wants "everyone who's been mean to me to feel bad." No apologies, no hesitations—Scarlett wants what she wants. She tries to hide herself behind convention to get what she wants, batting her eyelashes and being sweet when absolutely required. But just as Rhett can take her hand, turn it over, and see that Scarlett has been working in the fields, so the audience can take the sweet disguise, turn it over, and realize that Scarlett is play-acting at being a Good Girl. Calluses and character will out in the end. In contrast, Melanie is genuinely sweet and never narrows her eyes in jealousy or desire (unlike Scarlett), and as a consequence she has no good lines—but she *does* have for a husband the man Scarlett loves. Interestingly, Helen Taylor's study *Scarlett's Women: Gone With the Wind and Its Female Fans* presents responses to two questionnaires, one given to high school girls in 1957 and a follow-up given to high school girls in the mid-

1980s. In 1957, when tenth-grade students were asked which character they most identified with, eighty percent cited Melanie. In the later group, the vast majority of the girls expressed their allegiance to Scarlett. Clearly, Bad Girl Scarlett was always the object of attention in the film, but it was not until very recently that girls could declare openly their admiration for such a character. The Bad Girl has only recently been granted permission to be the heroine. However, the definition of fiction, to paraphrase Oscar Wilde, is that Good Girls end happily and Bad Girls end unhappily. In real life, to the great relief of most of us, the prizes are awarded more haphazardly.

The Patty Duke Show was not the first or the only version of this Good Girl/Bad Girl plot on television. In sixties television, for example, other humorous Good Girl/Bad Girl "doubles" occurred in the programs *Bewitched* and *I Dream of Jeannie*. In both these programs, the main female character had a Bad Girl double whose main function was to say all the things the Good Girl couldn't say. In *Jeannie,* Barbara Eden played a magical girl in a bottle attached to an unmagical military man. She was occasionally bottled up by a wicked double who was seductive and sarcastic. The nice Jeannie would beat tiny fists against the velvet-lined walls of her bottle until the military man realized the mistake and rebuked the substitute, getting back the sexy but subdued original whose bosom heaved only slightly under the veils, in contrast to her counterpart, whose bosom seemed, somehow, more prominent.

Samantha was the name of the sorceress-turned-good-wife played by Elizabeth Montgomery in *Bewitched*. Known as "Sam" (which made for some interesting mixups, of course, since her husband, Darren, often identified her to strangers by this name), this witch had promised her advertising-executive husband not to practice magic after their marriage. Sam swore that she'd play straight and give up all her supernatural powers in order to be a "regular" wife, like any other housewife on the block. It was important to Darren that his wife not be different—

in other words, not be an individual, but one of a type. It is tempting to equate marriage in *Bewitched* with the end of all magic or, even more precisely, to see Sam as symbolic of the woman who loses all her own power and personality after she walks down the aisle. Darren didn't want her to use her powers because it made her too different, too scary, too formidable a partner. He wanted a marriage of equals, with him on top, so to speak. Sam's powers made life too unfair. Darren wanted to rise to the top of his profession based on his own talent and not because his wife put him there. Sam had to cook meals legitimately, sew her own clothes, and save pennies even though she could have wrinkled her nose and ordered food in from Lutèce, clothes from Chanel, and jewels from Tiffany. If goodness depends on renunciation, then Sam was certainly a Good Girl.

But Sam had a dark-haired, nearly identical bitchy sister, Serena. Serena, also played by Montgomery, could be distinguished from Sam by her dark hair, great pop-culture clothes, miniskirts, and polka-dot vinyl boots, while Sam still wore Donna Reed dresses. Serena was definitely a Bad Girl, appearing in Darren's den uninvited, riding a Harley, and wearing leather shorts. Darren, unlike the male viewers of such a scene, did not appreciate Serena's presence, because she was a Bad Influence on his wife and represented the coven—a metaphoric as well as literal coven—of female relatives who might draw Sam back into using her magic. Serena particularly annoyed Darren by routinely saying all the things Sam couldn't say. For example, Darren would forbid (!) Sam to take offense at an offensive client. Serena would attend the dinner party, invisible, and make cutting remarks attributed unfairly to Sam. The dark sister made the jokes and had the fun. Sam smiled at the boss, smiled at her husband, and had her Bad Girl double make fun of them both. Serena would certainly make jokes herself, but she never took jokes very well. Serena, blissfully single, did not have to rein in her powers. Cross her, and you could end up as a poodle scratching on the patio door. Sometimes it was as if Serena acted the part of a ventriloquist, apparently putting wonderfully sarcastic and cutting remarks into the mouth of Good Girl Samantha. Sam, wrongly accused of saying something bitchy, would then have to rise to her own defense. Often Serena was a catalyst for Sam's speaking up for herself. Even when she didn't speak to the issues, Sam, like Annette, Cathy, and the other Good Girls, would frown at Bad Behavior and yet manage, somehow, to wink and nod in complicity. The Good Girl and Bad Girl are not as far apart as they might appear to be at first glance.

Control is the quality most explicitly associated with Good Girls. Like a beautiful vase, the Good Girl can be counted on to decorate any room without calling too much attention to herself. Decorum and poise, the ability to be both demure and self-possessed, these are the trademarks of the Good Girl. She is mature but never precocious. She is affable and easy to please. Immune to temptation, the Good Girl can be counted on to have a sobering influence on any group by her very presence. Good Girls don't swear, sweat, succumb, or satirize.

Does the Good Girl, in Fact, Exist?

We can deduce from this catalogue of characteristics that there are, in fact, no Good Girls in real life. Everybody sweats. We carry around with us the idea about what a Good Girl is meant to be, and this image torments us without giving us much help. It's like having a Barbie doll as a role model: attractive but sexless. Appealing but ultimately nongenerative. Nobody—nobody—looks like a Barbie. And nobody is a Good Girl all the time.

Bad Girls don't necessarily swear, sweat, succumb, or satirize (and only really Bad Girls do all four at once), but they can be counted on to make a little trouble. If the quality associated with Good Girls is control, then the quality most explicitly associated with Bad Girls is excess. Bad Girls overdo things, make messes, and are generally reluctant to control themselves. "Bad" can refer to more than toughness, smartness, or even sexual awareness. Being a Bad Girl can mean being anything "unfeminine"—messy, clumsy, loud, opinionated, physically strong, physically fit, angry, or frustrated. Anything, in other words, "human," as opposed to feminine. (However, it should be mentioned that as far back as Plato, people have been warned not to "abandon themselves to violent laughter." For Aristotle, the idea of excess was associated with vulgarity and was condemned. There is a long tradition behind the idea of laughter as dangerous, and this condemnation is compounded by the fact that what is dangerous or outrageous for a man is considered even worse in a woman.) Women are taught to be like Mrs. Kenny Rogers, described by Cathy—and Mo—in *The Cathy and Mo Show*. Mrs. Rogers is supposed to "be strong, in a weak and vulnerable kind of way," as well as being "independent, but without crossing that line to be unappealing." Women are supposed to be attractive without being disturbingly so, perceptive without being intelligent, and good at details without being practical. Women are never supposed to be too much of any one thing.

It is only through comedy that many women can be excessive and get away with it. This delight in excess is at the heart of a character like Lucy Ricardo in *I Love Lucy*. Lucy was indeed an interesting Bad Girl figure, because her character was presented as a good wife and loving mother, but these domestic elements did not prevent her from wanting *more*. (Lucille Ball has been quoted as saying "I believe a woman's place is in the home—or anyway, in some cozy nightclub.") Almost all episodes of *Lucy* deal with some manifestation of Lucy's excess— excess ambition (wanting to be in Ricky's chorus at the club or perhaps manufacturing her own line of salad dressing), excess desire for attention (wanting to be accepted by her insidiously self-controlled neighbors after they move to the country, wanting to be the lead in the community-charity pageant), excess jealousy, envy, suspicion, longing, desire. Lucy's character was built around her having to learn and relearn in each episode to contain herself or pay the price. The price was "learning the hard way": that is, Lucy tried and failed—much more like Bad Girl Patty than Cathy—despite her marriage and children. Lucy wanted to *do* things—she wasn't content only to play house with big and little Ricky, keeping the apartment clean and cooking balanced meals. That she wasn't content with domestic passivity is the source of the show's humor. Her desire for activity outside the domestic sphere was portrayed as funny, because surely a woman who had everything—husband, house, child, leisure—didn't need anything else. The mechanism of each plot had to take Lucy through her ambition and deposit her safely back into domesticity—at least until the next show. She had to learn, like Dorothy in *The Wizard of Oz,* that there's no place like home. She had to discover that she couldn't keep pace with the dancers or with the candy factory's assembly line when she and Ethel tried their hand at working for a living.

But there is an interesting paradox to all of this: it was Lucy's Bad side that endeared her to us. Her lack of self-control and her inability to contain herself in her role, no matter how hard she tried, made us watch her for thirty years. If she had been someone who just wanted to stay home, then there wouldn't have been a story. Nobody would have watched a show based on Cathy or a movie based on Melanie. The Bad Girls are the only ones with a story to tell. As the Victorian author George Eliot (Mary Ann Evans) wrote a hundred years ago, "The happiest women, like the happiest nations, have no history." The stories we want to hear are the ones where something happens. If something happens, you can be sure there's a Bad Girl somewhere in the picture.

Lucy's Bad Girl kept trying to push the Good Girl out of the way so that she could step into the spotlight. The recent TV program *Roseanne* takes up where *Lucy* left off. The show owes its popularity, at least in part, to Roseanne Barr's allowing the

Bad Girl to win in the struggle between Bad Girl and Good Wife in the character she portrays. Roseanne's character differs from Lucy's in that she doesn't even try to achieve perfection ("If it's five o'clock and those kids are still alive—hey, I've done my job"), and she doesn't have to be taught a lesson every week. Roseanne, with her acid tongue and hilariously bitter commentary, is more like the Bad Girl trying, if anything, to disguise her Good side.

Penny Marshall of the popular seventies television program *Laverne and Shirley,* and now one of the most successful Hollywood producers and directors (she directed *Big,* starring Tom Hanks), says that she found "that except for women like Lucille Ball or Carol Burnett, the girl was the neat and clean person. Mary Tyler Moore didn't fall down too much." Falling down is like laughing with your mouth open—it's one of the things girls aren't allowed to do. And although *The Mary Tyler Moore Show* broke a great many stereotypes about women and humor (an unmarried female character does not have to spend *all* her time looking for a boyfriend), it still presented Rhoda as a sort of Bad cousin to Mary. Mary wouldn't fall down or get dirty; she wouldn't break her diet or break her teacups. But Rhoda made jokes about applying the chocolate mousse directly to her thighs. Rhoda could overdo things by being too passionate, too eager, too hungry, too much herself. The Bad Girl/Good Girl split has been engraved in our hearts by years of television, movies, and books.

Bad Girls Initiate Humor

Bad Girls say what they think. This is particularly important because what the Bad Girl says out loud is usually the same thing that everybody else is thinking but is too ashamed to admit. This is often at the heart of women's humor—the ability to say out loud what nobody thought a girl was allowed to think, let alone say.

We were taught that only Bad Girls initiated humor. Or, to be more precise, Bad Girls used their humor when boys were around—because even Good Girls would risk a joke in an all-female group. An interesting point about this concept is that it is not particularly American. In communities throughout the world, according to the anthropologist Matadev Apte, women who tell jokes are regarded as sexually promiscuous. The connection between humor and sexual invitation is made up of many links, among them the thought that it takes a certain "fallen" knowledge to make a joke. Women in some Greek and Italian villages, for example, are considered less than virtuous if they so much as laugh aloud in mixed company. Only old women—or women who are somehow outside the sexual marketplace—are permitted to make lewd remarks. Their age diffuses the sexual implications and nullifies their mock "advances." The same thing seems to go on at any large wedding—don't the old aunts always make unbelievably personal remarks, which the bridesmaids would never risk in mixed company? The old aunts can joke about bringing five extra pairs of sheets on the honeymoon because they are out of the sexual race and can comment safely from the sidelines. In *Golden Girls,* the character of Sophia, the Sicilian mother of one of the retirement-age women, makes the most obviously and cynically sexual jokes. She shocks her fifty-year-old daughter with her uncensored remarks.

A similar pattern can be seen in the way early women comics, like Phyllis Diller or even the early Joan Rivers, set themselves up as unattractive, unappealing creatures. Any comedian knew, if she were sexy, she'd have to disguise the Miss America figure she had in order to be able to make self-deprecating jokes. Since they had turned themselves into "unattractive" characters, any sexual references could be seen as gratuitous, for purposes of amusement only.

A fairly recent example of the Good Girl/Bad Girl split, illustrating how the perception of a sarcastic wit is linked to an assumption of sexual knowledge, is in the character of Rizzo, played by Stockard Channing in the film *Grease*. Sandy, played by the superstar Good Girl Olivia Newton-John (Bad Girls never have hyphenated family names—she was made for the role), has to learn to be funny and sexy and Bad by the end of the film in order to capture the Bad Boy with a heart of gold. (By the way, Bad Girls can also have a heart of gold, but everybody's busy looking elsewhere.) Channing, who spent her energies working Rizzo into a three-dimensional character, has interesting insights into the Good Girl/Bad Girl split inside us all: "Rizzo's character was in the great tradition—the coquette, the wisecracking maid, the whore, the dark woman. . . . What's interesting to me is to take a little bit of the bad woman and a little bit of the pure angel and put them together and see what happens."

The Good Girl/Bad Girl division is not a modern phenomenon in literature. Writers such as Jane Austen created characters like Mary Crawford in *Mansfield Park* who break the rules by flirting and teasing without respect to rank or availability. When a young man begins telling her about the navy, for example, Mary replies that she has "heard enough of Rears and Vices," and that one line has sent Austen scholars on a critical debate lasting years. Mary Crawford, Austen's most self-consciously Bad Girl, is so unnervingly intelligent even in her most flagrant breaches of conduct that practically all the men in the novel fall in love with her. She completely outshines the angelic presence of the character who is supposedly the heroine, leaving the readers of Austen to argue over who emerges as the "true" heroine of the narrative.

Being a Secret Bad Girl

When Erica Jong writes in *Fear of Flying* that "Bigamy is having one husband too many. Monogamy is the same," we laugh out of a sense of recognition of our own secret thoughts. We wouldn't dare let ourselves think such a thing about our sweet spouses, but our laughter hints at some moment of doubt we have experienced somewhere over the years. When Cynthia Heimel writes an article called "Fear of Dating," she tells us, to our faces and without apology, all of our secret fears: "Not one thing on my mind will be a suitable topic of conversation. 'Do you think we'll sleep together tonight?' 'Are you one of those guys who can't make a commitment? Or can only make a commitment to a woman with really smooth, finely muscled thighs?' 'Is my deodorant working?' 'What kind of relationship did you have with your mother?' 'Do you like me?' 'How much do you like me?' 'Are you sure you really like me?' " We laugh at Heimel's remarks because we see mirrored in them the deepest of our own fears, those fears that can seem funny only when someone else says them aloud. If you are really worried about your own thighs, it's hard to laugh about them until you hear how funny it sounds when somebody else is worried about hers. When Glenda Jackson explains that "The important thing in acting is to be able to laugh and cry. If I have to cry, I think of my sex life. If I have to laugh, I think of my sex life," we laugh because she is exposing a feeling many women have shared, if not articulated.

When, as Julia Klein writes in *Ms.* magazine, Abby Stein does her stand-up routine, she expresses the sentiments felt but unspoken by many women in the audience. "I have this thing where I'm attracted to incredibly sleazy men," Stein confesses. She'd love to go to bed with one of them—"if I can shoot him in the head afterwards. Because if he tells anyone I slept with him, I'll have to move off *earth*." Women are not supposed to want to sleep with men whose overall demeanor horrifies them—women are not supposed to express desire for men based on physical needs alone.

By admitting her attraction to sleazy men, Stein identifies herself as a Bad Girl and enables us to share her censure of herself. She is immune from our genuine condemnation for two reasons: she told on herself first, and she admits out loud something we've all thought but would never admit aloud.

She's already in trouble for wanting to bed this character, but she's both better and worse for saying it out loud. She's worse because we're supposed to keep this stuff quiet and hidden. She's better because she's got the courage to say it and better because she lets us off the hook. We laugh at her and at ourselves, because by laughing we are once again showing that we got the joke. It wouldn't be funny if you never felt it, if there had never been a man you wanted desperately to kiss, in part just to keep him from saying something dumb. The comic Beverly Mickins makes fun of the lines men use to get women into bed—"Please, I'll only put it in for a minute." She replies with "What does he think I am, a microwave?" The laughter depends on our response of recognition. By recognizing her references, we're complying with the premise that we've gone through it too. Or at least that we understand it. We're Bad, and whoever is making us laugh is our group leader.

Shared Experiences as a Basis for Humor

In part, humor depends on our complicity, because so many of the workings of humor lose impact when they are explained. For the humor to work, there has to be a shared basis of particular experience—one of the reasons comedy doesn't seem as eternal as tragedy is because comedy often relies on getting a particular play with words or the overturning of a particular rule. It also depends on gauging your audience accurately. The shared experience of humor relies on the creation of the right sort of context. In her memoirs, *Kiss Hollywood Good-by*, Anita Loos discusses the film *Redheaded Woman*, which she scripted for MGM. Loos describes the movie as having outraged "ladies' clubs throughout the land" because "Our heroine, the bad girl of whom all good husbands dream, ended her career as many such scalawags do, rich, happy, and respected, without ever having paid for her sins." But, most important, the film became a major hit only after Loos included a prologue "to tip the audience off that the movie's a comedy." Since the plot centered on the breakup of a marriage, the preview audiences were not sure how to respond. Isn't such a topic tragic? One of the directors argued, "You can't make jokes about a girl who deliberately sets out to break up a family," to which Loos replied, "Look at the family! It deserves to be broken up!" Loos included a brief opening scene where the heroine, played by Jean Harlow, tries on a dress in a shop. She asks the saleswoman, "Is this dress too tight?" The clerk says that indeed it is, and Harlow replies "Good!" as she buys the garment. She then turns to the camera and winks, signaling a complicity between the main character and the audience members, as well as indicating that it's all in fun—if not necessarily all in "good" fun. The 1933 audience obviously felt better knowing it was okay to laugh. They had the film's permission to find laughable something usually considered an unfit topic for laughter.

When you realize why something is funny and then realize that you are permitted to laugh, the moment is characterized by a sense of delight and, importantly, relief. I remember all the years I grew up watching reruns of old Mae West movies without understanding them. I must have been about twelve—about the time of the auspicious, scientific slumber party—when the point (so to speak) of the line "Is that a pistol in your pocket or are you just happy to see me?" became clear.

Subverting Authority Through Laughter

We must be aware that when women use humor, there is always the risk of being misunderstood. There is also the even larger risk of not being understood at all, with the attendant danger of then having to explain what was so funny. Remember when you'd laugh at something forbidden in school—laugh when the teacher was talking or when a social studies film strip was being shown, when all the fruit flies died in science class, when the principal was giving a speech? You (and probably at least one other collaborator) would suddenly realize that you'd been caught. Then came the horrible, sweaty experience of having to reply to the question "All right, *young lady,* tell us all what exactly you find so funny in all of this. I'm sure we'd all like to laugh. . . ." But of course you couldn't explain anything; you felt as if you'd never be able to explain anything else as long as you lived, and for sure nothing ever would be funny again, ever.

There was irony, always, in being called a "young lady," because it was obvious that no *lady* would've laughed at the lines in Tennyson that read "the curse has come upon me." Or think that *Moby Dick* was really an amazing title for a book. You, your friend, and some weird boy from another neighborhood were the only ones who laughed, who couldn't control yourselves, even though *you knew for a fact* that every other kid in the class also snickered inside at the same lines. It was only that you dared to laugh out loud that got you into trouble—and only if you could be singled out as somebody who laughed either louder or longer than your peers. If you drew attention to yourself, seemed excessive, made a spectacle out of yourself, you called down the wrath of the authorities on your head.

Laughing out loud or making a joke in class, in front of adults (or, more often and more precisely, behind the backs of adults), showed "disrespect," that word that was always said in a hush to give it the full weight of disapproval. They were right, when you think about it; your laughter did show disrespect. It is evidence that you know enough not to take something too seriously, that you know enough to trust your own responses rather than to fear someone else's.

To return to an earlier example, you know it's a hand puppet instead of a monster, and your awareness is showing. If your sense of humor shows, it can endanger the authority of the hand puppet, because other people will realize that there's nothing to be afraid of. It's like the moment in *The Wizard of Oz* when they realize that the scary, smoky, gigantic wizard is just the machine controlled by an old man working some levers. "Ignore the man behind the curtain," shouts the wizard, but our fear has already been transformed into smiling relief, and the terror cannot reassert itself. You can imitate but not renew power once it is lost. Prolonged and outright laughter shows that you are able to let yourself lose control, if only for a moment, and therefore surprisingly illustrates how very much in control of yourself you really are. If you can laugh at your enemy, in other words, you are in the position of power.

There have been a number of theories concerning the laughter of the jailed against the jailors in both the literal and metaphoric sense. Nancy Walker, in her book *A Very Serious Thing: Women's Humor and American Culture*, devotes a chapter to the "Humor of the Minority." Professor Walker discusses the way women's humor, particularly humor created by women of color, operates by treating the dominant, white male culture as being a strict stereotype, allowing for a "we-they dialectic." Walker suggests that "Women's humor, like that of minorities, is usually expressed within the group, rather than in mixed company . . . and [when in print] in publications intended primarily for other women." Walker concludes that this sort of humor "is frequently a means of dealing with frustration or anger, rather than simply celebratory or fun." Dominique Moisi, deputy director of the French Institute of International Relations in Paris, argues that "the more you're scared, the more you have to create jokes," even, on occasion, jokes about your own oppression. Judith Wilt, a professor of English at Boston College, writes in a 1980 article titled "The Laughter of Maidens, the Cackle of Matriarchs" that "Comedy is an archetypal carrier of anger up to a point, the traditional protection against pain . . . [offering] solace, piling sandbags of wit against the flood of anger and pain."

And when women laugh at their enemies, the laughter is most often directed at authorities. Cathy and Mo open their show by portraying two angels creating human beings. The angels decide, committee format, how humans should reproduce ("If the females have the babies, the men will feel really inferior—we'll give them enormous egos to make up for it") and how humans should live. The angels want to create only one rule: "You can do whatever you want as long as you're willing to get up and do it." But the heavenly bosses, the Big Guy and Cliff, the rule overseer, don't think this rule is enough. When Cathy and Mo use humor, they direct it at any institutional, inflexible body of regulations—whether it's rules set out by God, the church, teenage peer groups, feminist support groups, or vegetarian restaurants. Any set of rules needs needling, needs the perspective that humor can offer. But such effective needling does indeed have an undercurrent of subversion. Those who fear it are right to do so.

Humor, however, is often read reductively as merely disrespect, aggression, or nastiness. This reduces it to a point where it can be easily dismissed, and this can be a problem in that our humor often does reflect larger issues. Anne Beatts, a former *Saturday Night Live* writer, clarifies this point. She also hints at why the case of "disrespect" seems worse in a girl than in a boy. Beatts explains that "When women are funny they're often called bitchy or catty. Women aren't encouraged to be funny. . . . They're afraid to speak out because they're afraid their humor won't be appreciated." She goes on to say that "A nice girl did not call attention to herself. . . . You were allowed to be 'pert'n'perky' but that was it. . . ."

A young director of comedy development for a major studio outlines part of the problem for women who make jokes: "If you've been in a situation where the woman is funny and the man is not, then the woman inevitably commands the attention—at a dinner party, with the relatives, wherever. It's a certain power, and a lot of men don't deal well with it. They'll like somebody else's wife or girlfriend to be funny, but they want boring."

Women Who Use Humor Are Women Who Use Power
· ·

This challenge to the traditional idea of masculine authority is what links the Bad Girl and the feminist—links them together so that, in fact, they are often one and the same person. The Bad Girl laughs at the rule makers and the teachers in this life, and refuses to take their (usually paternalistic) claim to power seriously. The Bad Girl has learned that for someone to have authority over you, you have to give it to him. Not only is she not the "young lady" who has to explain what she's laughing at, she's the one who makes everybody else in the room laugh, to the chagrin of the teacher. Remember when a whole roomful of kids would be laughing themselves sick and some adult was standing, back to the wall, yelling "That's not funny"? When you think about it, the line "That's not funny" makes almost no sense in a certain context. You only say "That's not funny" to people when they're laughing, so obviously there is indeed something funny going on. The point, then, is not to correct wrong information—something *is* undeniably funny—but that the person in the position of authority does not approve of the laughter.

The dynamic of the powerful authority versus the subversive voice is an important one to keep in mind here. The voice of authority, challenged by one joke maker, is different from the authority's own use of the joke against a powerless victim. For example, a teacher telling a group of thirty students "That's not funny" is quite dramatically removed from a single student telling the teacher "That's not funny." The voice of authority assumes control and offers definition; the voice of the minority suggests subversion and redefinition. Joking is a reaction that allows the joker to feel in control, however briefly. When someone in a powerless position laughs at the one holding the reins, the figure of authority is sometimes shocked into an awareness of the tenuous nature of any form of control.

The Bad Girl is going to challenge the emperor's new clothes and point out that he isn't wearing any, even when everybody else is saying how good he looks. The Bad Girl is going to speak up when some injustice is inflicted, when some arbitrary and capricious rule is being enforced. She's going to laugh at somebody who is trying to police her thoughts or actions, and she'll undercut the person's authority by refusing to take him or her seriously. Remember how the very worst thing you could do was laugh at your parents when they were yelling at you? That was the thing that made them the most angry, the thing they couldn't deal with. That's because laughter always indicates a refusal to take authority seriously.

I was at a conference in southern California about five years ago. Everybody was feeling pretty good, the end of the day was near, and we all had wine coolers—not to mention excellent tans. The group was a fair mix of senior academicians, junior faculty, and graduate students. One of the more entertaining of these students was discussing her reactions to Jane Austen's letters. Sharon was retelling some funny lines, we were all chuckling along, it was lovely. That is, until she got to the part where Austen—sweet, mannerly, nearly perfect Jane Austen—writes about a neighbor being "brought to bed yesterday of a dead child . . . owing to a fright." Austen goes on to speculate, "I suppose she happened unawares to look at her husband." It was a bitchy little remark, but we all laughed (more out of surprise than approval of Austen's sentiments)—all but one elderly gentleman, whose silence cut through our reactions like a hot knife through butter. He went red and said slowly but loudly, "That's not funny." It was an awful moment, returning us to that childhood sense of misbehavior in the face of adult disapproval. We shouldn't have laughed—but we all did. This time it wasn't just a private joke; it was public and shared by almost the whole group. But the fact that one of the "senior" people in the group said it wasn't funny made everyone else examine her or his response. It was especially difficult for Sharon, who had repeated the Austen remark. She sputtered and apologized to her professor, but she'd obviously lost points. But why did she lose points? The comment *was* funny until the gentleman scholar said it wasn't—everybody had been laughing or at least snickering. The student had only quoted from one of our most esteemed authors, quoting her at a moment when Austen was obviously herself, fully enjoying her role as a Bad Girl (in fact, Austen has many such moments, in her novels as well as her letters). It wasn't even as if Sharon was making up a story about Austen—she was using the author's own words. But it was not acceptable to this man to think that Austen was capable of such nasty comments or thoughts. It should not have been written, according to him; it certainly should not have been repeated; and, more than anything, it should not have been found funny even if Austen meant it to be. But the trouble with humor is that "should" doesn't operate. What was clear in the exchange was the professor's wish to silence Sharon, to censor Austen, and, in other words, to assert his version of Austen as the only correct one. Since he was the acknowledged authority, his version should not have been challenged, even by Austen herself.

When Men Don't Laugh

Women are often accused of being the ones who wish to repress jokes they find distasteful (and we'll deal with this concept in detail later on), but it has become apparent that at least as many men as women assert "That's not funny" in the face of evidence to the contrary. Said in loud and commanding tones, "That's not funny" is a line used by bullies, teachers, and irate spouses of either sex. Saying "That's not funny" to someone who's laughing is like saying "You're not going anywhere" to someone already out the door. It's a line of last resort, a futile attempt to contradict or deny what is obvious. If you make a joke or tell a comic story, you run the risk of such censure.

Mary Russo, a writer whose work is widely respected among feminists and nonfeminists alike, discusses the way in which making a joke, repeating a funny line, calling attention to yourself can be "dangerous" for a woman. Russo explains that "There is a phrase that still resonates from childhood. Who says it? The mother's voice—not my own mother perhaps, but the voice of an aunt, an older sister, or the mother of a friend. It is a harsh, matronizing phrase, and it is directed towards the behavior of other women." The phrase Russo refers to is "She [the other woman] is *making a spectacle out of herself.*"

Russo explains that "making a spectacle out of yourself" was applied only to women. "The danger," she writes, "was of an exposure. Men, I learned somewhat later in life, 'exposed themselves,' but that operation was quite deliberate. . . ." For women, the very act of getting attention is regarded with suspicion. Russo points out that the women who got attention were the "possessors of large, aging, and dimpled thighs displayed at the public beach, of overly rouged cheeks, of a voice shrill in laughter. . . ." The attention given to young and sweet girls was of a different order altogether—they were given attention that somehow was their due. As long as women were passive receivers of attention, rather than active seekers of it, that was fine. In other words, if you really needed attention and tried to get it, you were lost. Doomed. Not a Good Girl, not pleasant company. A spectacle. Any woman could make a spectacle out of herself by stepping out of line and becoming noticeable, an individual rather than a type.

Making a Joke Is Like Making a Pass
· ·

Making a joke is like making a pass—you take control, take a risk, and try to bring the house down. Good Girls just wait. But who wants to wait?

How much of women's humor is sexual? "More than most

men would imagine" is a coy and evasive but accurate answer to the question. Sexual humor per se will be dealt with in detail in a later chapter, but it is appropriate to bring up the question of how women's humor is linked to both sex and power. Erica Jong has been quoted as saying that if men knew what women laughed about, they would never sleep with us. Women's humor proceeds from women's power, and the idea of women having power is unnerving to many men. The blank-eyed, blue-eyeshadowed seventeen-year-old inhabiting the foldout dreams of men of all ages doesn't laugh, ever. She is an unpainted canvas, a sheet of paper without a mark. She could not possibly have a sense of humor, because she barely has a personality. Eve wouldn't have laughed in the garden before she met the snake. If you understand the punch line, you understand the basis for the joke: virgins don't laugh at small-penis jokes. Or they'll laugh along with everyone else, if they're good sports (most virgins are—they have to be) and then later ask what was so funny. Humor, like shame and wisdom, is a product of understanding. It can be said that humor is also a product of knowledge, sexual or otherwise. Getting it depends on knowing what It is.

When We Laugh Together, Are We All Laughing at the Same Things?

In a special issue devoted to comedy, the magazine *Gentleman's Quarterly* ran a double column comparing what men find funny to what women find funny. Since the magazine didn't list the source of the information, it is difficult to tell whether this was one editor's flight of fancy or the result of a national poll, but whatever the origin, the contrasts are illuminating. For example, whereas women found Oscar Wilde, *The Addams Family,* and *It Happened One Night* funny, men found Oscar Madison, *The Munsters,* and *Three Amigos* funny. Whereas women preferred

Roxanne, Judy Holliday, and drag to make them laugh, men preferred *The Jerk,* Marilyn Monroe, and sex-change operations for their comic material.

There are some solid data to back up the theory that men and women laugh at different matters, at different times, and even that they laugh at different elements in one joke. In a series of studies done by the folklore researcher Carol Mitchell, large numbers of female and male students were given a group of jokes and asked to rate them on a "funniness" scale. Mitchell came up with some fascinating conclusions, among them the observation that women's humor centers on female experience. For example, the following joke can be appreciated by men, but they might laugh at it for reasons different from the ones a woman will have: "A guy and a girl are in the front seat of a car adjusting themselves after a quickie. The guy looks a little uncomfortable and says to the girl, 'If I'd known you were a virgin I would have taken more time.' The girl looks back at him and says, 'If I'd known you weren't in such a hurry, I'd have taken off my panty hose." Men will laugh at the joke, according to Mitchell, although they won't laugh as much as women and they won't necessarily laugh at the same things. Men will laugh at what they might refer to as "the poor bastard's hurry," but they find the whole episode farfetched. The girls laughed, but for markedly different reasons—they thought this could happen quite easily. In addition, Mitchell argues that women are laughing at the panty hose side of the joke as well as the male hurry side of the joke. They are laughing in recognition of the difficulty of removing panty hose gracefully or sexily, knowing that panty hose in such a situation is a real problem. Most important, however, is that what women are often laughing at in such jokes are the problems men face when they don't consult a woman first, when they act on their own without considering a woman's needs, desires, opinions, or knowledge.

Daddy Doesn't Know Best
· · · · · · · · · · · · · · · · · · · ·

Many of the jokes listed by Mitchell have the issue of knowledge as power at the center. In many of the jokes rated highly by women, the man must learn that he is not as in control of the situation as he believes himself to be. He has to be taught a lesson by a woman who knows better than he does, although he doesn't initially believe it.

Mitchell found that women's humor often positions the women sexually or intellectually "ahead" of the male, as this story illustrates: "Once upon a time there was this couple that got married. And this man, he married this chick and she was really innocent or he thought she was. So the first time they got into bed, he pulls down his pants and he says, 'Now what's this?' And she says, 'That's a wee-wee.' And he says, 'No, that's a cock.' And she says, 'No, that's a wee-wee.' And he says, 'No, from now on you call that a cock.' And she says, 'No, I've seen a lot of cocks and that's a wee-wee.' " The joke here stems from the man's misperception of his wife's sexual experience as well as from his foolish attempt to "teach her" what she already knows. The joke is on him—she's the one in control of the situation. He thought he was teaching her, when in actuality she's judging him. It's a woman's joke made out of a man's nightmare, because it's more a joke about pedantry than about penis size. It's more a joke about a woman being knowledgeable and right than it is a joke about a man's penis being small.

A number of psychologists suggest, like Mitchell, that sexual humor and aggressive or hostile emotions are closely linked, especially for women. In a 1975 study published in *The Journal of Psychology*, Professor Frank Prerost found that while males in the study always preferred sexual jokes to any other form of humor, women preferred sexual jokes—particularly those directly joking about male sexual behavior—only when they were angry. Anger, suggested Prerost, might well cause women to "reject their role-expectant behavior," of being "passive-submissive," especially where sexual humor is concerned. Anger removes culturally imposed censoring mechanisms; one way we celebrate freedom from these restraints is by making and laughing at jokes considered "inappropriate" for ladies.

However, women often responded to sexual jokes made by men in a mixed group with jokes that were "anti-establishment" rather than sexual, even though they would then tell the sexual jokes to an all-female group. In part this is not because women are "shy" about revealing their sexual natures but because, as Mitchell argues, "Women are still less likely than men to use jokes for the purpose of embarrassing the listener." The men in the group might be embarrassed by the women's play on sexual matters, might feel that a joke about sexual inadequacy is directed at them. Women are often cautious about using humor around men, not because they perceive individual men as powerful, but because they perceive them as vulnerable, easily wounded. They do not want to embarrass the men in the group by telling them jokes that might undermine their self-confidence, despite the fact that men seem to have little difficulty in telling women jokes that might undermine theirs.

What? Afraid of Little Ol' Me?

Deanne Stillman, editor of *Titters: Humor by Women*, links men's refusal to see a tradition of women's humor with their fear that they will discover themselves to be the butt of the joke. Stillman argues that "Men are going around saying 'Chicks have no sense of humor' " because, if they admitted that women are funny, "they'd worry that we're going to laugh at the shirts they're wearing, which is probably true." She thinks that there are certain things women will laugh at that men won't understand: dress shields, for example. "People laugh at words that remind them of some awkward or funny experience they've had. So when you use a term like 'dress shields' you're gonna get a laugh . . . the fact that people invented dress shields in the first place is funny for women. Somebody actually sat around saying 'Hey, let's sell 'em dress shields. We've sold 'em Peds and spoolies—I'm sure they'll buy these useless patches of second-rate cotton and stick them under their arms.' "

In a recent interview, the British writer Margaret Drabble spoke about deciding to tell a large audience about her decision to remove her shoulder pads before she gave a reading of her new novel. Her husband was horrified by the idea that she would open her performance this way, but, according to Drabble, the audience loved it. "He just didn't understand about shoulder pads," said Drabble. "The women knew how complicated such a simple thing really is. Should we leave them in or not? Do they make us look more feminine or are they an attempt to make us look as much like men as possible? It's all terribly important."

Anne Beatts talks about how necessary it was for her to find another woman writer to work with at *Saturday Night Live* so that they could share "the same vocabulary and reference points." She describes a sketch that the two women wrote together that included "a line we thought was wonderful: 'Tell Granny Loopner only twenty-eight more cloves and the pomander ball will be finished.' " They tried the line out on a number of their male colleagues, none of whom thought it was funny. Finally Beatts asked one of them, "Do you know what a pomander ball is?" "No," he replied. Then she asked if he knew what a clove was and he answered, "Do you mean garlic cloves?" "So," Beatts said, "we went around and asked three different men . . . and none of them knew. Finally, we asked Lorne Michaels, the producer, and he said, 'Well, it's a spice, right?' I guess that's why he's the producer." Beatts goes on to speculate that "There's a woman's culture that men just don't know about. So when they say 'Hey, that joke's not funny,' it's sometimes because they don't understand the vocabulary." Beatts and her collaborator ended up removing the pomander ball line from the sketch, bowing to the concern that there might not be enough women in the audience to make it work.

Bad and Good Girls Do Laugh Out Loud— and Laugh Together
· ·

Nancy Walker discusses, in *A Very Serious Thing: Women's Humor and American Culture*, the growing understanding that "women can laugh about [the circumstances of their lives] without trivializing either the circumstances or the women themselves." When we laugh at ourselves, we can make sure that we do it from a perspective informed by acceptance and love rather than one fueled by self-anger and fear. Even when we joke about ourselves, it makes a difference whether we do it in such a way that the old stereotypes of women's weakness are reaffirmed or reevaluated.

If you lament, as did Dorothy Parker one Halloween, "Ducking for apples—change one letter and it's the story of my life," you trade on your own vulnerability. But in her poem "Comment" she questioned the larger issues of romance. "Oh, life is a glorious cycle of song/A medley of extemporania/And love is a thing that can never go wrong/And I am Marie of Romania," she wrote. In a book of poems titled *Enough Rope*, Parker included a poem called "Unfortunate Coincidence": "By the time you swear you're his/Shivering and sighing/And he vows his passion is/Infinite, undying—/Lady make a note of this:/One of you is lying." Parker attacks, not herself, but the romantic illusions fostered by our culture.

If women make fun of themselves in such a way that we devalue our own experiences, then we are harming ourselves—subtly and insidiously—in ways that may come back to haunt us. When we recognize the many sources of humor that are open to us, and that don't depend on self-deprecation or deprecation of other women, we open ourselves to whole new avenues of power and delight. When we see the humor that belongs to women, we can integrate our Good Girl and Bad Girl sides. Our Good Girl may help prevent our Bad Girl from taking any laugh just because it's easy and fun, even when it's at our own expense, and our Bad Girl can teach our Good Girl to let go, to discover the joys of excess and the breaking of taboos.

The enormously popular Lily Tomlin play *The Search for Signs of Intelligent Life in the Universe,* written by Jane Wagner, ends with such a scene. Several women—including a socialite, a bag lady, and a hooker—pass one another on a crowded New York street. It has begun to rain, and everyone is going about her own business, but the socialite stops and remembers "something I think it was Kafka wrote about having been filled with a sense of endless astonishment at simply seeing a group of people cheerfully assembled." She continues to describe her evening. "I saw this young man go up, obviously from out of town, and he asked them, 'How do I get to Carnegie Hall?' And the bag lady said 'Practice!' And we caught each other's eyes—the prostitutes, the bag lady, the young man and I. We all burst out laughing. There we were, laughing together, in the pouring rain. . . ." Once we catch the eye of another potential laugher, we find a conspirator and a colleague. We find reflected, even by a stranger, our deepest thoughts and reactions—the surprise we feel is the relief of finding that others also laugh.

We can see that there *are* enough other women in the room to make it worthwhile to say what we're thinking, to make the jokes we have inside us, to laugh out loud and with uncensored enjoyment at what gives us pleasure. There are enough other people in the room who will get the cloves reference, who also laughed at Tennyson's curse, who fall down and break china. "Our neighbor," writes Fay Weldon in *Letters to Alice,* "who we never thought would laugh with us, will." Once we recognize and appreciate the Bad Girl inside of ourselves and others, we can be less apologetic and gradually more empowered by the great lines we know we've always been able to come up with—even if we'd never had the nerve to say them aloud before.

Even if, in the worst of all possible cases, nobody else in the room is laughing at that particular moment, we have to stand assured that somewhere there are others who would have enjoyed the moment as much as we did, and not give ourselves all the old lines—that we're overdoing again, that we don't know what's funny from what's not, that we're only trying to get attention. "Only" trying to get attention is like "only" becoming a CEO—some things shouldn't ever have "only" in front of them, because they are too important. We are all both Good Girl and Bad Girl. And the teacher was right—although it would have killed him to know it—when he said that the young ladies should "be able to say what exactly we find so funny in all of this."

3

Putting a Punch in Your Punch Line

....

Strategies for Dealing with Aggressive Humor

When a man looks you in the eye after telling you an offensive and not even particularly funny story, and says, "It was only a joke," what he is really saying, according to Joanna Russ, is "*I* find jokes about you funny. Why don't *you* find jokes about you funny?" He might be genuinely puzzled. He might believe that the phrase "It was only a joke" means he can say anything and get away with it—a carte blanche for bad taste or hostility, a sort of "007" for offensive behavior. One thing is clear: very few jokes are "only" jokes. Most of them are emblems of larger issues, which is the reason it is important to see their social and psychological function.

We should also remember that even the "No, that's a wee-wee" jokes that make men bite their lower lip and drop their hands quickly can't hold a candle to the conflagration of anti-women jokes we've all heard from the cradle onward. The idea of humor-as-disguised-hostility is one of the reasons women have for so long been told they themselves can't laugh at a good joke: we've been hearing the underlying hostility of those jokes and have often been unable or unwilling to overcome our distress. It's difficult to hear the "funny part" when what you're really hearing is an attack. "It's only a joke" is an indirect accusation that we don't like to laugh at hostile jokes directed at groups of which we are part.

There are three ways aggression and humor can work together: Aggression in humor can be directed at you, it can be deflected by you, or it can be directed by you. Women's humor directs some of its most powerful material at men, questioning their authority and indicating a certain amount of aggression, but studies have shown that men's humor is much more hostile than women's. What strategies do we have for dealing with such humor?

The Booby-Trap Joke: Aggression Toward You

During the second week of my first job, I was having a chicken-salad sandwich in the official "old boys" lunchroom where the senior members of my department regularly gathered, rather like a herd around a kill. I was the only woman in the group, the only person under fifty, and the only new kid on the block. As you might imagine, being the new kid, I was eager to be accepted and liked, happy to be among these gentlemen, pleased to be listening to their talk, although I was not enormously eager to add to it myself. A pleasant, friendly atmosphere was then suddenly and subtly altered when one of the oldest, most respected of them started telling what he would have called an "off-color joke"—a joke with an obviously sexual innuendo. The men all listened and laughed, and I gritted my teeth, not sure how to respond. Do I laugh along—do I complain? This was clearly a test, whether or not it was stated as such, of my position in this group. The joke was undoubtedly offensive to women. I sat with a quiet smile and raised eyebrows, miserably unsure of what to do until the joke teller turned to me and with a sweetly paternalistic edge to his voice apologized for "telling a dirty joke in front of a lady." The rest of the group waited, sandwiches held aloft and poised in mid-bite, for my response.

Although I had been uncertain until that moment about how I should handle the situation, once he made the comment I knew what to say. I looked him in the eye and smiled broadly. "In fact, you did not tell a dirty joke *in front* of a lady," I replied in my most kindly professional tone, "you just told a dirty joke *to* a lady. Big difference." The rest of the group now laughed with me and at their respected colleague, and the tension in the room noticeably decreased. We all finished our food quite happily and had our coffee. On the way back to the office I was congratulated several times, with obvious sincerity, on my handling of the situation. I'd apparently passed some sort of initiation rite, even though it seemed a fairly obscure one, in being able to deal with a dirty joke told by someone who was essentially my "boss." My co-workers let me know that they were not bothered at all that I answered back (although I had worried about exactly that point as soon as I opened my mouth to speak), but rather they let me know that they were relieved that I could return fire for fire.

In this instance, the senior member of the department was using his privileged position to tell a joke that would make his subordinate uncomfortable, and so place that subordinate in a no-win situation. He was counting on the idea of my shame at hearing such a joke, counting on me to be too embarrassed to respond. He knew before he began telling the joke that it would have been equally disastrous in that situation for me to laugh or not to laugh. It was a booby trap. If I didn't laugh, then I proved that I was a humorless, sour-faced woman, precisely what they had all expected, just what they didn't want. If I did laugh, then I proved I was a pushover, a giggling lightweight who didn't dare name what offended her, and once again I'd be just what they didn't want. The senior department member was using humor as a form of aggression, and I was not the only one who recognized this. The silence that followed the laughter indicated that the rest of my new companions also understood the underlying confrontation between the joker and myself. The subtext, or hidden meaning, of his banter was this unspoken point: "I will tell a sexual joke to show how the men in this department really talk. If you want to invade our territory this way, you'll have to put up or shut up."

This gentleman's subtext was what can be categorized most clearly as a Dick Thing. A Dick Thing, or DT for short, is a phrase, gesture, action, mind-set, whatever, that is completely informed by the masculine nature of its possessor. A DT is a deflected power play, something that occurs because a man cannot actually take his penis out of his pants and wave it around. A DT, therefore, is that gesture sublimated. What are common DTs? Firecrackers. Corvettes. Excessively long electric guitar solos. All heavy-metal music. The NRA. Owning a very big dog. Drinking until you throw up. The Three Stooges. All tall buildings, especially round tall buildings with round bits on top. Being inordinately proud of knowing how to use chopsticks. Spitting.

So my response had to take into account my colleague's subtext as well as his text. To be effective my reply had to show him that I understood the gender-based difference that was at the heart of our relationship. His joke was a DT, and I had to respond to him in a way similar to the way I'd respond to a flasher on Seventh Avenue. My answer indicated that I was not simply a passive observer, like a bachelorette on *The Dating Game* who would put on the glassy stare and pretend not to understand. Instead I tried to make clear that I expected to be treated as a member of the group who would both listen to their humor and make some of her own.

In other words, I wanted to show them that I was someone who would use humor against them if they tried anything funny.

Is That a Laugh or a Growl?
. . . .

One theory about the origin of smiling is that we smile to show our teeth. The philosopher Albert Rapp believes that laughter originated as "the roar of triumph in an ancient jungle duel." The advocates of this line of thinking say that we smile widely to display our teeth as visible weaponry to a possible opponent, to warn them off any aggressive moves, to indicate that we can defend ourselves. This theory suggests that a laugh began as a growl. Whether or not this explanation of origins is valid, it certainly highlights something fundamental about using humor—much of the humor we use contains an element of aggression. A joke is often a disguised insult, laughter a socially acceptable way to define who is in the group and who is out. In this way joke telling is directly linked to power; the one telling the joke has command of the audience and controls its responses to a certain extent. Comedians know this very well. One of the standard stand-up ploys is to comment on any latecomer to the audience, to focus on that person who interrupts the show in order to show who is in command: "Whatsa matter, dearie, had to convince your date to be seen with you in public?" Teachers also know this ploy very well. Who hasn't had at least one teacher who took advantage of his or her powerful position in the front of the classroom to make fun of a student? Kate Hanson, a graduate student of psychology, has a vivid memory of one such incident that occurred some twenty years ago. She was slightly late for school in the seventh grade and tried to sneak into her large homeroom class without being noticed. The teacher, a man who would make Freddy Krueger seem like Santa Claus, could not let such an opportunity for ridicule slip by. "So, Miss Hanson," he began, as all eyes turned toward her, "you must have had a heavy date last night. Let's see, who could your date have been? Maybe Scott over here? Maybe Joey?" He kept naming boys, much to the amusement of the rest of the class. "What could I have done?" asks Kate. She remembers that she sat rigidly in her chair and looked at the blackboard until the bell rang for the next class. "He really had me. Of course everybody was going to laugh, even though they knew how nasty he was being. They would have felt terrible if it had been them, but since it was me—or anybody else—nobody felt any obligation not to laugh, let alone to rise to my defense. The worst part," Kate recalls, "is that even my best friends laughed. I was so mad I didn't call any of them for a week even after they apologized. I had to listen to wolf whistles in the halls for days." Such forms of joking are subject to wide abuse because they illustrate the power of the joker. Kate couldn't really talk back to him because he had too much authority over her, or so she perceived the situation.

How would the situation be different if a male student was the object of the teacher's sarcasm? For one thing, the boy's reputation would have been enhanced by the accusation of having had a "heavy date." The boys named by the teacher would all band together, look at one another, grin, and form a group; Kate was isolated by the teacher's humor, and clearly punished by his singling her out for attention that was both academic and sexual.

If the teacher had just called Kate a "tramp" or something clearly offensive, she could have gone to the principal's office and registered a complaint (which is what she wishes she had done anyway, being well within her rights). The other students would have gathered to her side and gone against the teacher. But since he used humor to distance her from the group, he solidified his relationship with the students and turned them against Kate. It is important to recognize that the responses to the joke tellers depend on the adequate disguise of the aggression. If the hostility or anger is too obvious, the joke won't work.

In a study done at the University of Southern California, psychologists found that the behavior of the "victim" of the joke, prior to its telling, is the most important in people's judgment of whether or not the joke was fair. In other words, if you pick on someone who has behaved well all along, it is likely that your joke will be considered unfunny, because it will be seen as an open act of hostility. But if you can turn humor on someone who has behaved badly, you will be perceived as "righting" an unjust situation. Your humor, according to Professors Gutman and Priest, would be enjoyed, even applauded, by others around you.

A graduate teaching assistant, a woman of twenty-eight whom I'll call Melanie, once told me a story remarkably similar to the one told by Kate. Melanie is interested in psychoanalytic readings of literature. In a class on the history of the novel, she brought up a point concerning Richardson's eighteenth-century novel *Clarissa*. In a letter to a friend, the heroine Clarissa talks of the hero's "great penetration," and Melanie wondered whether, unknown even to Richardson himself, there might be an unconscious association with sexuality. In asking her question, she acknowledged that there was no overt sexuality in the remark. But she also thought that such a word, when applied to one of the most famous rapists in literature, deserved critical attention. She made her remark quite seriously, applying legitimate reading tactics to the passage. But although her male professor seemed to listen thoughtfully, he immediately cut down her argument by replying, without missing a beat, that "Richardson was probably not thinking 'It takes two hands to handle a Whopper' as he wrote that section of the book." After he got the mild snickering he was hoping for from some of the students, he continued jokingly to advise her, "If you have any more suggestions along that line, you should censor them for the benefit of the more innocent members of the class." Even if Melanie's reading of Richardson was off the mark, she read clearly the significance of the professor's remarks: she saw in his belittling response that he was threatened not only by her bringing up a psychosexual interpretation (since he was strictly of the old school, which dismisses such "smutty stuff" and likes to stick to a "real" interpretation), but also that he saw her remark as somehow aggressive. He needed to make a joke to get the class back on his side, as if they would be swayed by her remarks. She felt the professor's response was inappropriate, because she was not making an aggressive statement; he reacted to her as if she were his enemy rather than his student. By reducing her comment to a simple "dirty joke" he effectively undercut her authority and kept his own without making his distress obvious. He acted out of fear. It's a very common gesture.

Can't You Take a Joke?

Many jokes about women are more hostile than any of us would like to face. The new gang of "shockucomics" like Sam Kinison and Andrew Dice Clay rely on jokes that bring the house down through sheer misogyny. Carl LaBove tells a sell-out crowd that the best thing to do with a boring date is to "snap off her left tit and leave her in the corner somewhere." Andrew Dice Clay will choose a woman from the audience and say that he can "see the stretch marks around her mouth." "Is she good in bed?" he'll ask her escort. "Yeah, so how'd she get that way?" Finally, according to Gerri Hirshey's article titled "The Comedy of Hate," which deals with these "shockucomics," Clay will apologize to the woman in the audience, offering her a toast. "Here's to you, sweetheart . . . Suckin' my dick!" According to Hirshey, these comics are playing to sold-out clubs, colleges, and concert halls. They have loyal followers who scream and bark loudly at each remark, especially relishing those directed against women. It would be comforting to tell ourselves that this is just a mutant moment in modern history, a phase bound to pass quickly. But is it? It seems as if there has always been a split between comedy that relies on vulgarity and comedy that treats its audience with more respect. "We can see [a] difference in old and new comedies," commented one critic. "For the writers of old comedy it was indecent language that was ridiculous, while those writing new comedy prefer innuendo." The critic was Aristotle, who lived from 384 to 322 B.C.

When someone tells a joke, he has to seem to be acting at least superficially "in fun." For example, if you went up to somebody and said "Boy, are you fat," it would be sheer hostility without any humor, and would be considered mean-spirited by anyone listening. The person who made the rude remark would be chastised and ostracized by the group for at least a short period of time. How could somebody be so downright mean, we would say to ourselves, and we would congratulate ourselves on the fact that we would never make a person feel bad about how he or she looked. We would be righteous in the knowledge that we would never insult someone vulnerable or easily hurt.

Wouldn't we? If the aggressive remark is couched in humor, it is sometimes difficult to resist, because it short-circuits our conscience. If an insult is disguised or dressed up as humor, then it is as if it becomes magically transformed into something acceptable, even attractive. If instead of saying "Boy, are you fat," someone says "Did you ever think of going on the television show *Eating for Dollars?*" then the ban on being nasty has been lifted, and the group will feel free to laugh. The object of the joke will be expected to take it as "only a joke" or "just kidding" and laugh along. The focus is placed on the object's reactions— the audience suddenly judges how s/he reacts, rather than judging the person who tells the joke. If the object bursts into tears, starts to yell, or stalks off, then everybody blames the victim. If someone tells a joke at your expense, it is quite literally that— you pay for it.

The joke depends, in a way, on the shame of the person who is the object. She should be ashamed enough, the implication goes, of her weight to let the comment pass rather than draw more attention to it. She should have been ashamed to have come late to class. She should be embarrassed to have raised a sexual interpretation of a text. I remember one friend at college who refused to be shamed into a response by a joker in our dorm. She had recently taken up with a really adorable hockey player, and everybody knew that he'd started spending the night in her room. This was not shocking in any way—most of us were pleased to have such a sweet man around. A guy from another floor, however, felt that his territory was being invaded and so decided to make Denise feel uncomfortable by joking about her new relationship. When she came downstairs just in time to get the last serving of breakfast one morning, this joker looked up with innocent eyes and said, "What kept you in bed for so long, Denise?" His snide tone implied that she should blush and stammer. Instead she looked him in the eye and said, "Charles kept me in bed, but he didn't have to try very hard." Because she rose to the challenge and refused to be ashamed, she effectively "won" the situation.

If you're embarrassed or sorry, it's difficult to defend yourself, and the joker holds all the cards. In this way the person telling the joke gets to act badly without risking his reputation. He, in fact, is the one person in the group who is triumphant, because he is the one who does not laugh; he retains the right to his self-control while the laughter of those around him signals that they have, for a moment, lost theirs. The person who is being made fun of suddenly becomes the focus of attention, and her reactions will be all-important. If she laughs she has, willingly or unwillingly, given herself over to the sexuality or hostility of the joke. It's like eating from a plate of food prepared by your least favorite neighbor at a block party: politeness causes you to join in so that everybody else doesn't feel uncomfortable; still, you find it hard to swallow.

Deflecting Aggressive Humor

We probably have all faced a situation where we know we're being cut down by someone else's laughter, where a joke is being told at our expense. The most overt example is the one described earlier—where a man tells a dirty joke to a woman. Half the fun in such an exercise is watching what the woman will do, as if the audience is counting on her to provide some of the entertainment by being shocked or outraged. Freud suggested that the excitement of telling a dirty joke to a woman springs from the expectation of her shocked and ashamed reaction. He argued that the power of the joke teller in that situation is derived from his ability to force a woman to "see" the sexual act as she hears the joke. The dynamic works as follows: the joke is told by one person to another person of the same sex, but its aggression is directed at the listener of the opposite sex.

"Smut is like an exposure of the sexually different person to whom it is directed," observes Freud. He goes on to explain that hearing the dirty joke "compels the person" who hears it "to imagine the part of the body or the procedure in question and shows her that the assailant [the joke teller] is himself imagining it." The "inactive listener," the third party, inevitably another man, is the one who enjoys the joke. The man who makes the joke, according to Freud, is pleased, and the one who listens is laughing. What about the woman? She's the object of their humor, but the joke calls for her to be shut out of pleasure. She's necessary to the joke, but her embarrassed response—the act of imagining, usually in silence—is all that's required.

Let's take a few liberties with Freud's theories and apply them practically to our current situation. Let's say you, a woman, are at a bar when a group of guys—whom you are already beginning to think of as your erstwhile friends—begins telling dirty jokes. The first thing you'll notice, if you haven't noticed it already, is that you are "not one of the guys" in such a situation, even if you've seemed to be on an equal footing until that moment. All eyes will turn to you when the punch line is delivered, and never before will the phrase "punch line" have as much meaning. That last line, usually the one that clarifies the sexual and aggressive nature of the joke, really is like a punch, a slap, a hostile act. The audience, in this case these pals of yours, wants to see how you'll respond. Will you react as a Good Girl who keeps her mouth shut and doesn't say anything to make anyone uncomfortable? Or will you react as a Bad Girl?

As a Bad Girl you can react in one of two ways. You can laugh at the joke and so admit sexual, "fallen" knowledge that makes you part of the group ("You can tell a dirty joke around Hilary, and she'll laugh as loudly as anybody"), even though you are most certainly not part of the group at this juncture. This point is important: you are not part of the group, or one of the boys. They are very aware of your difference, and you should be equally aware of it. To laugh uproariously is the typical Bad Girl reaction, and it makes life pretty easy on the guys because it relieves them of their guilt. What you're probably doing to yourself at this point is quite convoluted, however. You are, in effect, neutering yourself into a non-gendered being by disassociating yourself from the generic "woman" of the joke. In other words, the reasoning process goes something like this: "Women, as defined by your stories, are all sluts or bimbos. I am not a slut or a bimbo. Therefore I am not a woman according to your definition." Hence, the joke doesn't apply to you or your friends, so you can go ahead and laugh as if you belonged to another sex altogether—which you don't, not even by these guys' standards.

When somebody looks you in the eye and says "Don't take this personally," you know better than to take it any other way, right? The same principle applies here. All those comments and slights directed toward that unknown category of human beings, "women in general," are really directed toward us, each one of us, personally. When you walk into a room, men see you as a woman. They do not see you first of all as an accountant, social worker, or pilot, they see you as a woman. When you walk out of your executive office suite and onto the sidewalk, the guys working in construction do not see a senior vice president, they see a babe, a chick, or something even less polite. They respond to you first as a woman. When they tell jokes about women, they mean you, too, even if to your face they say otherwise. Often when we see derogatory images of women, we disassociate ourselves from them—we're not like that. We're the bright exceptions that prove the rules, right? We've grown familiar with that refrain, but it's simply untrue. We have to learn to realign ourselves with ourselves—with women in general. I first became aware of this at the nearly all-male college I attended during my wonder years. As a member of one of the first classes of women, I tried to fit in by playing well with the boys, by learning their game and trying to be a "good sport." I sang all the old college songs, even the one about the team invading college towns and telling the inhabitants to "run, girls, run" because the boys were in town for "fun, girls, fun." That was the refrain, and I sang it as loudly as any of my peers, thinking that those girls at women's colleges couldn't take a joke when they got angry at the lyrics. One night in the bathroom, the only single-sex part of the dorm, a visitor from a women's college told me that she thought it was weird for me to sing a song essentially about rape. It caught me short because I'd never thought of the song as being about rape—although it was, because the fun they were talking about obviously wasn't a coed volleyball game—and I spent about ten minutes trying to convince her that it was all in fun. At one point, however, I really listened to what I was saying. I was repeating the justifications I'd heard, but I could see that none of them were good enough. I'd tried to align myself with the dominant group, but was doing so at my own expense.

A more effective Bad Girl frame of mind will indicate to your pals that you're going to make trouble for them by refusing to act as if you're one of the boys. For example, you can make trouble by not laughing or not smiling if you find the joke too hostile to be acceptable. To return to the earlier analogy, you can refuse to eat from the plate of food prepared by your least favorite neighbor. Let the others partake, you'll wait for another entrée. Or you can really confuse the audience by making a comeback of your own, a response to show that you're not just a passive recipient of the joke's hostility. If you can find a way to draw attention to the joke's hostility, then you're in the best position, because you'll be able to defuse the booby trap.

Let's try a worst-case scenario. Say you've left this jolly group in the bar for a minute to go to the bathroom and return to find that your pals have placed a wrapped condom underneath your glass so that when you pick up your drink for the first time after your return, you see a Fiesta package smiling up at you. All eyes are turned your way. What are your options? You can say, with perfect authority, "That's not funny," because it really is pretty low on wit. You can giggle and push it to the far end of the counter and pretend the whole thing never happened. Or you can turn to the man on your left and smile sweetly as you hold the package lightly between your fingers, saying "What's the matter, J.B.? Wanted to make sure a live woman actually saw one of these before the expiration date runs out?" as you put it in his shirt pocket. It doesn't matter whether it was his or not; you were representative of woman, which is why the joke was played on you, and it's only fair that one of the guys can represent all men for the same purpose.

Humor can be used to disguise hostility directed against you; you can use humor to avoid or sidestep hostility; you can use it to disguise your own hostility toward someone else. Or, of course, you can use it to return hostile fire. Margaret Thatcher, not known for her feminist sensibilities, has nevertheless had to deal with her share of "only joking" remarks from friends and foes alike. When, for example, she received the following backhanded, ironic compliment from a Labour Party official, "May I congratulate you on being the only man on your team?" she replied unhesitatingly, "That's one more than you've got on yours!" Thomas Hobbes, the seventeenth-century British philosopher, said that laughter arises from a feeling of "sudden glory" when we best our opponent with a comment. Laughter arises from the feeling of smugness that the Labour Party official must have felt when he made his comment to Thatcher. But when Thatcher won the competition by using his own words against him, she proved herself to be the better-equipped duelist. In such cases, Hobbes's theory obviously applies—laughter here arises from comparing our wit with a well-matched opponent and winning.

Joking and Bonding

Those who laugh at the joke feel part of the club—there's even the old routine about the folks stuck on a desert island who'd all heard the same jokes so many times they would refer to them by number and say simply "Number 33" and everybody would laugh. Kids know this instinctively, and often an "in" joke will define the current list of who is considered hip. Teenagers often will repeat only the punch line to one another as a kind of shorthand for the initiated. The group gathers around a common pool of information and a shared perspective. If you and your pals laugh at Helen Keller jokes and the new girl refuses to laugh, or tells you off for being mean, she's unlikely to be welcomed into the group.

Adults, of course, also have their in jokes. Elaine, a Brooklyn social worker, explains how a joke came to be adopted for professional use in her office, although of course everyone involved would be horrified if anyone outside the group knew. "There are three men waiting to get into heaven," Elaine begins. "Saint Peter asks the first one whether he was a good man. 'Yes,' he replies, 'I did a lot of charity work and helped the destitute and homeless.' Saint Peter then asks whether the man was faithful to his wife. 'Yes,' the man replies, 'from the day we first met until my last moment I never looked at another woman.' Saint Peter looks pleased and tells the man that he can ride around heaven in a new Mercedes-Benz. The next man up is asked the same questions. He replies that he was a pretty good guy, and helped his family and neighbors, cheating on his wife only when he was away at conventions. Saint Peter looks resigned and tells the man he can drive around heaven in a 1981 Buick. The third man is less pleasant. 'I looked out for number one, me, myself, and I. Faithful to my wife? Are you kidding? Every chance I got, I got lucky.' Saint Peter tells the man sternly that he is permitted to drive around heaven only in a 1972 Pinto with denim seat covers. A year later, the guy in the Pinto sees the guy in the Mercedes crying. 'What can you be crying about?' shouts the guy from the Pinto. 'You're driving around for eternity in a Mercedes-Benz.' 'Yeah,' the other man replies, wiping his eyes, 'but I've just seen my wife and she's on skates!' " Elaine explains that she and the other workers now refer to unfaithful spouses they treat as "on skates." Obviously the joke has become a shorthand for the in group.

To Laugh or Not to Laugh, That Is the Question

Since humor cements bonds between group members, it is no surprise that male humor has traditionally relied on this ingroup mentality. The clichéd scene puts men around a bar, telling jokes and slamming each other on the back as they laugh uproariously. This sort of masculine scenario is reflective not only of general good fun and camaraderie, but of something else, which usually remains unspoken: a sense of competition—especially when the jokes are of a sexual nature. These guys tell jokes to amuse one another, but they also try to outdo one another. Not to come up with another, better, dirtier joke is to these guys like not being able to come at all. This is the sort of behavior that is particularly interesting because it is almost never present in all-female groups. Much male humor is both sexual and aggressive, adding insult to injury where women are concerned. Since women are traditionally brought up to believe that they should be neither aggressive nor overtly sexual, it is difficult to develop a strategy for dealing with the sexually aggressive nature of "traditional" humor. A woman probably would not choose to be in the middle of that particular bar scene, at least not on her own, because she would be the one the male gaze would address when the punch line was told. Even if she could hold her own—and in such company even an innocent phrase would receive a great deal of comment—the atmosphere would hardly allow her to feel comfortable about herself, because she would on some level realize how hostile the jokes about women really are.

Think about it for a minute, however uncomfortable that minute might be. Think of the first dirty joke you heard, the first one told to you by a boy in front of another boy or in front of a group. Remember not knowing where to look, or whether to laugh? I remember the horrible feeling of realizing that this was not a cute-dirty joke (like "What do WASPs say after making love?" "Thank you") but a real dirty joke. This fourteen-year-old kid who thought he was John Travolta (considered, without irony, to be a terrific hero by my age group at that time) was sitting at "our" cafeteria table. He wasn't really part of "our" group, but it was some sort of religious holiday, so only certain kids showed up and the usual crowd wasn't really present. My friend Bonnie and I were brown-bagging it as usual, and this kind-of-cute guy sat down and we were pretty happy about it. But then he told this joke. "You know what the perfect woman is?"

We waited, smiling, anticipating something a little dirty but maybe flattering, too. "The perfect woman is waist high, has no teeth, and she's got a flat head so you can put your drink down somewhere." I could feel the flush that went from my ankles to my forehead. Bonnie kicked me hard under the table, but we didn't look at each other. The other boys laughed a little, some halfheartedly, looking at us, not being sure what we'd do. It would have been kinder for the joke teller to bash us on the heads with a metal tray or pour hot coffee on our spring skirts. We couldn't wait to get away and we never laughed at the joke, even by ourselves, although strangely enough we both told it to other girls. I think we wanted to see what they would say. None of them laughed either. That was the first experience I ever had of a joke as a form of violation. It was not the last. The joke told to me when I was new at my first job was a replay of that scene, although the joke was more sophisticated. But, if anything, the gesture behind the joke was even meaner than it was in junior high. The teenager had the excuse of not really knowing any better; he was repeating what somebody else had said. His own idea of the perfect woman would have been one who actually went out with him. But when the senior department member told his joke, he was behind it a hundred percent.

Freudian Slippage

Psychologists have offered a number of theories to explain the origin and the importance of humor. Many of these theories link humor to aggression. But, interestingly, not one of the well-established, traditional theories discusses in any detail gender differences in the initiation or perception of humor, except to point out that women don't use humor as well or as often as men. Since this assessment applies to nearly every human action of significance—women don't do it, or don't do it well—its application to humor should not surprise us. What is significant, however, is the fact that this pronouncement has only recently been challenged.

Freud's theories have made a great impact on how we think about humor, whether or not we've even realized his influence. One way Freud has influenced the American culture's view of humor is by sanctifying hostile humor as "cathartic." Aggressive jokes are a mechanism whereby people "let off steam" and so ultimately behave better. Clinical research over the last twenty-five years, however, does not generally confirm Freud's theories concerning the cathartic powers of aggressive humor. Much of it, in fact, suggests that aggressive humor leads not to civility or serenity, but to increased aggression. Freud also underscores the notion that women produce fewer and less effective jokes than men because they have, according to him, a less complex superego structure. Women, according to Freud, don't have as great a need to make jokes as men; they do not have as sophisticated a psychological alarm system, since they do not go through the same Oedipal struggle as the male child. They do not need, therefore, to manufacture humor to escape setting off the alarms.

Freud's general concern with humor is reflected in his study *Jokes and the Unconscious*, where he declares his commitment to understand the psychological implications of humor: "Is the subject of jokes worth so much trouble? There can, I think, be no doubt of it." Freud's is a fascinating, if brief, book, full of remarkably poor examples of comedy. His examples include a large number of what we would now call ethnic jokes ("Two Jews met in the neighborhood of the bathhouse. 'Have you taken a bath?' asked one of them. 'What?' asked the other in return. 'Is there one missing?' "). Freud's study also includes an interesting array of anti-women jokes ("The bridegroom was most disagreeably surprised when the bride was introduced to him and drew the marriage broker on one side and whispered his remonstrances: 'Why have you brought me here? She's ugly and old, she squints and has bad teeth and bleary eyes . . .' 'You needn't lower your voice,' interrupted the broker, 'she's deaf as well' "). And it includes a great number of sexual jokes ("A Royal gentleman was making a tour through the provinces and noticed a man in the crowd who bore a striking resemblance to his own exalted person. He beckoned to him and asked: 'Was your mother at one time in the service of the Palace?' 'No, your Highness' was the reply, 'but my father was' "). Freud emphasized that jokes are a way that people can approach taboo subjects—like the ones just mentioned of race, sex, and questionable paternity—that would otherwise be out of bounds. Jokes can make light of the most serious subjects or can even bring to light subjects that are otherwise shrouded by society.

Whether or not we think Freud would have wowed them doing stand-up routines at The Improv, his ideas have had a great impact on the way that humor is regarded by most people. For example, Freud argued that humor lets off steam socially and psychologically. Freud attempted to demonstrate how people get to have the thrill of being aggressive or sexually aroused in a safe situation where there is little danger of our signals being misinterpreted. His discussion of humor pivots on the "It's only a joke" disclaimer. As we've seen, Freud's theory is that our need to joke is entangled with the development of our conscience, and that joking is a way to get around the defense mechanisms protecting us from our "base" impulses. Humor, then, is a way to defy Big Brother (or, in the case of Freud, we should probably use the term "Big Daddy"). However, according to Freud, the ultimate end of this excursion into the forbidden is a safe return to the protective fold, shepherded by our guilt. We use humor not to overturn society's conventions, according to Freud, but ultimately to reaffirm its dominant values. Jokes allow a little taboo bashing as long as it doesn't get out of hand. Jokes, therefore, end up being another method of control, in this case controlling one's self.

Regarding humor and hostility, Freud argues that in the same way human beings learn to repress their sexual feelings, so they learn to repress hostile or aggressive feelings as well. "By making our enemy small," Freud writes, "inferior, despicable or comic, we achieve in a roundabout way the enjoyment of overcoming him." He goes on to state that "One can make a person comic in order to make him become contemptible, to deprive him of his claim to dignity and authority." Change "him" to "her" in these last quotations, and we can see how Freud's remarks apply to the way women have been portrayed as the generic "enemy" who must be overcome. It is infuriating to be reduced to a series of characteristics—breasts, buttocks, loud mouth, or menstrual cramps—as it would be to have one's face cut out of a photograph or to have a paper bag put over one's head. "Did you hear the one about the woman who . . ." seems to apply to all women generally, so that we feel like shouting in response "Don't call me 'women'!" when we hear it, as if the label "women" was itself insulting.

Playful vs. Hostile Humor

The important point is to recognize that humor in certain situations can move quickly from being playful to being aggressive. This is especially true when the joking remark touches on a sensitive point, such as weight, age, ethnicity, class, or, of course, gender. For example, a man I know who would rather set himself on fire than admit to racist or sexist thoughts told the following joke after a dinner meeting: "What's the difference," he asked, "between a Pygmy village and an all-women's track team?" From the outset, I was pretty sure I wasn't going to like this joke, and our black colleague didn't look too thrilled either. But the joke teller continued, not picking up on our signals. He was enjoying himself. "What's the difference between a Pygmy village and an all-women's track team? The Pygmies are a cunning bunch of runts!" Now, this is a guy who has probably never said the word "cunt" out loud in his entire life, but he feels perfectly comfortable telling a joke where the word "cunt" is central to its effect even if it remains unspoken. It's all okay because it's a joke—geddit? A few folks in the group laughed, more moaned, some stayed quiet and prayed for the moment to pass. Subsequently, this friend was congratulated for his economy of gesture—he successfully offended whole groups of people at the same time. He was horrified to think that there was anything insulting in his joke, but his unawareness did not, in fact, make the joke any less offensive. He did not see the joke as either racist or sexist, and he did not see the "colonial" mentality that put both blacks and women in a debased category. Dividing people into either runts or cunts didn't strike him as what the joke was about, although both the spoken and unspoken punch lines revolved around this idea.

Freud would have argued that this man told the joke to release hostility toward the two groups he felt threatened by, without admitting even to himself that he was engaged in such an operation. He would have been miserable if he had had to analyze the joke's content, embarrassed at the underlying meanings. He would have denied that there was any hostility in the joke at all and he would have meant it sincerely. But he would have been covering up the real meanings out of a need to appear like a "good guy" in his own estimation of himself. He would have "displaced" his anger or fear so effectively that he would have been unable to recognize it, even though it became obvious to the people around him. This is a bad moment for the person telling the joke—the time when a witticism or story doesn't elicit laughter because the underlying meanings have not been well enough disguised.

Freud and his followers believed that women don't really need a sense of humor, because they have fewer strong feelings to repress, and this is where traditional theories about humor fail in relationship to women. The argument runs that women need to be naughty less because they are psychologically less complex. If a joke hides sexual or aggressive impulses, the line of reasoning goes, then girls will not make many jokes, since they do not have either sexual or aggressive impulses. The only response to such an argument at this point is a loud "HA!" Supplying a perhaps more convincing response to Freud's theory of penis envy is one told by a psychology professor at the beginning of every introductory course: A little girl and a little boy are in a sandbox. The little boy wants to compete with the girl, and so he tells her about how his family owns a color TV set. The girl says *her* parents own a color TV set. He says they own a boat. She replies that her parents also own a boat. He pulls down his trousers and declares, "*I* have *this*!" She pulls down her pants, looks, and runs home crying. The next day they are back in the sandbox. Having enjoyed himself the previous day, the little boy says that his parents have two cars. She replies that *her* parents have two cars. He says that they have a big house. She counters that her family too has a big house. Figuring that it worked before, the little boy pulls down his pants. The little girl looks him in the eye and says, "My mommy says that when I'm big *I* can have as many of *those* as I want!" This joke often unnerves the professor's male students, but it gives them all an irreverent perspective on Freud's theory of penis envy.

Using Aggressive Humor

So far we've been looking at situations where humor disguises hostility directed against us, and have seen the ways we can deal with this combination. But what about when we have hostile, angry, or fearful thoughts and want to use humor ourselves to give vent to these uncomfortable feelings?

There is a difference between using humor defensively and using it aggressively. When the actress Judy Holliday was being chased around the room by an aroused casting director, she finally stopped running and removed the "falsies" she had tucked into her bra. "Here," she told him, handing him two spheres of foam rubber, "I believe it's these you're after." However, when an old lover walks into a fancy restaurant with a new date and ignores us and we shout out (following an example set by Tallulah Bankhead) "What's the matter, darling, don't you recognize me with my clothes on?" we have just used humor as aggression. To make such a remark is as effective as overturning a glass of red wine on a white tuxedo jacket—the stain is hard to remove, everybody else can see it, and the perpetrator gets to walk away unsullied.

Or does she? This is one of the tricky parts: when men use humor to mask their anger, they are rewarded for resorting *only* to verbal aggression rather than acting it out physically. The implication is that the man is using language instead of his fists, playing out the thought that the first man to hurl an insult instead of a spear is the one who founded civilization. The subtext is that when a man demonstrates his anger through humor, he is showing self-control, because he could be acting destructively instead of just speaking destructively.

When a woman demonstrates her anger through humor, however, she is seen as losing self-control, because she isn't meant to have any angry feelings in the first place. A man's joke is seen as a legitimate way for him to disguise feelings; a woman's joke is seen as evidence of feelings she's not supposed to have in the first place. The understanding is that women employ humor as a last resort rather than as a first step, and so a woman's humor is seen as evidence of the fact that she is "unfeminine" in wishing to challenge someone. This sort of thinking can go back to the playgrounds of our childhood. If two little boys started taunting each other, nobody thought worse of it, because they were still considered to be behaving themselves. They might have even been congratulated for having kept the fight on such a calm level, their parents demonstrating approval of the grown-up use of words over violence.

In contrast, if two little girls started flinging nasty words at each another, their argument would be considered bad behavior. Cynthia Heimel describes a scene in *Sex Tips for Girls* under the heading "Faulty Upbringing": "Being a good little Everygirl meant shutting up and pleasing others. 'But Johnny hit his friend over the head with a baseball bat and you didn't lock him in the attic for three months,' Everygirl complained to her mom. 'But Johnny is a boy, dear. . . . Johnny gets to do stuff like that because when he grows up to be a man he will have to be strong and brave and hit other men over the head with a baseball bat when they try to steal his TV set.' 'What'll I do when someone tries to steal my TV set?' Everygirl wondered. 'You'll get your man to hit him over the head with a baseball bat,' Mom answered promptly." Heimel's scene points to the fact that boys are congratulated for engaging in violence as well as avoiding it. They are meant to rise to a challenge. A woman is meant to avoid challenges, and when one presents itself as unavoidable, she's supposed to find some man to rise to it for her, not to confront it herself. If she rises to the challenge herself, she is unfeminine. If she can defend herself, she raises all sorts of suspicions. In other words, if she can indeed defend herself, nobody congratulates her. Instead they wonder why she is so defensive.

How does this play out in adult life? Judy Tenuta states, "You can probably tell just by looking at me that I want to be a wife and mother. Oh, I really mean it. I want to be tied to the stove, making pancakes for some plumber." Very anti-male, right? Compare this to Andrew Dice Clay's routine about "sticking my tongue up some chick's ass while she's waiting on line at the bank." Women's comic comments about men are rarely, if ever, as violent in their revulsion for the opposite sex as those delivered by men. Yet female comics are often accused by male critics as "unfairly" critical of men. In everyday conversation, when men engage in repartee with one another, they are considered urbane and witty. When women engage in repartee, they are considered bitchy.

Which, of course, is no reason not to engage in repartee. Using humor as a way of showing your anger or resentment is not wrong. While making aggressive jokes is certainly less acceptable for women than keeping quiet altogether—impossible for any creature actually breathing and moving around—it is less unacceptable than other forms of self-expression for women, like crying or screaming. This is not to underestimate the power of crying and screaming, both critically important methods of getting one's point across in a pinch. Instead, this is to suggest that the strategic use of humor by a woman backed into a literal or figurative corner can have enormously positive results.

The most satisfying results occur, as we've already seen, when you can hold your own in response to an aggressive remark. For example, when Liz Carpenter, the former White House staff director for Lady Bird Johnson, published her book *Ruffles and Flourishes*, she came in for a number of remarks from male colleagues. When Arthur Schlesinger, Jr., stopped Carpenter to make the following comment, "I liked your book, Liz. Who wrote it for you?" she replied brightly, "I'm glad you liked it, Arthur. Who read it to you?" The man who believes he runs no risk when he launches a joke at a woman should be made to reevaluate his situation. The reason most men feel comfortable making jokes directed at women is that they do not expect any viable retort. They are more prepared for a hurt look than a quick reply, and to be able to take them off guard with the woman's own humor is to move in from a position of advantage. Susie Essman, a New York comic who has appeared on HBO and *Comic Strip Live,* identifies her use of humor as "a way to have the last word. When I was a kid my father used to say I had 'last-word-itis.' " She sees her humor as a positive form of armor, a device that allows her to take risks yet remain unscathed. "I see myself as a warrior when I go out there, because comedy is a pretty aggressive act. But I also know that when I'm being my best—being myself and being funny—I've got a lot of power. And," she adds, "that's pretty sexy." She rarely has trouble with hecklers, because "They just know they won't win. They know that with my sense of humor—and it's my job, after all—I always will have the last word."

Florynce Kennedy, a gay black activist, is noted for her ability to get to the heart of the matter. For example, when a male heckler called out "Are you a lesbian?" she immediately replied, "Are you my alternative?" Kennedy tells one story that categorizes the need for women's awareness of the power we have once we recognize it: "There's a lady in the dentist's chair who is pretty nervous about what's going on. The dentist works on her for about three minutes and all of a sudden he realizes that she has managed to obtain a very tight grip on his testicles, and she's squeezing just short of agony. So he stops and says, 'What is this?' and she says, 'We are not going to hurt each other, are we, doctor?' " Kennedy uses this example, she says, to underscore the idea that "Anyone that's close enough to hurt you can be hurt." In other words, when someone tries to take advantage of you, verbally as well as physically, you have a right to protect yourself.

This is especially the case when the joke or remark is one used as a form of violation, perhaps when a dirty joke is told or an overly familiar remark is made. Diana Dors, an English actress known as a Platinum Bombshell in the 1950s, came in for her share of sexual remarks even when she was not playing a role. When, at a dinner given in her honor, a fellow actor toasted her by saying "I cannot claim to know Miss Dors well but I should like to—and when we met this evening she gave me the eye and I could hear her saying to herself 'There's a man I'd like to be made love to by,' " Dors rose to the occasion and replied, "I protest at what the speaker has just said. He knows perfectly well that, even when talking to myself, I should never end a sentence with two prepositions." Dors finessed the situation by first recognizing that the personal nature of such a remark meant that she was in an antagonistic relationship to the man making it. This man was not flattering her by such a comment. Rather, he was metaphorically sticking his hand up her dress in public. She retaliated by attacking a vulnerable spot, much like Flo Kennedy's dental patient. She used humor to her advantage by building up to her comment, because surely when she said, "I protest at what the speaker has just said," the audience expected indignation at the sexual overtones and smug nature of the actor's toast. Instead of supplying what they expected, she used sarcasm to point to his weakness rather than relying on indignation, which would have underscored his ability to make her uncomfortable.

If and when you decide to use aggressive humor, you have to be sure to do it with finesse. It has to appear not to matter to you at all, otherwise it won't work. Like any joke, it depends on concealing the true feelings underneath. If the feelings show through too obviously, then you'll lose the sympathy of your observers. Unless you perfect the art of seeming cool when you are in a murderous rage, it is unlikely that any useful comeback will come to you. This is why most people spend their time wishing that they'd said something clever the moment they were verbally assaulted—but the emotion of the moment is blinding in its intensity and so prevents us from thinking of anything useful. This is the factor that makes it difficult to come up with a terrifically amusing response when your heart is breaking. Probably best not to try it. You can always write a letter later on or, better yet, a novel. Look how well Nora Ephron did with *Heartburn*. Using anger, hurt, or the desire for revenge to propel yourself into an activity is not the worst that can happen. As the writer Naomi Bliven has pointed out, "Behind almost every woman you ever heard of stands a man who let her down."

But those minor annoyances of life—the guys at the bar, the nasty co-worker, the snotty salesman—these can and should be countered by a battery of humorous responses you can cultivate like a beautiful and slightly poisonous garden. When a construction worker shouts at you as you walk down the street, "Hey, honey, I want to get into your pants," by all means shout back, "Nah, I got one asshole in there already." His pals will give him a hard time all day, and they might even applaud you. They are unlikely to give you any more problems, and you don't have to spend the next twenty minutes fuming about the way men can yell things at women but women can't yell back. Yell back—just attack him with a joke he can't answer. Making a joke at the joker's expense is like making a cheat pay the tab when he thought he was going to be the one who got the free meal.

When your co-worker sneeringly tells you that he never argues with a lady, answer, à la Mae West, "Playing safe, huh?" If your significant other has been watching too much television and comes to you accusingly with a shirt that has "ring around the collar," point out, à la Erma Bombeck, that it happens to match the one around his neck. When snotty second cousins ask "So when are *you* going to get married?" answer with Mae West's immortal line "Marriage is a great institution, but I'm not ready for an institution yet." Follow the example of Dorothy Parker when someone is flirting too openly and aggressively with your date, and coolly mention to him that you've heard that "She speaks eighteen languages, and she can't say 'no' in any of them. . . ." After you've gotten over the initial trauma, explain to your friend that your lover left you for a much younger woman so that he could save money by buying all those half-fare plane tickets. Or that he wanted a nice girl, someone who wouldn't point out that it was odd for a man to have penis envy. Or, à la stand-up comic Diane Ford, you could do a routine on the idea of his leaving. The sweet-faced LA comedian who looks like the original Good Girl (she *is* from Minnesota) begins by explaining, "I had to hold down three jobs to put him through school. Then when I turned twenty-six and thought that I should go back to college," she continues, her voice getting lower and faster as she speaks, "he divorced me. For a nineteen-year-old bimbette with straw for brains who walks seven feet behind him so that when he stops to read a road map she wipes his butt." At this point she hesitates, smiles a smile full of sunshine and dimples, and comments, "But I'm not bitter." The laughter that greeted this routine when she did it on the HBO *Women of the Night* special was evidence that the audience understood fully the embittered nature of her diatribe as well as the need to smile and lie, dimples and all. The combination of Good Girl and Bad made for enormously effective comedy. For a throw-away line after the laughter she smiled conspiratorially and said, "Sometimes I do them just for me," indicating that this particular story arrived in her repertoire the hard way, through experience. When you can begin to do "routines" or make stories out of your most painful moments, you are well on the way to recovery. You'll begin to notice one thing: using humor to air your anger will make you feel better. The one thing to avoid, however, is using humor to be hostile to yourself.

Playing Against the House

When you turn back upon yourself the anger you have toward another person, you are playing a losing game. Women tend to turn their anger against themselves, psychologists argue, since women are taught that it is unfeminine to show anger at anyone else. Phyllis Diller says that "Comedy is a hostile act," and that she attacks herself because "that's what got the laughs." If instead of seeing that the reason you are mad has less to do with your own inner self than it has to do with reacting to outside forces, then you can begin to challenge that which is making you angry. When a guy shouts to you on the street and you feel bad about having provoked such a comment, you should stop and think about the dynamics of the situation. This guy is not even seeing you as a person, he's eyeing you as sexual fast food. Therefore you don't have to examine yourself to see whether you've done anything to bring this on yourself. You haven't. You are therefore allowed to respond to him as fair game, as somebody who has violated you verbally, and you are allowed to respond in kind. I know a woman who was once so angry at such a comment that she screamed back "If your mouth is so big, your dick must be real small" and then spent the rest of the day worried—honest to God—in case he really did have a small dick. Believe me, this is misplaced compassion. When you respond with a bitchy, funny remark, you are not so much being hostile as asserting your right to be heard. You are making sure that you have the last word. And the last laugh.

4

The Laughter in the Kitchen

....

Growing Up Female and Funny

Keeping It to Ourselves
....

There were maybe ten to fifteen women between the ages of eighteen and eighty-three in that basement kitchen every Sunday afternoon. Only women. The men would be upstairs doing whatever they did; nobody expressed much interest. The women would have all gone to church on their own, the men treating God as if He were one of their wives' relatives that only the wives had to visit. The husbands stayed home to wash the cars. After church, the women came home to cook. Having served the requisite amount of church time, the women would feel a little reckless, a little lighthearted. They would joke around, sometimes not too kindly, about their lives, their husbands and children, and their neighbors. By the time the veal cutlets were ready, the noise level would have reached majestic proportions. It looked like, and sounded like, an opera. Aunt Josie would be holding her sides, the shiny material of her black dress stretched to bursting by her laughter. Aunt Lucy would be mimicking the snooty salesgirl at A&S, with her facility for reproducing every move perfectly. Aunt Marie would be wiping the tears away, being a silent laugher all her life, unable to stop herself from crying if she laughed, as if to appease the gods, who wouldn't want her to be too happy. Then cousin Nina would start on her husband's habit of falling asleep when they had company, and we would understand and laugh. Everyone spoke at once, everyone shrieked at a particularly wicked line. And then the most amazing thing would happen. When the food was brought upstairs and we sat down with the men, all the laughing stopped. We all smiled, but all traces of conspiracy and the raucous, unholy enjoyment of the steamy kitchen were completely removed. The serious talk began—money, cars, jobs. Nobody made wicked remarks. Nobody shrieked. And if one of the uncles asked, friendly and sincere, what we had all been laughing at downstairs, the only answer anyone ever gave—ever—was "Oh, nothing."

What Our Mothers Taught Us

Many of us grew up listening to the laughter in the kitchen. Even as little girls we knew that our mothers, aunts, neighbors, friend's mothers, women in general, were pretty funny. We listened to funny conversations while hiding under the tablecloths, overheard one-sided phone calls that were funny despite the absence of half the dialogue. Nicole Hollander, the cartoonist and creator of "Sylvia" (a cartoon syndicated in several countries, translated into many languages) explains, "My grandmother, my mother and all her friends were witty; in my neighborhood, women had all the best lines." Similarly, Marilyn Sokel, whose appearances on *The Tonight Show* and on Broadway have won her a large following, says that her sense of comedy "came from my mother—she had a bawdy sense of humor. There were more women than men in my family and when we all got together there would be my sister, my cousin Betty, my Aunt Lillian, my Aunt Mabel, my mother. . . . Most people go into comedy because they made their friends and relatives laugh. . . ." Gilda Radner has told very much the same tale: "I'll interview my mother. 'Why am I funny?' She'll tell me stories about my grandmother." The playwright Wendy Wasserstein also remembers thinking as a child "that my family was very funny. I think this was because my mother was somewhat eccentric." Wasserstein describes how she learned to use her writing talents to her advantage in high school. It's not exactly about becoming head cheerleader, but about using her talents to get her out of something rather than into something. She recalls, "I figured out that one of the ways I could get out of gym was if I wrote something called the Mother-Daughter Fashion Show. I know very little about fashion, but they used to have this Mother-Daughter Fashion Show once a year at the Plaza Hotel, and you got to leave school for the fashion show. But if you wrote [the show] you didn't have to go to gym for like two or three weeks, it was fantastic." Wasserstein got out of gym, but she also got to write early on for an all-female audience that could appreciate her particular kind of humor. Women learn from an early age that making other women laugh is more than an acceptable idea—it's a good one. The common denominator among women who have grown up with a keen and active sense of humor is their identification of a humorous female influence early in their lives. It is no secret to women that women have a sense of humor.

Yes, women's lines have always gotten a laugh—but only in secret. "Secret" meant just what the deodorant ad told us: "Secret" meant "for women only." It's as if women saw the same sort of "glass ceiling" between the kitchen—or the private world of women—and the "upstairs" public world of men, as women have seen in the workplace. According to the authors of *Breaking the Glass Ceiling*, women place restrictions on their behavior because of a fear of being perceived as too aggressive or because they believe that they cannot act themselves in a public setting. It seems as if this anxiety about performing in public has implications for the way women are taught to use—or not to use—humor. According to recent research, women generally rate themselves as most comfortable when telling jokes to a very small group of close friends, whereas men feel comfortable telling their jokes to groups of a much larger size. This follows the patterns set by traditional expectations, which lead us to anticipate that men would be out in the public world dealing daily with groups of strangers, whereas women would inhabit a smaller, essentially private world, composed of family, neighbors, and friends. Women also prefer to tell jokes to a group composed of other women. Most of our everyday experiences will confirm this theory. As soon as a man entered the picture, most of us will remember hearing the laughter in all female groups stop altogether or, even more confusingly, "change" into a softer, less active or assertive, style. We began to notice that after a certain age even our brothers weren't safe to laugh around anymore. At about the same time that our brothers could no longer be allowed to go to the ladies' room, the laughter stopped or changed when they were present. It is no surprise, then, that men have thought women have very little sense of humor. They have certainly been privy to very little of it. Women's humor was shut away from them, sealed off as tightly as bologna in a Tupperware container, all the better to preserve it for later.

Older women taught us, by their example, the code that indicated when the tone of the conversation had to shift—like a quick change of scenery between acts—to accommodate the arrival of a man. There was more smiling but less laughing around men. Smiling and laughing represent very different experiences—a smile, especially for a woman, is seen as an act of supplication, whereas a laugh is often read as a challenge. When we plug in the general, all-purpose smile, we signal, effectively, "I'm not looking for trouble. Just be nice to me." When we smile that all-purpose smile, many of us look down or in some manner avert our gaze so that we do not make direct eye contact. When you laugh with someone, in contrast, the instinctive response is to look directly into the eyes of the person with whom you share that moment. You've connected. You're standing on the same turf. Laughing together is as close as you can get to a hug without touching.

The Smile Is Generic, the Laugh Is Specific

The glazed smile is generic, the laugh is specific. You can smile at any time, keeping the expression in place under a number of circumstances. When you laugh, you are reacting to a moment. A good, hearty laugh is one of the most difficult things to manufacture if the genuine impulse is not present. A smile is easier to manufacture because it is a general, rather than specific, response. The smile is passive—not so much a statement as an expected reply.

A smile also remains ambiguous, and women have been taught to believe that there is strength in uncertainty. Too clear a statement of like or dislike is frowned upon. Mystery, intrigue, elusiveness—these were all traditionally considered positive attributes in a woman. The *Mona Lisa* is considered one of the greatest images of woman. Like the *Mona Lisa,* a woman with a smile is seen as a woman with a hint of mystery. The smile of *Mona Lisa* has been the focus of great speculation: Is she pregnant? Is she in love? Is she getting paid a hefty fee to sit there and smile? The riddle of her smile has made the figure a public icon, and a model for women. We're supposed to keep our thoughts to ourselves and only hint at what's really going on inside our heads, in order to give us that air of secrecy men have been taught to desire. When a woman laughs out loud, the mystery is replaced by certainty. Everyone around you knows precisely how you feel—you're having a good time and reacting impulsively and intensely to a specific moment. You've lost that sweet uncertainty and have replaced it with a pungent sense of self. If you suddenly laugh without explanation, people will be made very nervous—it's just not done. In contrast, if you smile and don't explain yourself, that's elusive and seductive—because it's traditionally "feminine." That women are supposed to smile without a reason is fine, because it's a woman's role to be pleased and pleasant at all times. She doesn't need a reason, because the script calls for her perpetual, unquestioning delight. A woman is expected to smile, even required to smile, around men. But her laughter will often come as a surprise, even when there's an obvious and good reason for it. Why?

Humor in All-Female vs. Mixed-Sex Groups

Why has the feminine tradition of humor, ubiquitous as it is, remained essentially hidden from the mainstream? In part it is due to the Tupperware mentality that sought to preserve humor by keeping it away from the potentially hazardous male gaze. If men didn't find funny what we found funny, then they would think we were foolish. If they thought our joking was foolish, we might learn to like it less ourselves. It wasn't worth the risk. One of the other answers is a paradox: when women joke—as we all know women do and do well—they are exploring a particularly feminine tradition of humor. The laughter in the kitchen, dorm room, and locker room is evidence of women's ability to joke and appreciate joking in an all-female group. They are exploring, in their laughter, female territory. The idea that women have their own humor, that a feminine tradition of humor could exist apart from the "traditional" masculine version, is not considered a viable possibility, and so women who initiate humor are seen as acting like men.

In a 1976 study done on joke telling in mixed-sex groups, a team of psychologists from the University of Maryland found that "It seems reasonable to propose that attempting a witty remark is often an intrusive, disturbing and aggressive act, and within this culture, probably unacceptable for a female." No wonder the only acceptable answer to "What's so funny?" was always "Nothing." No other explanation would have allowed the women to remain "feminine." To deny the entire experience in front of men was the only way these women thought they could protect the experience. "Maybe Rose laughed a little when I spilled some sauce," my grandmother would offer apologetically, and I would be kicked under the table by someone's black orthopedic shoe if I betrayed the women by looking surprised or, God forbid, by giggling.

How do we learn what's "appropriate" behavior? Certainly we learn it by watching the older people in our families. But there are, of course, other pervasive, and broader, influences. Studies have been done by sociologists and psychologists that go far in proving what we've all suspected—namely, "that society may hold different expectations regarding boys' and girls' humor." These social norms, argues the psychologist Paul McGhee, dictate that "Males should be the initiators of humor, while females should be responders." McGhee outlines the ways in which early childhood experiences form the expectations we have concerning how men and women use humor. McGhee theorizes that "Humor in interpersonal interaction serves as a means of gaining or maintaining dominance or control over the social situation. Because of the power associated with the successful use of humor, as we have seen, the initiation of humor has become associated with other traditionally masculine characteristics, such as aggressiveness, dominance, and assertiveness."

Hence, when a girl makes a joke, she is seen to be acting like a boy. When a girl uses humor, she makes those around her nervous because her use of humor indicates that she is unwilling to accept her role as passive onlooker. A little girl is not often rewarded for her funny behavior, in contrast to the approval generally awarded to a boy whose antics amuse his elders. If a boy came into a room full of adults to show them how he had put a rubber elephant nose on his dog, the adults would probably laugh more overtly at his action than they would had a girl done the same thing. She would be seen as unfeminine in acting out such "unmaternal" instincts. She should know better than to make the dog uncomfortable just to get a laugh—she's supposed to care about others. The boy, in contrast, would be more easily forgiven for having put the comic moment before the dog's well-being, so long as no serious damage was done. By using humor to get attention, the girl shows that she wants—consciously or unconsciously—to break with society's expectations and that she is demanding a more active role than the one scripted for her. If a girl initiates humor, she is probably learning at an early age to use humor to make those around her uncomfortable, rather than using what is seen as more typically "feminine" humor to put them more at ease. If she learns to be amused, then she'll make people comfortable.

Self-deprecating humor is acceptable as feminine, of course, as we've already seen. That making fun of yourself or, by extension, of other women, is okay comes across clearly to young women. Penny Marshall claims, "I would make fun of myself before anybody else could. I had braces and my hair in a ponytail—real attractive. . . . So I would always hit before anyone could hit me. Self-defacing humor is my forte." The very word choice of "self-defacing" is interesting here, since, by using a comic mask, Marshall seems to have found a way early in life to put on a new face. If Marshall's story resembles the earlier one told by Gilda Radner about her childhood, this is not surprising. Many funny women found out in childhood or early adolescence that self-deprecating humor can draw fire. Phyllis Diller said that becoming funny was her way of "adjusting to puberty. When I reached that self-conscious age where I looked like Olive Oyl and wanted to look like Jean Harlow, I knew something had to be done. From twelve on, the only way to handle the terror of social situations was comedy—break the ice, make everybody laugh. I did it to make people feel more relaxed, including myself." Jay Presson Allen, a playwright and screenwriter whose credits include the screenplays of *The Prime of Miss Jean Brodie* and *Funny Lady,* says, "Humor comes out of hostility. Men feel threatened by this from women—unless they turn it on themselves."

So we grow up learning that we can defuse a situation by turning ourselves into a self-effacing diversion, taking a little bit out of ourselves in order to make others happy. Wendy Wasserstein makes a distinction between being funny and being pleasing. "There's a line about Janie in 'Isn't It Romantic?' that says, 'That's the thing about Janie, she's not threatening to anybody. That's her gift.' " Wasserstein sees herself as basically shy, although, she says, "Sometimes I can be funny." When talking to the interviewer Esther Cohen, Wasserstein explained, "I can be funny with a girlfriend. I can be very sarcastic. . . . I know how to make friends, get on with people, because I could be funny . . . in a non-threatening, likeable way." We try to develop our abilities, but only within the perimeters set by society as acceptable.

But we also learn to be careful with whatever ability we do discover. We don't want to draw too much attention to ourselves or "take over" a situation by being funny. In *The Cathy and Mo Show* the girl who wants to grow up to be Mrs. Kenny Rogers knows that she needs to be "independent, without crossing that line to be unappealing," and in the same way, girls know they want to be amusing without crossing that line to being obnoxious. Remember "obnoxious"? "Obnoxious," like "immature," was a high school word directed at those unattractive creatures who had to get attention in ways other than being hip and cool. Girls who were too loud or made too many crass jokes could easily be labeled by other girls as "obnoxious." (Boys who were obnoxious were the ones who kept asking you out even after you told them you didn't want to go out with them. Boys who were immature were the ones who didn't ask you out at all.)

Girls learn early on that they get social points for directing humor against themselves and negative points for directing it against others—especially if the others are male. But some girls also learn early to use humor to defend themselves against the humor of others, to deflect the aggressive tendencies that, as we've seen, inform a great deal of what is considered comic. Judy Tenuta, the stand-up comedian whose radical act seeks to convert her audience to her own religion of Judyism, grew up in a religious Polish-Italian household with her six brothers and one sister ("My mother . . . is very religious. On special holidays she will still drive to have the cardinal bless the groceries"). In a recent interview her mother claims, "Judy was a sweet and quiet child. There was never any sign that she would be a comedian. In some ways, her brothers were funnier." What kind of humor did she grow up around—what was this humor of her brothers? According to the story reported in *GQ*, Judy was originally the butt of her brothers' jokes rather than the initiator of her own. "When she was four," writes the reporter Marcia Froelke Coburn, "one of her brothers taught her that her last name was Tenuta-Fish. Then he lost her in the park. She told the policeman her name and phone number and he called her mother. 'Hello, Mrs. Fish? We have your daughter.' When the squad car pulled up in front of her house," explains Coburn, "her family was outside, laughing." Enough to make any girl learn to manufacture her own jokes before anyone else could foist theirs on her. Making your own jokes is equivalent to taking control over your life—and usually that means taking control away from someone else.

If these psychologists are right, and "The witty person in a natural group is among the most powerful members of the group," then it is not in society's interest to allow girls to learn to use humor unless it is willing to accept that, by doing so, girls will be learning to use power. Many stand-up performers have learned to command authority in other settings before facing an audience. The comedian Joy Behar, whose insights into male-female relationships are consistently profound, brings the authority she once used in an inner-city classroom to the stage. Having taught in a school where "they sent kids who would otherwise be behind bars" to her classroom, Behar translates her self-assurance to other areas of life. There is no hesitation in her remarks, no self-effacement. You can see that she is in control, and that her intelligence sharpens the edge of her wit. When she comments that, since women's liberation, men are no longer sure what they should do and not do, she gives them clear instructions. "A lot of men are confused about what their role is. What do you do? When the check comes when you're on a date, do you pay it? Yes, you do. Do you hold doors open, pull out chairs? No, you don't. Do you still have to kill the big bug in the kitchen? Yes, you do." Behar's comedy proceeds from her personal authority and power. This is, once again, the equation that makes women's humor subversive—the equation between women using humor and women using power. Sometimes this means a clear understanding on the girl's part that her power comes from her difference—that even if others are not laughing, she has the right to her own assessments and her own responses.

Who Else Is Laughing?

The nineteenth-century philosopher Henri Bergson, whose work on laughter remains one of the most important discussions of the subject, knew that a person would "hardly appreciate the comic if you felt yourself isolated from others. Laughter appears to stand in need of an echo." Bergson went on to argue that "Laughter is always the laughter of a group. It may . . . have happened to you, when seated in a railway carriage or at a table d'hôte, to hear travellers relating to one another stories which must have been comic for them, for they laughed heartily. Had you been one of their company, you would have laughed like them, but, as you were not, you had no desire whatever to do so. A man who was once asked why he did not weep at a sermon when everybody else was shedding tears replied: 'I don't belong to the parish!' What that man thought of tears would be still more true of laughter . . . laughter always implies a kind of freemasonry, or even complicity, with other laughers." The philosopher's point is that the experience of laughter implies a community of shared values. What happens, however, when a group is excluded from the mainstream? Will this group ignore the mainstream's values and develop values of its own?

Certainly girls are not brought up to ignore mainstream values—quite the contrary. One of the compelling findings from studies done on early childhood influences on the development of humor in girls is the assertion that girls seem to be more aware than boys of the reactions of other people around them. Studies have found that girls will look and listen for the reactions of other audience members more than their male counterparts. Girls are trained to be aware of social reactions—girls are encouraged to be on the lookout for the needs and wishes of others, even if it means putting the needs of others before their own. Girls are therefore less likely to laugh if no one else is laughing, because they are acutely aware that no one is sharing their response. They are made uneasy, and even if they would laugh on their own, they are unlikely to laugh in a group if their response would be markedly different from those around them. But if boys and girls find different things funny, and the boys aren't laughing, in most cases a girl's laughter will be drastically inhibited. Even if there are other girls in the room, each will have listened before laughing, so it becomes a vicious cycle that no one is able to break. Until girls can start to laugh in the assurance that there are others who share their responses, the only reply will be the silence of the half-smile.

Growing up, a girl learns to distrust her own instincts in a mixed-sex group, especially one that is predominantly male. "Oh," she thinks, "this word play must not be very funny, because nobody else (not one of the boys in the room) is laughing. I guess I should be quiet and not embarrass myself. Oh, this eye poking (pie throwing, mud wrestling) must be funny, because everybody else (every boy in the room) is laughing. I guess I should laugh, too, otherwise they'll think I have no sense of humor." Girls learn to listen before they laugh because girls are brought up to believe that they need guidance in their responses. They are trained to be aware of what their male counterparts are doing; they are aware that their behavior will be judged according to the standards set by the men—they learn that masculine behavior is "universal" and applies across the board. Put most simply, girls are taught to be led, not to lead.

Learning to Lead

Mary Davis, a senior vice president of Time-Warner, Inc., defines herself as having been a "good girl" all through her childhood and schooldays. She had to learn to use her natural sense of humor as she grew into her leadership position. She would certainly support the theory that the witty person in a group is among the most powerful members of the group. The strategic use of humor is one of the identifying factors of the so-called natural leaders. Davis explains, "The funny boys were always the class leaders. Joking wasn't something you got points for as a good girl." Davis had, early on, repressed her gift for laughter because, especially as a girl growing up in the South, she'd been taught to act like a lady. In her seventeen-year voyage through the ranks of Time-Warner, she gradually learned to have more confidence in her sense of humor, even though it was often difficult to overcome inhibitions. "It took me a long time to understand that if I was comfortable enough to laugh and joke around people, they would then feel easier around me. Feeling easier around me makes them feel good about themselves. As a consequence, my humor lets them associate my way of working with an efficient, fun and satisfying way of getting things done." Mary believes that using wit is as effective a leadership tool for women as it is for men, but that women have to unlearn what they learned as girls in order to implement useful strategies for using humor.

When a woman thinks about making a joke during the opening moments of a small meeting, for example, she probably encounters—if not consciously, then unconsciously—what psychologists would call "old information." This is a term for the unpacked emotional baggage we carry around with us from our younger days. Old information has an effect on what we do even—or especially—when we are least aware of it. It's the collection of fears and worries left over from childhood training. When four of your co-workers happen to be wearing white-and-green ties and you want to say something about them looking like the Dartmouth Ping-Pong team, you hesitate. The remark, trivial and lighthearted as it is, just won't come out of your mouth. You're afraid they won't get it. You worry that they won't like it if you try to show off by calling attention to yourself. You're afraid that maybe you're misremembering the Dartmouth colors. Maybe they'll resent your calling attention to their attire. Worst of all, none of them will laugh and they'll look at you with that puzzled, wide-eyed expression indicating that they think you've really lost it this time. So you shut up. Your worries win and keep you quiet. All this takes no more than a couple of seconds, and the thought process is almost automatic—you don't really think it through point by point. At the same moment, the man sitting next to you calls out, "Hey, what are you guys, anyway? The Dartmouth tiddlywinks team?" And they all laugh and say what a riot it is for this guy always to have something funny to say. What a funny guy he is, how they can count on him to break the ice. What would meetings be like without him? This man sitting next to you did not have to go through the same old information you did. He did not have to confront the same worries, because he grew up knowing that this kind of comment would get a favorable response. And meanwhile you're still sitting on your hands, letting all those old fears keep you from speaking up.

Unlearning Old Patterns
. . . .

Early fears should no more prevent us from appreciating our own humor than they should stop us finding jobs or playing squash. Because most of us have to discover our own abilities in terms of humor doesn't mean we should listen to the old information that tells us not to bother trying. Studies have shown that girls who learn to initiate humor also show other patterns of assertive behavior—a willingness to break away from the culture's expectations. Since most of us have had to break away from early training in passivity, it is not surprising that acquiring our own uses of humor is a gradual process. We have to unlearn the old habits that keep us quiet. Women need to have a better understanding of how their early experiences might still prevent them from exercising their sense of humor even when it is most appropriate.

A girl learns not to trust her instincts in terms of humor. Because the standards set for what is considered funny have been set without her in mind, she is aware of laughing in the "wrong" places. If she doesn't laugh at the farting scene in *Blazing Saddles,* for example, she'll be considered humorless by her date. If, however, she laughs too loudly or enthusiastically at Madeline Kahn's song in the same film—a song that hilariously complains in a Marlene Dietrich style about men who come too soon but never enough with the women they bed— then she might be accused of being one of those women who like anti-male jokes. If she prefers the comedy of Claudette Colbert in *It Happened One Night* to the comedy of Jerry Lewis in *Cinderfella,* she might not pass the "test" of humor set by a guy who has been unchallenged since he was twelve. We've all been conditioned to believe that there's something wrong with us if we don't laugh along, so we do.

We produce nervous laughter—that particularly falsified response—to any number of situations. We're especially likely to laugh nervously when we're attempting to conceal what we think is an inappropriate reaction. "See?" you're trying to signal, "I'm really enjoying myself, honestly." This scene of someone miserably self-conscious trying to appear self-confident by laughing is a standard of situation comedies and funny films. It's what Shelley Long, playing Diane Chambers in *Cheers*, would do whenever she felt particularly out of place. It's what Lucy would do to a hysterical degree when faced with a movie-star companion of Ricky's. It's what Patty always did—and what Cathy never did—on *The Patty Duke Show*. It's what all the women do on *The Newlywed Game* if they're not whacking their husbands. False laughter has become so familiar on the screen because it already is so familiar in life, especially for women. If women are indeed concerned with making sure that everyone around them is comfortable, then a woman will try doubly hard not to make anyone uncomfortable through an expression of her own discomfort.

The trouble is that it's nearly impossible to fake laughter convincingly. Did you ever have to laugh as part of a role in a school play? It's easier for most amateur actors to cry—produce tears, sobs, sniffles—than it is for them to laugh. Or, in that situation so familiar to most of us, did you ever try to laugh at his jokes even when you didn't find them funny? Really laugh? You probably made a strange strangled sound, as little like your real laugh as a sneeze.

Faking a Laugh Is Like Faking an Orgasm

Women fake laughter for the same reasons we sometimes fake orgasms—to make somebody else feel comfortable by pretending we're comfortable. It's probably even easier to fake an orgasm than it is to fake a laugh, as the film *When Harry Met Sally . . .* has shown. But faking either one is unhealthy, because faking a sustained response with any regularity tends to confuse boundaries between what's real and what's pretend. At some point you'll give up locating your genuine response and give in to the pressure to react as you think you're meant to. The scene for both sorts of faking works this way: The woman sees that her companion is waiting for her response. She feels that if she doesn't respond as he hopes, he'll feel let down and embarrassed. Instead of allowing him to feel bad, the woman pretends to be delighted spontaneously, and tells herself that it can't hurt to make him happy. But faking a response is just another version of "putting out," in that charming phrase. . . . Laughing at something that isn't funny is just another version of "putting out." You're concerned with appearing to produce the right response. You want to seem like a good sport. Sure, at some point, reading from the script becomes easier than inventing your own dialogue, but it's never a good idea. We need to find our own definitions and boundaries for what really delights us— if we're only doing what's expected, we can't expect very much.

Finding Other Women Funny

Women seem to know what will make other women laugh. Now, this concept seems so basic it appears unnecessary to defend it. But like fashions designed by men for women built like men— six feet tall, no breasts or hips, shoulders that make it difficult to enter a doorway without turning sideways—comedy has traditionally been written by men, even when it has been directed at an audience of women. Only within the last fifteen years or so has the creation of a particularly "feminine" comedy been seen as profitable by those in the business. In a field almost completely dominated by men, we've seen finally the ascendancy of cartoonists such as Nicole Hollander, Cathy Guisewite, Lynda Barry, and Roz Chast. With a new wave of women comedians and comic actresses, as well as women screenwriters and directors, we are gradually watching the formation of a distinctly women-centered comedy, which emerges from the kitchen and makes its way onto the stage or screen without losing any of its flavor.

"I always write the same thing," says Susan Silver, whose early scripts for *The Mary Tyler Moore Show* and other comedies have won her acclaim, "from my own life, myself. . . . I went into the MTM offices with six stories from my life and they thought they were fantastic. They weren't really. They were women's stories that any woman could tell you, but the business had been so male dominated that men weren't even thinking along those lines. They thought I knew some great secret." The great secret that's hit television and film in the last ten years or so is the awareness that women find other's women's material funny—that there are distinctly feminine plots, style, and tone. For one thing, there has been a growing interest in feminine material that is also feminist. As Lisa Merrill, a professor of speech and communication arts at Hofstra University, has argued, "A feminist comic sensibility would be one in which the details of women's lives were presented in such a manner as to allow the female audience to mock our traditional roles." Such a revisionary vision would "affirm women's experience rather than denigrate it."

Where men hear something funny and want to "top it" with one of their own stories, women hear a funny story and think "Oh, thank God, that happened to you, too! It means I'm not crazy!" Women are more concerned with integrating a story into their own lives than competing to see whether they can come up with a better one. Where men tell jokes, women tell stories, usually stories about themselves or their friends, and, not surprisingly, these will concern issues of particular importance to women. The humor present in these stories will uncover or explore feminine responses to the world, and by hearing the woman's side of things, women will respond strongly. That's why it might be dangerous to watch a *Mary Tyler Moore* rerun with a new boyfriend, in case he doesn't get the jokes, and then you've got to explain what's funny, and everything gets confused. However, as time goes by, he should indeed be able to appreciate, if not actually share, the feminine perspective on humor. If he doesn't find you at all funny, or if you can't share at least some of your laughter with him, it's unlikely that the relationship has a future.

One clear-cut test of a man's reactions to what is a quintessential piece of feminine humor can be administered by reading him aloud from Dorothy Parker's immortal short story "A Telephone Call." The story, which is essentially a monologue, has been worshiped by generations of women. It begins "Please, God, let him telephone me now. Dear God, let him call me now. I won't ask anything else of You, truly I won't. It isn't very much to ask. It would be so little to You. . . . If I didn't think about it, maybe the telephone might ring. Sometimes it does that. If I could think of something else. If I could think of something else. Maybe if I counted to five hundred by fives, it might ring by that time." There are very few women who have not had similar monologues running through their minds, and so the Parker story appeals to them through its confrontation with one of the most painful, powerless moments of their lives. "He couldn't have minded me calling him up. I know you shouldn't keep telephoning them—I know they don't like that. When you do that they know you are thinking about them and wanting them, and that makes them hate you. . . . And all I did was ask him how he was; it was the way anybody might have called him up. He couldn't have minded that."

As we continue reading, we recognize the disturbing realism behind Parker's words. We can laugh at the helplessness of her character because we can see, when it's presented by another woman, how we create our own self-destructive, torturous thoughts. Parker tells us to our faces that she knows about all those moments we try to disguise. She exposes all the little games, the secret fictions we tell ourselves to make ourselves feel better when we know the situation is desperate. "I'll be so sweet to him if he calls me. If he says he can't see me tonight, I'll say, 'Why, that's all right, dear. Why, of course it's all right.' I'll be the way I was when I first met him. Then maybe he'll like me again. I was always sweet, at first. Oh, it's easy to be sweet to people before you love them." Parker holds a mirror up to our self-delusions, forcing a laugh on us even when we're miserable.

I remember a friend reading me the Parker story while I waited for a long-distance phone call from a dubious boyfriend, sitting in a pale green dorm room on a frigid winter night, and the two of us hysterical even as I knew the silent "pleasegodlethimcall" refrain was rubbing itself against the back of my laughter. It was wonderful to hear that Parker felt in 1923 exactly what I was feeling in 1978. If I was being foolish, as I knew I was, at least I wasn't crazy. Parker and my pal both reassured me that from one angle at least what was going on was both typical enough to be understood by others and absurd enough to be comic. The laughter provided by the situation afforded me a feeling of community that got me through the worst part of waiting. However, I made the mistake, when the sacred call actually arrived, hours later, of reading to my beloved part of what I'd just been laughing at. I figured that he'd be amused and that it would help him to understand how much I'd been looking forward to his call. I read a few sentences and waited to hear his welcome, throaty laugh. Nothing. Finally he said, "Ah, yeah. Okay, is that the end?" without providing so much as a chuckle. Then he supplied the killer line, "Seems kind of sad that this lady had nothing else to do besides wait for the phone to ring," and I felt a rush of resentment that made the lights in the room flicker. He was telling me "That's not funny," but at that moment I knew he was wrong—it *was* funny. He didn't get it—he missed the funny part—but that didn't mean it wasn't a terrifically comic piece of writing. I was sure, at that moment, that I at least knew what was funny and what wasn't. I knew that, even for him, I wasn't going to say what was expected. I knew that I just couldn't simper and say "You're right, it's pretty sad for somebody to sit around and wait for the phone to ring, how stupid. I don't even remember why I thought it was funny," because I'd be denying myself something important, my right to my own responses.

Coming Out of the Kitchen

There comes a moment, finally, when we all get tired of answering "Nothing" to a man's question of "What's so funny?" A great deal around us is funny, and we've always laughed about it when we've been with other women. What makes us laugh is worth talking about. Our humor is worth sharing openly, with enthusiasm and confidence, with a generosity that will make our laughter easy to join. It's now up to the men who are listening to try to get the jokes we make, and no doubt most of them will try and succeed. It's certainly time for us to stop apologizing for, or repressing, our laughter. When we take the laughter out of the kitchen, we'll find that, like all the other good things that kitchen has yielded up over the years, it's nourishing and healthy—and that there's enough to go around.

5

Laughing All the Way to the Bank

•••••••••••••••••••••

Humor and Strategies for Success

Do Good Executives Laugh with Their Mouths Open?

When Margo Shaw began her job as a systems analyst for a major publishing firm in Chicago, she believed in a number of myths. She swore by the following maxims: 1) For a woman to be taken seriously, she must be serious at all times. 2) Business and pleasure do not mix. 3) Success requires unwavering attention to the goal—any diversion becomes an obstacle. Shaw believed that, as Claire Lehan Harragan had dictated in *Games Mother Never Taught You: Corporate Gamesmanship for Women*, "Not a single phrase or idiom [of management prose] is witty or amusing. The language of business is deadly serious." Shaw subscribed to Harragan's theory that any young executive "who dares laugh or poke fun at a business communiqué may expect to be told to 'get down to business,' that is, be serious." Shaw adopted a gleam in her eye and tightened her mouth, so that what passed as her smile looked like the shortest line between two points. In the same way that she subscribed to the dictum that to get ahead she had to play strictly according to the rules, erasing her own intuition and perspective in order to adopt the larger "game plan" of the corporation, she believed that her own sense of humor had to give way to the pressures of being accepted as a serious participant in office politics.

Like Mary Jane Genova, a communications consultant in Stamford who wrote an Op-Ed piece for *The New York Times* in 1988 entitled "Wit Can Undermine a Woman's Career," Shaw believed that wit and laughter in the workplace could "undermine a woman's business career" the same way that "those other things" could—the other things being "fat, profanity, too little or too much makeup, a jerk for a husband and undue aggressiveness." Shaw bought Genova's line of reasoning, which suggested women in business do not laugh out loud, "just like, at one time, 'nice' girls did not have sex before marriage or at least they didn't broadcast it," and that "for women serious about careers, laughter seems to be a pleasure that is off limits." Shaw thought that she had to repress her sense of humor so that, in Genova's words, she rarely sees "humor in anything, even when I'm out of my power suit and off-duty." Shaw avoided bantering in the boardroom or bathroom; she wasn't about to risk her hard-won position in the company for a few light moments.

After all this planning and self-denial, did Shaw's decision to siphon humor out of her professional life help her? Did being deadly serious and consistently humorless propel her onto a fast track reserved for those who could forgo pleasure for business?

Humorlessness Equals Powerlessness

Absolutely not. To say that women must be serious at all times is as tyrannical and misleading as to say that they should smile at all times. Both prescriptions tell women to reject their responses in order to provide a consistent, unchanging, and impersonal public identity not of their own making. Both prescriptions force women to forfeit intellectual, instinctive, and emotional reactions and replace them with a script dictated by a prejudicial power system that is only just learning to value women's concerns.

The woman who is unable either to joke or to appreciate a joke is a woman who has not learned to trust herself. The woman who presents herself as humorless also appears to be unwilling to take risks, assert herself, or initiate change. For a woman to be afraid of risk, self-assertion, or change translates, in professional terms, to a woman who is afraid of, or at least unwilling to pursue, success. The research of John B. Miner, a professor of management at Georgia State University, indicates that when women are placed in positions of power they are less likely than their male counterparts to take risks and act on their own unless specifically instructed to do so, and that this un-willingness to take risks contributes to their being undervalued in corporate life. In other words, unless women are able to challenge the power structure on some level, they are regarded as ineligible for admission into its upper ranks. If you can't talk back to the boss, you'll never be the boss.

Marilyn Loden's book *Feminine Leadership, or How to Suc-ceed in Business Without Being One of the Boys* (a wonderful title that itself effectively demonstrates the appeal of humor) records an important observation by Columbe Nicholas, pres-ident of Christian Dior, who attributed her power in the business community to her "ability to interact." Nicholas stressed that "You don't have to conform to some stereotype of a tough-minded executive in order to have and use power. In the final analysis," this formidable woman advised, "you have to be yourself." Higher-status jobs require less conformity and require more originality from the members of the inner circle. Humor may be tolerated in lower-level positions but it will be demanded in higher ones, because humor appears as evidence of intelli-gence, personal strength, and quick thinking. When a student asked me to write her a letter of recommendation, I was sur-prised and elated to see that the application form for the pres-tigious Wharton Business School asked that the candidate be evaluated on her sense of humor, as well as on the more traditional qualities of perseverance and maturity. Jane Trahey, in *Women and Power*, quotes the film producer Jacqueline Babbin on what she expects to see when she interviews someone for an executive position: "A person with humor. Oh, God, I can't tell you how important humor is on sixteen-hour days."

Paradoxically, those women who appear to be able to treat themselves and the business they're in with the perspective offered by humor appear to be those who are most seriously competing for the top rung of the ladder. The woman who can successfully employ humor in the workplace is one who will achieve, efficiently and effectively, the sort of important leadership position that requires quick thinking and a sense of authority.

Margo Shaw played the games by the rules set out by the men around her and never let her humor get the better of her or anyone else. Her self-restraint contributed to her stagnation and defeat. It would have been better for Shaw if she'd learned to see humor as a way to display her intelligence and her ability to respond to situations quickly and appropriately. Intelligence and humor are connected in a number of ways, not the least of which is in the ability of the possessor of these qualities to assume a novel perspective on a problem or situation. Applying humor to a situation is like applying lateral thinking—it allows you to see things from a new angle. The successful corporate executive has been defined as someone who "enjoys new ideas, new techniques, fresh approaches and shortcuts. His [sic] talk and his thinking are terse, dynamic, sometimes playful and come in quick flashes." Although this description, offered by a book narrowly titled *The Gamesman*, refers to male workers, the same expectations are held up for female workers.

Shaw's set of beliefs allowed her to think that as long as she played along, she would be accepted. She got the acceptance, but not more; she was considered a good team player, but she was not seen as a leader. She was congratulated on her good work, but not on her initiative—since she rarely displayed any. Too often when she attempted to teach a new worker the ropes or to resolve a conflict with a co-worker, her unwavering seriousness made her seem inaccessible and judgmental. Shaw would never even kid around about the company's new advertising campaign involving kangaroos or about the plastic ferns in the lobby. She just didn't joke, because she mistakenly assumed that wit could undermine a woman's career.

And because she seemed unwilling to take any risks by lightening up, no one lightened up around her. Her colleagues often responded to her entrance into a room by quieting down. She was considered a bad sport even if she was a team player, someone whose distant observation would rule out any fun, even if that fun was intellectually stimulating and creatively productive. Does she sound like a successful woman to you? It's pretty safe to say that she doesn't.

She doesn't sound like a successful woman to Mary Davis, either. This senior vice president at Time-Warner suggests, as we've seen earlier, that a sense of humor is as much a tool for, and an indication of, leadership in a woman as it is in a man. "When you meet a woman who has a sense of humor, you know immediately that you're in the company of someone who has enough confidence *in* herself to *be* herself—she shows that she's not uptight or nervous even when she's in a new or challenging situation. She can allow herself the room to make a witty comment because she knows that she's in control. And people will admire her for that, and—even more importantly—they will trust her. The people working with her will have as much confidence in her abilities as she does." Davis views a woman's sense of humor as evidence of her ability to cope effectively in the corporate world. Lois Wyse's book *The Six-Figure Woman (and How to Be One)* supports this conclusion. Wyse suggests that women using the "female style" of management can enhance the corporate climate by "using humor to reduce tensions at meetings," and make work more pleasant generally.

Disturbing Stereotypes
. . . .

Women do need to guard against the stereotype of the "giggler," whose indiscriminate and shrill response undermines everyone else's legitimate laughter and humor. In *Breaking the Glass Ceiling*, Ann Morrison, Randall White, and Ellen Van Velsor refer to one woman executive as not having "a good rapport with customers. She's a giggler—she has a grating giggle that gets in her way. She comes across as a little girl. She loses presence power. She lacks poise with customers." This woman's laughter was seen as evidence of her insecurity rather than of her self-confidence. The giggler has no belief in her own ability either to make or to get a joke, and since she doesn't trust her own sense of humor, she feels she must laugh at everything everyone says, just in case. She's slipped so far from any intelligent or sensitive response of her own that her giggle begins to seem more like a nervous twitch than the spontaneous and sincere appreciation of the moment. She'll be discounted by her colleagues because they'll see the little girl behind the giggle, and little girls aren't allowed to play in big offices.

The other negative stereotype associated with women's humor in the workplace is the viciously bitchy woman. Unlike the giggling little girl, this stereotype reinforces the idea that women cannot be put into positions of power—not because they'll be too weak, but because they'll become power hungry and "castrating" in their quest for supremacy. Too often any woman's humor is categorized by her opponents as bitchy. However, in the same way that we have to be careful about who will hear our complaints, we must be careful about who will hear our sarcastic or cutting humor, because there is the possibility that it will be taken drastically out of context. No one wants to be caught having to say "But it was only a joke" and being put right back in the powerless position of having to defend, explain, or apologize for what was probably a minor incident. There is enough humor to enliven and empower us without resorting to the remarks that can bury us after the laughter has died down.

The way to avoid falling into either of these stereotypes is to recognize that they proceed out of a definition of women that assumes we will somehow be unable to use our own cleverness in moderation and with confidence. To fall into one of these stereotypes is to fall into patterns as outdated as the black-and-white television on which we first saw these stereotypes portrayed. We should work on translating our own humor, rather than any misrepresentative cartoon version of it, to the office.

From the Kitchen to the Boardroom

Once women's humor has been taken out of the kitchen, it becomes apparent that a good place to transplant it to is the workplace. The humor that made "private" work in the home tolerable for women over the years is similar to the humor that makes "public" work in the corporation effective. Moving women's humor from the private to the public sphere enables women to exercise their capacities for perspective and invention. As we've seen, much of women's humor is directed at the supposedly unchanging and unchangeable institutions of our culture. Many of these sacred cows have their feeding grounds in the corporate world. It is no wonder, then, that it's in the interests of the men who maintain these institutions to be particularly wary of women's humor and to discourage it whenever possible. Consider again how many experts have commented on what they perceive to be men's fear of women's humor.

It is not surprising that men in positions of power should be particularly fearful of women's humor in the workplace, since women are seen as alien creatures in such environments to begin with. A group of women executives laughing together no doubt conjures up visions of the three witches from *Macbeth* cackling over a caldron—and in that caldron, no doubt, the male co-worker sees himself stewing. Does this mean that women should respond to the possibility of male fear by repressing their own humor? You already know the answer to that one—of course not. The man who fears the laughter of women is the man who fears the power of women. Unless you're willing to make yourself powerless, you might as well give up on making yourself humorless. The only way to make such a man happy is to sink back into the typing pool, permanently. Since you're unwilling to take this route, you might as well get him used to the idea of your own importance.

When Harragan wrote her book *Games Mother Never Taught You: Corporate Gamesmanship for Women* in 1977, women only recently had acknowledged a desire for achievement and learned to savor the pleasures of ambition. Harragan was talking to women who had to wear pin-striped suits with paisley bows at the throat in order for their colleagues to speak to them as human beings. In the intervening thirteen years, the position of women in the corporate structure has changed considerably, if not radically. Women no longer have to "pass" as male clones. The women who started out fifteen years ago and have succeeded in their professions show, in fact, a profound respect for the uses and effects of humor in the workplace. They feel humor cannot be overestimated as an effective strategy for dealing with myriad stresses and conflicts. Good executives can and do laugh with their mouths open.

Humor Should Express Self-confidence

Since women's humor can and often does proceed from a basis of confidence and personal strength, women should no longer worry that wit or laughter will make them seem "lightweight." However, it should be noted that feeling lightweight is prevalent among even obviously accomplished women. As Dr. Joan Harvey has explored in her research on the "Impostor Phenomenon," even solidly successful women tend to harbor "a secret sense of being a fraud" and live with the "constant fear of being exposed." In her book *If I'm So Successful, Why Do I Feel Like a Fake?* Dr. Harvey suggests that the most effective way to cope with feelings of inadequacy is to find ways of gaining control over a situation, and to recognize that feelings of inadequacy often arise from low self-esteem rather than from any genuine inability to perform well. She deals with the ways in which women undervalue their achievements and minimize their accomplishments. Although Harvey doesn't mention it as such, it is clear that self-deprecating humor falls into the pattern of undervaluing one's self. When your humor is misdirected at yourself or is in some way self-demeaning, it would logically serve the negative function of undermining your confidence and heightening your feelings of incompetence.

If we mistakenly associate women's humor with the self-deprecating remarks of early comediennes, then of course such humor will backfire in the workplace. If the humor used in the workplace is like the humor used by Helen, the legal assistant in a large Wall Street firm who waited for people to contradict her when she used her favorite line, "Gosh, I'm such a dumb blonde," then it will damage all women's reputation for competence. Helen used tactics taken from the characters portrayed in the television programs of her childhood or from those lovable but fictional discussions of the incompetence described by Jean Kerr and Erma Bombeck in their earlier days—the women who made millions writing as if they had nothing else to do between the spin and fluff-dry laundry cycles. Even the traditional "domestic" humorists are no longer taking a self-effacing stance as a matter of course. Women's work, including women's work in the home, is the subject of a non-self-effacing tradition. Erma Bombeck also produces humor that challenges the underlying assumptions of traditional domesticity. While some of it can be placed in the self-effacing tradition ("After marriage, I added thirty pounds in nine months, which seemed to indicate that I was either pregnant or going a little heavy on the gravy"), she also writes essays with less sympathy and with more of a bite than the conventional "good mother" is meant to possess: "So you swallowed the plastic dinosaur out of the cereal box. What do you want me to do, call a vet?" When Bombeck writes "I don't think women outlive men. . . . It only seems longer," she challenges the system that would have us believe women live easy lives. When Jean Kerr, author of *Please Don't Eat the Daisies*, writes that the reason men and women have trouble getting along is because "most men insist on behaving as though this were an orderly, sensible universe, which naturally makes them hard to live with," she is raising, in a different context, the same sorts of questions Lily Tomlin and Jane Wagner raise in *The Search for Signs of Intelligent Life in the Universe*. Indeed, women writers have always suggested that a keen sense of the absurdity of one's life ensures a measured sense of sanity. Louisa May Alcott, best known for *Little Women*, wrote in 1872 that "a sense of the ludicrous supported me through many trying scenes."

We should delete self-deprecating humor from our repertoire, especially at work. It becomes clear that self-effacing humor must be avoided especially at those moments when we are most tempted to use it. If your design for a project is rejected, for example, you should avoid making jokes about it at your own expense. If a memo comes back saying "No good. What were you thinking?" you should *not* automatically reply, "Thinking? If I had been thinking, I wouldn't have been so dumb," even if at the moment such a remark lets off steam or makes you feel momentarily more comfortable. Your wit should give evidence of your strength, not of your vulnerability. A more effective remark would acknowledge the breakdown of communication without creating unnecessary guilt and embarrassment. The return memo might read "What was lost between thinking and writing yesterday could be made up by speaking today. Please give me a call when you have a minute and I will explain the idea more fully."

Humor as Signature
· · · · · · · · · · · · · · · · ·

Your sense of humor is like your signature—a unique sign representing yourself. If you're like my friend Rose, your wit will present itself like a gourmet meal, generous and obvious, essentially optimistic and loving. You never make a joke at anyone's expense and rarely if ever use irony. Your laughter is straightforward and unmediated, and you gather people together under its aegis. If you're like my friend Bette, however, your humor will be more like the perfect martini, dry and with a twist. Your sense of irony and of the absurd will be highly polished. Rather than laugh along at your own jokes, you'll play it straight and let others respond once they get the rather complex meaning behind your subtle commentary. Those who get your jokes congratulate themselves enormously; those who don't, spend a great deal of time wondering what they missed and trying to keep up. Your laughter will be light and sharp, used as much to keep some away as to draw others in.

Lynette Lager, an executive at Dean Witter and one of the leaders of the Financial Women's Association, attributes at least some of her success to her own very personal wit. "I have sort of a strange sense of humor," admits Lager, "so people know right away what they're in for. On my last trip to Chicago, for example, one of the men we were dealing with seemed hard to reach until I made some funny remarks—we were the only two who laughed (I usually laugh at my own jokes), but he saw that as a sign. He felt that it meant we'd work well together in the future. It helped our dealings enormously."

One of the most reassuring passages concerning women's effective use of humor in business is presented by Claire Lehan Harragan, the author of *Games Mother Never Taught You: Corporate Gamesmanship for Women*. When Harragan presents the reader with the possibility of being faced during an interview with questions obviously sex biased, the responses she suggests women give are witty indeed. Harragan points out that a prospective employer has the right to ask any questions he wishes as long as every potential employee is similarly evaluated. Harragan goes on to say, "That would mean that every interviewer who poses the question to you has amassed a pile of statistics on the topic," and she suggests that when faced with an unfair question, the woman might respond in the following manner: "How interesting that you asked about contraceptives. I've been doing some research myself. What form do you find most popular with employees of this company?" Or she might say "I've noticed that five of your questions have had a direct or indirect sexual focus. Would you mind reviewing the prerequisites of the job you have in mind for me? I'm wondering if there's more here than meets the eye about the proposed job duties." The last example is an especially effective use of humor because it responds to the interviewer's subtext by turning the hostile subtext of the interviewer's question back on him. Harragan, as the saying goes, "puts the ball in his court." Obviously Harragan herself is not averse to women using humor—as long as it works well.

Three Ways Humor Works at Work

In an article called "Friends, Enemies and the Polite Fiction," the sociologist Tom Burns discusses humor in the workplace and suggests that it can 1) reinforce the rules and boundaries of an established group, 2) help to break down the boundaries of a group into which you'd like to be accepted, and 3) ease tensions between groups. Burns argues, "In all societies, the joke is the shortcut to consensus."

Humor can help to confirm the rules and the boundaries of your in-group through its "tacit delineation of mutually accepted norms of behavior." Humor can and does reinforce the rules of the group. When someone consistently spends more time at lunch than her peers, for example, her co-workers' "good-natured" joking about it when she comes in serves to reinforce the consensus of the group that lunch should, in fact, take no more than an hour and a half. "Claire got another cabdriver who just refused to listen to her directions—again! Strange how you can get a staff of sixteen to listen to your every word but can't find one cabbie to pay attention."

Professor William Martineau, a sociologist and anthropologist who specializes in humor, affirms that this situation—an individual's lack of punctuality—is a particularly emblematic example of the way humor reaffirms a group's standards. "If one is caught being late, the joking relationship is usually invoked immediately . . . the function of humor in most instances is to arrive at, or return to, a state of consensus about, and conformity among, members. Humor is used to express grievances or can be directed at someone in the group who has not learned or who has violated the norms of the group." In this way, humor allows the group members to air their concerns and resentments without openly challenging an individual and so allow things to continue "as normal," without obvious conflict. To put it another way, the group's teasing is a way of reaffirming the rules without getting "serious" about it; if Claire is smart, she'll listen to the subtext of the kidding and take her cue from the underlying meanings rather than the lighthearted tone.

Another interesting dynamic concerning this sort of joking relationship depends on the willingness of the object of the joke to play along without changing the game. For example, I once worked with a woman named Jane who could not have told an interesting story if her life had been held in the balance. She would have been burned at the stake after the eighth set of "then-I-said-and-then-he-said," however great her desire to live. But since she loved to tell these stories, and since she was part of the group, we all tacitly agreed to listen as long as we could reserve the right to kid her about it, the way you'd kid someone who is always late. She would be beginning a story about her brother-in-law's podiatrist, and we'd put down our work, fold our hands, and say "Let 'er rip, Jane."

But one day when she was in the middle of one of her monotonous monologues, a messenger came into the office to deliver a package to one of the other women. One of our group exchanged a few words with the kid delivering the parcel, and Jane suddenly got very huffy. "Please," she said, shrill as somebody's eighth-grade teacher, "I'm trying to tell a story here." Suddenly Jane had switched codes, and instead of being playful she became very self-righteous. The parcel-holding woman then said, "Jane, if you'd stop *trying* to tell stories and actually learned *how* to tell one, we'd all be enormously grateful." This exchange obviously broke down the joking relationship that had, until this point, allowed the friction to remain inert. Jane could no more return to the position where her unending stories would be tolerated than the other woman could pretend to listen to them. The joking relationship, fragile as an ego, was irreparably damaged.

Us-vs.-Them Humor

Another way that humor solidifies a group is by producing what one researcher has called "simultaneously a strong fellow-feeling [*sic*] among participants and joint aggressiveness against outsiders. . . . Laughter forms a bond and simultaneously draws a line." If your group's joking tends to focus on the foibles of another group's style or structure, you're using humor to cement the bond between you and your colleagues by contrasting your "right" way of doing things against your opponents' "wrong" way.

For example, if you're working on a group project that will eventually compete with a project proposed by another group, no doubt at least some of your humor will be directed at the poor performance—or at least differing performance—of your competitors. Let's say your group is characterized by a sophisticated, fast-moving, fast-talking style. Although it won't help you achieve your goal in any direct way, poking fun at the opposition will enhance your feelings of solidarity and confidence. It's one of the things every politician knows instinctively: Throw a joke that sticks to the opponent, and it'll seem like you've won a victory.

So what will you say about the competition? Interestingly enough, you'll probably pick on fairly personal items, rather than on the large issues dividing you. You'll describe the competition as being straight out of *Hee-Haw*, and perhaps make reference to the way you fall asleep between their sentences. You'll describe the way the head of their committee buys only suits that'll "wash nicely at home and still keep the crease" or say, "To these guys, L. L. Bean is Giorgio Armani. If they can't get it out of a catalogue, they won't buy it." By treating your competitors as an unworthy, foolish bunch of know-nothings, you've helped to underscore a feeling of solidarity among your own group members. None of you would ever be so silly, none of you would exhibit such poor taste. You're all hip and savvy, right? This sort of humor goes back through seventh grade, when you'd define someone outside the group as someone with "cooties," and back through the cave, where the guys who couldn't make their own fire just weren't with it. It's enormously reassuring and primitive, quite a powerful combination. If you can learn to employ this method of drawing the members of your group together, you've gained an effective management tool.

An interesting side product of this kind of humor is the effect of making a participant feel less bad about besting someone on the other side. Joking someone out of a feeling of guilt can be accomplished by reassuring her that she deserved her success—

that the right group won. Like the woman who was worried about shouting back a response to a guy on the street who yelled vulgarities after her, worrying that he might indeed have a small cock, some women are particularly susceptible to what is essentially a misdirected concern. They spend a great deal of time worrying about what the competition thinks—or, more important, feels. Some of these are, of course, genuine and laudable feelings. But they can also be carried to a self-sabotaging extreme, where the woman is ready to forfeit her own success so that someone else will not have to forfeit his or hers.

Carole DeSanti, who worked at a major publishing company, tells a story about hiring an assistant. "The young men who applied for this job all came up and declared 'I'm the one for you,' whereas the young women all apologized for their inexpertise. One woman even told me that, despite the fact that this was her dream job, I shouldn't worry about not hiring her if someone else was more qualified. Amazing." If you have a group member who fits this pattern, you might be able to help her when she's feeling bad by kidding her out of her guilt or anxiety. You might exaggerate it to the point where she can see how ineffective a method of coping it really is. I once hired a research assistant who was so efficient that she had me reading until three A.M. just to keep up with all the materials she found relating to the obscure subject on which I was then working. But her concern was that I'd hired her out of a sense of obligation or because she'd thrust herself on me. I reassured her several times, but she returned to the thought that somewhere there was another person who'd be better for the job. The only thing that finally convinced her to accept the accolades she merited was my jokingly telling her about the follies of my earlier assistants—the way I would tell them to find me an article on how little girls dress from six to ten, and they'd bring me articles on evening wear for children. By creating a context for joking about her anxieties, by offering her a place to put herself, I was able to relieve her of her worries.

Boundary-Breaking Humor
. . . .

Humor can help to break the boundaries of a group that ex-
cludes you. Quick-witted and amusing talk can help you integrate yourself into another set of peers. It can signal your
readiness to be accepted into another group without seeming to
betray the one you're in. In an interesting exercise conducted
by a number of corporations, a group of executive trainees was
asked to lock arms to exclude an outsider. Observers of the
exercise agreed that "Invariably . . . men will use force to break
through. Women on the other hand will talk their way in."

Let's say that you're new to a job and want to start having
lunch with a group of interesting and impressive colleagues.
What should you do? For one thing, you should remember the
seventh-grade lunchroom, where you knew you'd never get to
sit with the hip kids by going over and saying "May I join you?"
You knew that even if they let you sit down, you'd remain an
outsider. You have to think of a way to make your new colleagues want you to be part of their group. You have to indicate
what you can offer to their hour of extra-office conversation.
Obviously, using humor is one of the most effective strategies
in such a situation, but your humor has to be perfectly tuned
to their tone and style. Since you'll have done your homework
and know something about the tastes and interests of these folks,
you'll be able to find an opening or—replicating the pattern of
the game—a way of talking your way into the circle.

Such a dynamic is emblematic of the way women can use
their intellectual and personal strength to maneuver themselves
into a desirable situation. "Too many women think they have
to discount their cleverness in order to be perceived as serious,"
declares Nancy Taylor, a senior administrator for a large urban
hospital, "but it isn't the case. Women should take more advantage of the pathways opened by the judicious use of humor,
especially when they're in a liminal situation—let's say when
trying to ease their way out of their present position into one

with more responsibility—and humor can help to ease that transition."

Easing Tensions Through Humor

We've already seen that humor allows us to vent or deflect aggression, and it is important to underscore that humor also plays a role in our coping with other forms of stress.

For example, when a woman gets a promotion, she will need to form an effective strategy for dealing with those individuals who have to adjust to her new status. Mary Davis argues that those working with a woman who has a healthy sense of humor will be particularly appreciative of "her willingness to remain 'human' even when she's the boss." Davis's conclusion affirms the findings of the sociologist Tom Burns, who argues that "Embarrassments are usually attendant upon change of role, which may have to be overcome by banter and irony." Again, humor will allow your colleagues to express approval, envy, or even resentment without disrupting the flow of work. They will be able to tease you about your new status ("Will you ever come to visit us in our lowly environs? It'll be a little dusty and grimy for you down here after the jet stream of your new job"), but such joking will reinforce both your new status and the awareness of your former group that you have left them in good standing.

When Anne Groulx won one of her company's most prestigious awards, she told her friends that she'd had to spend so much time completing the paperwork demanded by the bureaucracy of the award committee that she didn't have time to work anymore. She allowed her peers to laugh off the edge to their envy, because there is something in everyone that has trouble with someone else's astonishing success. Groulx's lighthearted treatment of her accomplishment in no way resembled self-deprecation. She didn't say, for example, "They only gave it to me because my new hairdo got their attention," which would have implied that her own abilities were not sufficient reason for her to win the award. She made a humorous remark that turned the glare of attention away from her winning but without taking the shine off her achievement.

Easing Tensions Between Groups

Humor can also ease tensions between groups—especially when you are a member of two groups simultaneously. Picture yourself as the first woman manager of a production unit within a large organization. Most of your employees are female, while all your new peers are male. You belong to both groups simultaneously—you're part of the woman's group by definition of your gender and of the manager's group by definition of your position. This can raise complex tensions, among them divided loyalties. When one of the women comes to you and complains about the slave-driver mentality of one of your new colleagues, how do you handle the situation? Obviously a great deal of attention should be paid over a period of time, but what do you do when this woman hangs on to your cuff in the bathroom in order to complain at length? Of course you have the right, as her boss, to tell her to send you a memo about it and leave it at that. But if this is a woman whom you like and respect, one on whom you depend, a person you want to take seriously, you need a strategy to deal with her immediate anger and defuse the sense of crisis she feels.

One way to handle effectively such a tricky situation is to use humor in order to negotiate time and space for yourself and to help her move to a sense of perspective. If she says with vehemence "I don't know what I'm going to do about David. I'll kill him the next time he makes a crack about how messy my desk is," you can say with a smile "But then the body would clutter up your office even more. You have little enough room as it is, which is what the problem is really about. We'll have to work on getting you moved to a better spot. Until then, keep your hands away from the letter opener when you're near him, just to be safe."

Your humor should defuse her anger and allow her to switch gears, moving her from anger to a position where she can listen to your suggestions. You've taken her threat and exaggerated it to the point where she can laugh at it, but at the same time you've indicated to her that you understand her anger, and that you've listened to her. Playing on her own idea is a way of showing that you've at least heard her idea. It is important to make clear by your tone and expression that you're not dismissing her complaint, but that you want to keep things calm and work on the problem at a later, more appropriate moment. Your humor will allow you to remain within the circle of both groups, having not offended anyone. When there are bulls in fields on either side, sitting on the fence is your safest bet. If you can develop a method of making the sort of remark that will break the tension in a stressful situation without alienating people in the process, then you will have developed a crucial managerial skill.

Creating Consensus Through Humor

If you can make people laugh with you, you have won them over, however briefly, to your side. You have created an atmosphere of consensus, a moment of agreement when everyone is in sync. Humor functions as a sort of social cement, especially in tense or competitive work situations. Sociologists have found that laughing together "creates and reinforces a sense of solidarity and intimacy within groups." Humor can effectively create a situation where those individuals who might be on opposite sides of an issue can at least share a moment where their perspectives are aligned.

Suppose you're working in an industrial setting where you and your boss are often at odds concerning how available bonus funds should be allocated. She thinks that workers should be compensated by seniority, while you believe they should be paid on a scale graded by productivity. Your boss appears immovable on this issue. You are about to leave her office on fairly bad terms, but you decided to switch gears before you leave. As you collect your files, you make a joke about how the company photocopying machine has been around since they invented electricity and has yet to work for an entire day without breaking down. Your boss laughs for a moment, and even if it's only for a moment, you've shared something. You've indicated that you'll go out of your way to find a common territory, or at least a briefly met agreement. You pick a harmless scapegoat—the photocopying machine—and both of you can agree on how awful it is without compromising either of your positions. You give the office equipment a significance it otherwise would not have, and by exaggerating its poor qualities, you draw fire away from the issue where you and your boss are divided, although you still make an implicit point concerning the importance of rewarding efficiency. No doubt you'll return and do battle over this issue time and time again, but your use of humor indicates that you intend to keep a reasonable perspective on the matter, as well as subtly indicating that you expect her to do the same. Your humor shows that you expect her to be able to switch from an antagonistic mode into a friendly one without losing a beat, as you've obviously been able to do.

The Icing on the Cake

Mary Davis believes that a sense of humor is the "icing on the cake," the ultimate flourish provided by a winning combination of intelligence and quick thinking. Davis argues that it's often the last thing to fall into place, the final proof that a job candidate is an especially smart businesswoman and a desirable catch. "Someone describing an excellent new worker might finish off the usual litany of praise by adding, '*And* she's got a sense of humor!' as if it's proof positive that she's great, as if with that final kicker no one in her right mind would turn her down." While Davis would remind us that business "isn't exactly one big slumber party," she would definitely encourage women to explore humor as a strategy for success, as one way to make sure we're laughing all the way to the bank.

6

"It's Hard to Be Funny When You Have to Be Clean"

....

Sexual Differences in Humor Appreciation/Differences in Sexual Humor Appreciation

Are You a Man or a Woman? Send Stamped,
Self-addressed Envelope for Answer
....

Nicole Hollander, whose "Sylvia" cartoon series is widely syndicated, has drawn a two-frame summary of the differences between what men and women find funny. The first frame shows, simply, a clipboard with the phrase "Gender Differences in Humor" written across it. The second frame shows us Sylvia. Sylvia is, of course, in the bathtub, her hair wrapped in a turban; the perpetual cigarette dangles from her lips as she hits the keys, having conveniently located her typewriter on a board across the bathtub. Sylvia, that mistress of logic, has devised a quiz to settle all questions of sexuality. "Are you a man or a woman?" she asks. "Check the things you find funny: 1. Larry, Moe, and Curly. 2. Men dressed as women, but with their hairy legs showing. 3. The disparity between the ideal and the real." She then instructs us to enclose a stamped, self-addressed envelope for the results. By taking the differences in humor as a definition of gender, Hollander exaggerates but nevertheless illustrates the way in which our differences inform our responses. But what are some of the reasons why men and women find different things funny?

Help! Why Don't I Laugh at Benny Hill?

When I lived in England, I was shown *The Benny Hill Show* the way visitors to the Tibetan mountains would be shown footprints of the abominable snowman—given the near impossibility that such a thing actually existed, proof was necessary. I watched my first *Benny Hill* openmouthed and unlaughing. I saw my first episode with a group of medical students in the hospital canteen, and they kept turning to me to see whether I was finally going to giggle, wanting me to appreciate the absurd—but to their eyes lovable—skits. I wanted to laugh too, especially since my date had been the one to suggest the idea that I would be the one American to find Benny Hill funny and so redeem a national reputation. He was counting on me. He was looking at me the way a gambler looks at a greyhound at the starting gate, uncertain but hopeful. One of the problems was that I'd already given them a whole routine about women who faked their laughter. My boyfriend was pretty much in tune with my reactions—even if I could pass in front of his friends, he'd know if I was not really enjoying myself. It's nearly impossible, as we all know, to let go under pressure, but for me it was totally impossible to laugh at Benny Hill.

Now, I was always the first one to laugh at any and all Monty Python sketches, even the one where the grotesquely fat man explodes in the restaurant after eating too much ("Have a mint, sir? It's only wafer thin"). I liked *The Life of Brian*. I loved Rowen Atkinson, and had even smiled through a theater evening of *No Sex Please, We're British* when somebody else paid for the tickets. All of this was evidence enough that I was capable of laughing when something was funny and proof that I was even willing to be a good enough cultural ambassador to laugh when I knew I was really meant to. But laugh at Benny Hill? Big-bosomed women in halter tops bending over melons while the shopkeeper made comments about firmness and ripeness? Men dressed as schoolgirls bending over a desk to be hit by a big-bosomed teacher who holds an enormous ruler? Jokes about using garter belts as dental floss? None of the women had more than two or three lines. They were represented by their body parts, like chickens in the supermarket, all breasts and thighs. The sophistication level of the dialogue made the book *Truly Tasteless Jokes* read like P. G. Wodehouse. It just wasn't funny. Like Queen Victoria, I was not amused. I tried to be, but I wasn't.

When I asked a woman friend in the group who was clearly enjoying herself whether she really liked the show, she unhesitatingly replied yes. She liked it because it was "so bloody daft." "Didn't you even like when 'Wanda the Whip Lady' was chasing the little old man in the wheelchair?" she implored. I smiled weakly and decided that Benny Hill was something British I couldn't learn to love. Even though I'd become quite accustomed to warm beer and cold houses, this was one aspect of life in England to which I could not adjust.

It occurred to me that maybe my English counterpart thought that Benny Hill was funny because she was more used to the kind of T-and-A (translated as tits-and-ass) humor than I was. Surprisingly, the reserved British have an uncensored appetite for breasts that would put a red-blooded thirteen-year-old American boy to shame. The girls grow up faced with the infamous "page three" ladies: bare-breasted, bare-bottomed six-teen-year-olds gracing the third page of one of the nation's most popular daily newspapers. The first time I was confronted with one of these, I was more shocked than any Victorian woman was shocked by bawdy music-hall dance numbers. I simply couldn't believe that there, next to the weather, after the national news and before the local, near the comics and beside an advertisement for twenty pence off Heinz tomato paste, was a nearly naked teenager, inevitably described as someone from Somerset, who wanted to be a model and work as a travel agent. Back in the States (as I had already learned to call home), copies of *Playboy* were kept neatly stacked out of reach behind the news vendor's counter. But in England, it seemed, T-and-A was pretty standard fare. No need to be shocked by boob jokes on *Benny Hill* when you've been faced since birth with a pair over your corn flakes, my friend explained to me, thus illustrating the point that Freud made about sixty years earlier—namely, that "Every joke calls for a public of its own." There are jokes that don't translate between groups because of different social structures and expectations.

I decided that there were real differences between our nations. The way that Americans "run for office" while the British "stand for office," the way that Americans try to "get it on" with each other while the English try to "get it off"—there were some interesting junctions at which we parted ways. *Benny Hill*, I told myself, just wouldn't translate, showing that for once Americans exhibited better taste than the Brits. Imagine my disappointment in finding that *The Benny Hill Show* is now widely syndicated in the United States, and has quite a large (one wouldn't want to use the word "respectable" in this context) cult following.

The Effect of Money on What's Funny

But for the most part the show remains a cult item, because the humor really doesn't appeal to most Americans. Benny Hill's humor, for one thing, is almost completely and relentlessly male defined. To go back to the point made by Hollander's cartoon, such humor relies for standard fare on men dressed as women but with their hairy legs showing, and does sincere homage to the kind of eye-poking fun that made the Three Stooges famous.

But the humor of the Three Stooges no longer seems to hold the appeal it once had, and this is in part because our "national" humor is no longer an essentially "masculine" humor. Even male viewers might show some mild embarrassment at admitting they're Hill fans. Our cultural perimeters have changed over the years, and a program that might have been mainstream twenty years ago can no longer cut it with today's audience. Benny Hill seemed anachronistic, part of a time warp that had passed over Britain without making a dent in it. They could get away with material that could no longer draw a substantial following over here. A culture can change, especially when there are economics involved.

The American "viewing audience" is increasingly, and now predominantly, female. In addition, and in contrast to fifteen or twenty years ago, there are more female heads of the household, controlling the family purse. This is important, because when women have economic pull, they pull things in their own direction. They can choose not to watch certain programs, for example, and advertisers are aware of such viewing patterns even when the audience reaction is passive withdrawal rather than active revulsion. We mustn't get too excited by such progress too soon, however. It doesn't mean, for example, that someone like Johnny Carson must avoid making anachronistic jokes. When the Miss America contest announced that there would be less sexism in the 1989 pageant than ever before, Carson could still quip "In other words, they're ruining it." There are moments when American television dives as far down as possible.

But any measure of economic control has an impact. Economic control has been one important reason so many more programs, films, and even stage performances have been geared toward women in the last few years. "It used to be that when a couple came to a club, the guy always paid," explains Joy Behar. "So that meant he controlled where they went and that meant they'd go see comedians he thought were funny. If she's deciding where to go because she's either splitting the bill or paying for both of them, she's got the right to say, 'Hey, this is the stuff *I* think is funny.' And it might well be different from what he would have chosen. She wants to enjoy herself, not just watch him enjoying himself."

Some of the differences between men's comedy and women's comedy have already been discussed—the idea that women's humor doesn't work off finding a victim to be the target of hostile jokes; the idea that, for the most part, women tell stories rather than one-liners; the idea that women's humor picks on the powerful rather than the pitiful. But we should add to this one important difference, rarely discussed in the accepted literature about comedy, and that is the idea of the differences in sexual humor—not the sexual differences in humor, but the difference in what men and women find funny about sex.

What's So Funny About Sex?

Nearly everything about sex can be seen as funny, if you're in the right frame of mind, or, to put it another way, in the right position. One of the typical childhood reactions to a first official description of sex is to share the information as quickly as possible with a friend—a discussion that often leads to a sort of nervous laughter, no doubt born of fear and disbelief, but nevertheless effectively links public discussions of sex and laughter. You keep a straight face when the adult explains various functions, but then you run and relate the details through convulsive giggles to your pals as you try to picture every grown-up you know doing things to/with/on every other grown-up you know. You have an instinctive desire to render the information funny so that it won't be scary or bizarre. You want to make a joke out of your own uneasiness in order to control your feelings.

We laugh at sexual matters in a group, especially at those

details that terrify us the most, because suddenly we feel like we're all in it together. Being in a group relieves us of the singularity of our embarrassment or admission of knowledge, since it helps us to understand that we're no longer the lone bachelorette in the *Dating Game* spotlight. Laughing in a group at sexual jokes or stories means that nobody has to take personal responsibility for breaking the taboo—everybody admits to having the same feelings all at once.

Sharing sexual stories and jokes has long been an underground activity for women, a private set of experiences monitored as fiercely as our weight and kept just about as secret. These stories could never make it to the light of day. We all promised one another that the stories would go to our graves with us, crossing our hearts and hoping to die every night as we pulled our nightgowns over our knees, brought the popcorn closer, opened another six-pack of Fresca and/or Bud Lite, to listen to somebody else's hysterical defloration story, first-period story, premature-ejaculation story, and, of course, everyone's tiny- or enormous-penis story. The first session where everyone admits to losing her virginity is a landmark event in any girl's life. It's like a baptism into adulthood, a celebration of your femininity, especially if you can giggle at and share the anxiety of the event. Occasionally there will be a girl in the group whose holier-than-thou attitude threatens to undermine the coziness of the event. I remember one friend's reaction to such a situation. We were sitting there in the middle of the night, eating Sara Lee cheesecakes (still frozen, when their flavor is at a peak), swapping stories. One little blonde, with tiny eyes and a nose so upturned it resembled a ski lift rather than a ski jump, said, rather archly, that where she came from Good Girls didn't sleep with their boyfriends. Without missing a beat, my pal met her beady eyes and replied, "In my neighborhood, Good Girls sleep *only* with their boyfriends." The conversation proceeded without further sanctimonious interruption, and even the little blonde had lightened up by the end of the evening, laughing if not actually joining in. Maybe she had started to feel as if she'd been missing out instead of holding out.

These conversations are important because women's experiences have traditionally been regarded as less than "universally" interesting—so women often reach an understanding of the significance of their own private experiences in single-sex groups. Virginia Woolf argues that women's lives have not been explored much in public: "It has been common knowledge for ages that women exist, bear children, have no beards and seldom go bald; but save in these respects, and in others where they are said to be identical with men, we know little of them and have little sound evidence upon which to base our conclusions." Woolf also wrote, "The values of women differ very often from the values . . . [of men]. . . . Yet it is the masculine values that prevail. Speaking crudely, football and sports are 'important'; the worship of fashion, the buying of clothes 'trivial.' And these values are inevitably transferred from life to fiction. This is an important book because it deals with war. This is an insignificant book because it deals with the feelings of women. . . ." The author Mary Gordon comments on this double standard in a 1980 essay when she writes "It was all right for the young men I knew . . . to write about the hymens they had broken, the diner waitresses they had seduced. Those experiences were significant. But we were not to write about our broken hearts, the married men we loved disastrously, about our mothers or our children. . . . Our desire to write about these experiences only revealed our shallowness; it was suggested that we would, in time, get over it."

How Small Was It?

Every sexually active young woman has her own stories, of course, and it's exactly that information that keeps men suspicious of all-female gatherings. Men worry that when we get together we'll talk about our lovers. This is a good worry. This is worry with some substance behind it.

In this case, men are absolutely right—we do talk about our lovers. Interestingly, most women are especially willing to discuss their ex-lovers in the greatest detail, perhaps as a way of regaining a sense of control. Since there's usually something even the best lover can be faulted on, these faults become the topic of conversation for the duration of post-breakup trauma. Libby Reid asks in the "Bitter Woman Test" in her book of cartoons titled *You Don't Have to Pet to Be Popular,* "The quickest way to a man's heart is a knife in his back: True or False?" The joke, at the man's expense, is the final knife in his back—usually fairly painless for him, since your girlfriends are unlikely to report back what you've said. Possibly this kind of humor is used by women as a way of breaking the final taboo— the revelation of shared secrets. Nora Ephron ends her brilliant novel *Heartburn* with a list of reasons why it's absolutely essential to "turn everything into a story" when a friend questions why she has to give a funny answer to even the most serious questions. "So I told her why," says Rachel, whose husband has just left her for another woman. "Because if I tell the story, I control the version. Because if I tell the story, I can make you laugh, and I would rather have you laugh than feel sorry for me. Because if I tell the story, it doesn't hurt as much. Because if I tell the story, I can get on with it."

But until very recently, this talk remained dorm talk, telephone talk, late-night-bar-in-another-city talk, and breaking-up-with-the-bastard talk (where you relate, in Technicolor detail and with graphs, if possible, each and every one of his sexual misdemeanors, from the way he wheezes when he bends to take off his mismatched socks to the way he keeps checking the digital clock to see how well he's doing, etc.). Until these last few years, women's experience of public sexual humor was an experience of male sexual humor. Only recently has women's sexual humor been explored in public—on television, in clubs—in other words, in front of men who are often surprised to find that women have been making jokes at the men's expense.

Male Sexual Humor
. . . .

In an 800-page book, *No Laughing Matter*, first published in 1968, G. Legman catalogues literally hundreds of sexual jokes and analyzes them under such headings as "The Overlarge Vagina" and "Jealousy of Male Urination." Legman's book is certainly thorough. It is also unhesitatingly, unapologetically, and so therefore unimaginatively, masculine. The sexual jokes are male-centered sexual jokes. Women are completely "Other," in that they are the object of the jokes told, participants who are not invited to partake of the laughter. Typical of the sort of stories discussed by Legman is the following, which appears under the subheading "Rape": "The bellboy is accused of having raped the chambermaid by catching her with her head out the window watching a parade, locking her head there by pulling down the window, and having intercourse with her from behind. 'Why didn't you call for help?' asks the judge. 'Well, Judge, I didn't want people to think I was cheering for a Republican parade.' " This is one of the least offensive of Legman's collection. And while it is clear that the answer the maid gives is funny, the scenario is obviously a gender-specific, male fantasy where the woman being raped turns out to enjoy the experience and so doesn't scream. What at first glance seems merely witty, at second glance appears fairly insidious.

Legman doesn't hesitate to offer his "psychological" explanations for why jokes work, as well as to offer other pieces of wisdom, like "Maybe the ugly girls really are more likely to be willing to 'whet the vigor of a mutual,' etc. Hard to know. Certainly many insecure seducers prey on fat girls . . . and are cynically advised to do so, on the grounds that fat girls are easy lays (because nobody pays any sexual attention to them) . . . ." For anyone who doubts the gender-specific nature of "traditional" comedy, Legman's work will render such doubts embarrassingly impossible.

And Legman's book is, of course, only one among many—and one scholarly one among many less dainty in their approach. Typical *Playboy* jokes, turning as they do on the withholding nature of attractive women and the unappeasable nature of unattractive ones, are less varied in their approach to sex. And, as we've already seen, few of the jokes in print can compete with the overtly misogynist nature of the humor of stand-up comics like Kinison and Clay. In fact, next to this lineup, Benny Hill starts to sound like a friend of Gloria Steinem's, socially aware and intellectually sound. Male humor offers us the following: "What's got eighteen legs and two tits? The Supreme Court," as well as the grandfather of all male sexual humor—"Why do women have vaginas? So that men will talk to them" and "How can you tell when a woman comes? Who cares?" There is little to be said about such humor except to emphasize that it is pervasive, learned by rote by most boys in the United States. It's no longer acceptable to repeat these jokes and expect women to laugh, but apparently the jokes are still staples among all-male groups, if my spies can be trusted. Nearly all men I've asked know the "Why do women have vaginas" line—but some of them have trouble understanding why it's considered a joke.

How Ugly Is She?

But since we're surrounded by male-centered sexual jokes, and have been for as long as we can remember, these sound as if they're the only "real" jokes. When any two-bit performer can still get an audience to yell out in approval and recognition "How ugly is she?" when he begins his routine by saying "My wife is sooo ugly . . . ," we can see that the traditions have held fast. The other night I went to a fairly sophisticated club where a man who worked the circuit (good clubs in New York and Los Angeles, as well as in Atlantic City and Las Vegas—someone who had even appeared on Johnny Carson) told a string of my-wife-is-so-ugly jokes that could have been written in 1953. They might well have been. The problem, if we can call it that, was that the audience seemed to go along with it. Granted that the place seemed to have an unusually high number of lime-green-sports-coat, angora-mock-turtleneck types, it still struck a jarring note to hear applause greeting lines such as "She was so ugly, even the gynecologist had to have somebody else look for him." And, once again, women seemed to be laughing along, or at least smiling enough not to make an issue out of it, so as not to make their unease apparent. This is humor, right? This is a night out at a comedy club? The pained smiles of the women in the audience seemed to say "What can you expect?"

Even the women working such venues expect that they'll have to deal with traditional male humor—not from other performers, but from guys in the audience. Lara Kightlinger, a young stand-up comic who was described by a producer as "one of the most attractive women in the business," has had to deal with her share of harassment from the audience. In the middle of her act, one guy at a front table kept shouting "Take it off," as if this were the height of urbane and sophisticated repartee. Finally Kightlinger turned to him and said, "Look, I know it's a new experience for you, seeing a woman who isn't behind Plexiglas, but you'll just have to deal with it," very politely. Interestingly, the audience then turned against her for being "nasty" to the guy who'd kept telling her to strip. The audience, spurred on by this guy's buddies at the table, blamed Kightlinger for casting aspersions on the heckler's sexual prowess, as if it wasn't fair for her to make fun of him. What did they expect her to do, be flattered by the attention? Take the guy's number? Take off her clothes in order for this jerk to be quiet and pay attention to her subtle and intelligent humor?

Women are taught to expect that any assault on male sexual self-esteem will be turned against them. Of course we're supposed to listen to jokes at our expense when we hear comedy.

Of course Eddie Murphy is going to make a joke about some woman's "fine ass," and Henny Youngman is going to beg, "Take my wife, please." We're accustomed to this material, familiar as an old rag and just about as imaginative. We nod in acknowledgment and try to get through the time as quickly as possible, because listening to such jokes is about as interesting and useful as waiting on the longest checkout line in a supermarket.

Changing Our Expectations

For one thing, women can start to change what's expected from comedy. Over the last few years, women have made a real difference in shaping the profile of public humor. Women fans made Roseanne Barr famous, applauding her "domestic goddess" routine with a vigor they never brought to a comic who started his set by saying "My wife is sooo fat . . ." Women have found in comediennes like Carol Leifer, Joy Behar, Susie Essman, Elayne Boosler, and Rita Rudner a mirror to familiar experiences, comedy that reflects the feminine perspective—especially the feminine perspective on sexual experience.

Typical Differences

And there certainly *is* a decidedly feminine perspective on sexual experience reflected in women's humor. If the typical masculine sex joke relies on the teller's implicit or explicit contempt for women, or anger at women ("What's the difference between your job and your wife? After five years, your job still sucks"; "What are the three things a woman can do that a man can't? Have a period, have a baby, and get laid when she's dead"), then women's humor relies on a reversal of that contempt and anger, aiming it at men ("I married beneath me. All women do"; "Do you know why women have poor spatial perceptions? Because we've always been told that this [hold up fingers three inches apart] is ten inches"). If male sexual humor relies on brag stories of prowess or potency ("After a week in the hotel without going out, the groom decides to take his bride to a movie. He calls to her in the bathroom, 'Honey, would you like to see *Oliver Twist?*' 'No thanks, I've seen it do everything else"), then women's sexual humor relies on the undercutting of the male brag (" 'Quick, quick,' I told him as he came into the kitchen, 'I want you to make mad passionate love to me.' 'Can't resist me, can you?' he said. 'Actually, I want to cook an egg and I don't like them to boil for more than twenty-seven seconds"). If male humor reinforces stereotypes of female submissiveness ("Why is the new contraceptive sponge such a great idea? Because after sex your wife can get up and wash the dishes"), then female humor reinforces the stereotypes of male impotence— sexual and otherwise ("Why don't you come up and see me sometime? Come up on Wednesday, that's amateur night," and, to a suspicious lover, "Trust me. Hundreds already have"). Certainly women's humor is open to the criticism that it is as unfair about men as men's humor is unfair about women—but the way to deal with that statement is to make sure it is read as what it is, an observation. Yes, that's right, women's humor is as unfair about men as men's is about women. This having been said, it is time to examine women's sexual humor in detail.

Women's Sexual Humor

Mae West's line "Is that a pistol in your pocket or are you just happy to see me?" is quintessentially feminine humor in its playful undercutting of the masculine role of stealthy aggressor. By calling attention to her suitor's erection, West puts herself in the position of the observer and judge—or perhaps "umpire" would be a better term. She's certainly established that she's the one watching the plays and deciding who's out and who can come home. West's line has captured the public imagination and entered the language as a cliché because it is both so obvious and so deadpan that it's the perfect test. If you get it, you've already shown your colors. Of course, West would prefer a "real man" showing off his own piece rather than some gun, identifying masculinity with sex rather than violence. She says what is meant to remain unspoken, looks at what you're not supposed to notice, asks the unaskable, gives herself an active role in choosing what she likes instead of simply hoping to get it by default. Perfect Bad Girl stuff. Perfect women's sexual humor. In the same category are other West gems: "It's not the men in my life, it's the life in my men"; "When women go wrong, men go right after them"; "A hard man is good to find"; "He who hesitates is last"; "Give a man a free hand and he'll run it all over you." West said that "It's hard to be funny when you have to be clean," in response to the censors' demands that she avoid overtly sexual humor. But she also asked "Why should I be good when I'm packing them in by being bad?" West's humor almost never attacked other women. It focused on the assumptions behind the typical sexual encounter and subverted them. Her humor was sexy as well as sexual—a wry, clipped, and confident commentary on our sexual manners and styles.

A more contemporary example, Cynthia Heimel's brilliant book *Sex Tips for Girls*, is the perfect combination of sex and humor. Heimel offers a wonderful illustration of particularly feminine approaches to both subjects. Heimel doesn't rely on jokes, she tells stories. She comes up with principles and examples. She grounds her humor in intelligence and insight. Added to all this, it really *is* a book of sex tips, including "Zen and the Art of Diaphragm Insertion" and what to do with first-night impotence ("What one must not do, no matter what, is to keep kneading the penis as if one were preparing dinner rolls. This will only make him sad"), as well as a discussion of the larger issues facing women today—such as "The Perils of Obsession" and "The Great Boyfriend Crunch." Heimel instructs her readers on the proper manners for sex: "Be polite, be pleasant. It is not polite to: —laugh and point at the penile member; —break into prolonged, spasmodic sobbing; —say that your husband did it the same way . . . ; —ask if it's in yet." Heimel catalogues the dos and don'ts with affection and enthusiasm.

Heimel certainly grapples with the heart of the matter (so to speak) in sections such as "Does a Man's Size Have Anything to Do with a Woman's Pleasure?" In that particular subchapter Heimel addresses every woman's secret question and every man's secret fear by reporting that when a "group of girls get together around closing time at some sleazy joint with plenty of Hank Williams on the jukebox" they will "come clean." When most of the women admit they like "big ones," they also know that this satisfies more of a psychological than physical need. (Big penises are what the cartoonist Libby Reid refers to as "Oh-So-Fine Genetic Code Delivery System.") But, as one of the friends in Heimel's book theorizes, it's okay to like big penises, since, she argues, "What good do big tits do? None. But most men crave them." Heimel brilliantly illustrates the particular ways women deal humorously with sexual matters. By saying out loud what we've all thought but dared not admit, she makes us realize once again that the Bad Girls have all the good lines.

Like Heimel, Joy Behar deals with sexual matters by coming at them from a decidedly feminine angle. "Sure I want a man in my life," says Behar, "but not in my house. I want him to hook up the VCR and leave. Why should I want him in the house?" "Where Joan Rivers used to do a routine about getting the ring," says Behar, "I say 'live alone'—things have changed over the years." Behar's humor doesn't exclude men, she explains, but instead deals with the relationships between men and women in general—without making anyone into a victim. Examining a healthy relationship doesn't threaten it, and joking about a relationship should make everyone take a judicious look at its covert sexual dynamics.

Aren't Your Ears Cold?
· · · · · · · · · · · · · · · ·

One particularly interesting pattern to emerge from any extensive research into women's sexual humor is an emphasis on cunnilingus. In fact, jokes about cunnilingus are found in an astonishing number of women's books, routines, novels—everywhere. They are the one set of jokes to rely quite often on sexual aggressiveness, if not coercion, on the part of the woman. Women are determined, it seems, to have men go down on them no matter what. One short joke appears to sum up the unequal situation many women seem to find themselves in: "What's a sixty-eight? That's where you go down on him and he owes you one." Apparently a lot of women are interested in foreclosing on those outstanding debts.

Lenny Bruce used to do a routine where he asked how many men in the audience had ever had a blow job in their lives. The majority of men raised their hands. When he then asked how many women had given blow jobs, no woman put her hand up. Bruce looked around the audience and concluded, "Somebody's lying." Women, of course, are conditioned not to admit to performing any sort of sexual activity, especially one involving pleasure at the expense of procreation. But even more outré, more unacceptable, is for women to admit to wanting such an activity performed on them. Talking a woman into *administering* oral sex seems to be one thing, perfectly acceptable to most men. That they see as a perfectly legitimate request, even in light of the fact that it's pretty unladylike. When comedian Diane Ford's husband tells her that belching and swearing aren't ladylike, she replies, "Neither is a blow job, but you don't complain about that." But for a woman to demand reciprocal treatment? Ask a man to go down on her? It's enough to make you laugh. It's also enough to lead to a whole subcategory of women's sexual humor. There are scores of cunnilingus jokes told by women to other women, with the underlying understanding that men just don't understand how women feel about it. These are, apparently, jokes that are rarely told in mixed-sex groups because of the suspicion that men will react negatively, especially in a public setting. Some women admit to telling these privately to their lovers, in hopes of conveying their desires in a lighthearted fashion. Whatever the reason, it is a curiously pervasive genre of joke.

Listen to Deanne Stillman in her play *Girls in Suits at Lunch*. One of her characters suggests, "Instead of prenuptial agreements, you could urge paranoid clients to have sex contracts. The groom relinquishes all claim to his wife's body if cunnilingus is not performed on the wedding night." Heimel suggests that if you find a man who likes to go down on you, "Treat him well. Feed him caviar and expensive brandy and don't let your girlfriends catch a glimpse of him." Diane Ford, when talking about her horror at the idea of being out in public wearing a panty shield that breathes, says that such a contraption had to be designed by a man. "If a woman had designed it, she wouldn't have made it breathe, after all. She would have put little tongues in there or something." The women in the audience laugh, screech, bang the table in recognition. Who would dare say this out loud?

One joke popular when I was an undergraduate in a cold climate was the following: "A guy and a girl get a flat tire one blizzardy night. The guy goes out to change the tire but he has no gloves and after a while his hands start to get blue, so he comes back into the car. 'Put your hands between my thighs and that'll warm them up,' invites the girl. He does, and pretty soon his hands recover and he goes back outside. After a while longer, his hands get cold again and once again she suggests that he warm them between her thighs. He does so, and returns to finish putting on the spare. When he comes back into the car triumphant, she looks at him and asks 'Aren't your ears cold?' "

A joke included in *Truly Tasteless Jokes* is a revision of an old fairytale. "Little Red Riding Hood goes out into the forest, but this time she's hiding a .44 in her package of goodies, ready for action. The wolf follows her into the woods and grabs her from behind. 'Now that I've got you I'm going to fuck you until dawn,' he growls. But Little Red Riding Hood pulls out the .44, holds it to his head and announces calmly, 'No you're not. You're going to eat me like the story said.' " This is one of the few jokes I've come across that puts the female in the violently assertive position, demanding oral sex backed up by threats of violence.

Such joking remarks are prevalent in women's everyday conversation, of course. When one woman who had recently decided that she was gay rather than bisexual was setting up a straight friend of hers with an old boyfriend, the friend, delighted, looked up and said, "Oh, and if he was *your* boyfriend, you must have trained him correctly! How marvelous!" If you can convince your partner that the worst thing about oral sex is the view, then you can tell him these jokes without risk of offending him. For many men, it seems, become uneasy at the very mention of the subject. For women, couching the discussion of cunnilingus in humorous terms might be a way of dealing with their own anxiety about their desire for something, a desire that men sometimes appear unwilling to fullfill. Male jokes about cunnilingus are tedious repetitions concerning saltiness and discomfort, reinforcing the idea of the male's unwillingness to perform this act. It is no surprise then that Stillman should suggest making cunnilingus part of the contract—until that time, however, joking about it might help to make women's desires public without making anybody feel too bad about it. As with a number of other sticky subjects, introducing the idea through humor might increase the possibility of change.

Another joke, popular when I was in college, has a senior woman chatting up an enthusiastic and handsome, if unsophisticated, new freshman. After they've been talking a while, she asks him "Do you know the difference between tortellini and cunnilingus?" "No," he replies. "Good," she says, "let's go to dinner!" This joke is interesting because it has the woman playing on the man's naiveté, and procuring his sexual favors by bribing him with dinner. When I've repeated this story to men, they tell me a version of this joke involving a male boss and a new female secretary—and they tell me that their version is the "right" one. This in itself is interesting—the male listeners are frustrated by the form of the joke being violated, they insist, rather than by the change in the power positions. They are terribly earnest and sincere as they attempt to correct me, and have the full weight of authority behind them as they attempt to convince me that the joke doesn't work with a woman in the inviting position. When women hear the joke, they don't question the premise. They just laugh. They get it without any hesitation, just as I did when it was first told to me.

No woman I know has ever complained that the joke doesn't sound "right"—since that complaint seems to belong only to men, I have to conclude that it is a male reaction to the sexual dynamics of a situation in which they find themselves uncomfortable. Being uncomfortable in the situation, they try not to remedy their own discomfort ("Why does this make me feel so bad? Can I do anything to make myself feel better—such as go down on my girlfriend once in a while so that I don't sound like all the jerks in these jokes?") but instead to make the situation appear "unnatural" and so in need of correction ("That joke isn't funny. Women are plenty satisfied with what they get and it's men who really need to ask for oral sex. The way you tell the story just isn't funny—you can see that I'm not laughing, which is proof that the joke isn't funny—because no woman really feels that way. I know my girlfriend doesn't want anything else, despite what she says"). The answer to this is, of course, "Not only do real men eat quiche—real men eat anything."

In the Preston Sturges film *Sullivan's Travels,* Veronica Lake tells the man for whom she's buying breakfast, "The good thing about buying a man food is that you don't have to laugh at his jokes." The joke about the senior woman and the freshman also suggests that not only don't you have to laugh at his jokes, he might well have to laugh at yours. It may be unpleasant to suggest finally that sexual power is inextricably linked to economic control, but it is not inaccurate. Perhaps the idea of women exercising sexual ambitions along with monetary ones scares some men?

Certainly men are uncomfortable around these jokes. Their own discomfort (Dare I call it a sheepish sense of guilt? A haunting sense of acts undone? Need I go on?) gets in the way of their ability to find the joke funny. You can't really laugh if you feel defensive, because the joke swerves too closely to your own concerns. When things come too close to home is when most folks resort to invoking the teacher-voiced response "That's not funny."

To Boldly Go Where No Man Has Gone

Women have managed to explore a number of other difficult sexual subjects publicly through humor. There are, for instance, masturbation jokes that live nicely alongside cunnilingus jokes ("Why did God invent men? Because your fingers can't mow the lawn"). There are a growing number of jokes about women's desire for younger men ("I'm only thirty," one woman explained, "so younger to me means about paper-boy age." Phyllis Diller argues that the only men who are too young are ones who write their love letters in crayon, wear pajamas with feet, or fly for half fare. As Bette Midler pointed out when asked about old men marrying young women, versus old women marrying young men, "Twenty goes into sixty a lot more times than sixty goes into twenty"). We've always laughed about such things in private, but to hear them discussed "out loud"—in front of a group, even a large all-female group—is a surprising experience for most women. It validates our private experiences to hear them said aloud. If you can see that *every*body's being "bad," then you can start to feel good—you can see that you're not feeling a certain way because you're different from everyone else. In fact, you feel the way almost every other woman feels— and it's an enormous relief for most of us to understand this. I remember vividly the first time I heard my mother laugh at a dirty joke. I was about fourteen at the time, and had picked up a secret and tattered copy of *Lady Chatterley's Lover*. It just so happened that soon after I began reading the book, some pretentious talk-show host was discussing D. H. Lawrence with a guest. I blushed because I felt that while I'd be privy to their conversation, my mother would not be, having kept away from such novels. When the guest was asked whether he'd let his wife read *Lady Chatterley's Lover*, he replied, "Of course I would." He paused for a moment, and then added, "But I wouldn't let my gardener read it."

While *I* was old enough to understand the joke, with all the audacity of the young teenager, I didn't really think *she'd* get it. She was my mother, after all, and mothers don't laugh at such jokes. It seemed to be in their contract to disapprove of them. I waited to see what she'd do. I was shocked, absolutely and profoundly shocked, to see her laugh, but then in the next moment I was delighted. I saw her laughing as a person, as a woman, not reacting just in her role as a mother. I remember that she laughed, then looked at me, covered her mouth to try to make her laughter less obvious, and then gave up trying to hide it altogether. It let me off the hook, and I could finally laugh with her. Of course she had read the book years before, and this moment of laughter broke the taboo between us that said we couldn't talk about such things.

Seeing other women laugh is a liberating experience. When appearing on the Phil Donahue Show, Mo and Cathy did their sketch about a woman's embarrassment about asking another woman for a tampon ("Do you have any *lipstick*?" asks one woman, winking and nodding her head so that her co-worker will understand her hidden meaning. "Oh, this shade is *super*," she says, giggling at her double entendre, and they laugh covertly). It was particularly interesting to watch the shots of the audience reaction to such material. The generally female, middle-aged, middle-America group that constitutes the studio audience laughed delightedly. The men in the audience, however, seemed to be at a loss. It was the only time I saw that glazed, unspecific smile on men's faces—they didn't know whether or not to laugh. The men appeared to be at a curious disadvantage. Women know that we're supposed to laugh even when we're not sure we get it, even when we're not included in it, even when we don't think it's funny. These men had no idea what they were supposed to do. They all looked like the bachelorettes on *The Dating Game,* insecure and uncertain what their reaction should be. Most laughed a little nervously, looking at the women to their right for a signal.

In a piece that seems a presage to Mo and Cathy's sketch, Gloria Steinem wrote an essay in 1978 called "If Men Could Menstruate." Steinem posed a situation where "if suddenly, magically, men could menstruate and women could not." What would happen? According to Steinem, "Menstruation would become an enviable, boast-worthy" event. Steinem goes on to describe a world where men would "brag about how long and how much. Boys would mark the onset of menses, that longed-for proof of manhood, with religious ritual and stag parties. . . . Military men, right-wing politicians, and religious fundamentalists would cite menstruation ('*men*-struation') as proof that only men could serve in the Army ('You have to give blood to take blood'), occupy political office ('Can women be aggressive without that steadfast cycle governed by the planet Mars?'), be priests and ministers ('How could a woman give her blood for our sins?') or rabbis ('Without the monthly loss of impurities, women remain unclean')." Steinem's essay emphasizes the way in which the rules could be—and usually are—changed to suit the powers that be. She brings menstruation out of the whispered conversations of our adolescence by naturalizing it through humor.

Steinem's position is seductive because it clearly delineates the false logic of the arguments used against women. By turning each point around, she illustrates the way that the "obvious" is really just a disguise for the convenient. By satirizing the assumptions about menstruation, she raises a number of political issues that might otherwise seem too "dangerous" for anyone besides a committed feminist. Joy Behar agrees, arguing that humor is one of the most effective ways to get an important point across to an audience. "You can't just go out there and vote for so-and-so. You've got to be funny to get them interested, to get them to go along with you. You make your point as you go along, but you never let the point eclipse the humor." Humor allows ideas to shift and alter by what seems like an effortless process. Rather than dragging someone into your frame of reference, you include them by *assuming* they will laugh along with you.

By the Way, Feminism Isn't for Women Only

Ben Elton, a British comic whose material is noted for its conspicuous absence of sexist or racist jokes, declares at the end of his routine that "sexism in comedy, sexism everywhere, we've got to get together and beat it together." Elton redeems British comedy by turning his lens on the "best gag in the world" material that typically debases women. He says that he'll never be able to be really funny because obviously he'll never possess the one thing everybody seems to find hysterically amusing—big tits. "Big tits," he says ironically, "are the best gag in the world—or so it seems, if you watch British situation comedies." He goes on to repeat the dialogue from one Benny Hill type of program, and of course the material seems unfunny, offensive, and astonishingly stupid. The success of Elton's comedy is based on the fact that, close up, certain anachronistic forms of comedy just don't work. When presented without the laugh tracks and rolling eyes, the dirty jokes told about big breasts are flat. By examining them under the light of intelligence and awareness, Elton does a terrific job of showing the way a male comic can do feminist humor, if feminist humor is defined as humor that does not debase women but instead values a feminine perspective.

The American comedian Jay Leno is another male comic whose work is sympathetic toward women. Leno often offers a perspective on material that women can applaud. For example, Leno does a routine about the Tom Hanks/Penny Marshall movie *Big* where he suggests that the premise of the movie, a thirty-year-old man acting as if he were thirteen, isn't exactly unfamiliar to most women. "The women are out there saying, why doesn't somebody make a *real* science-fiction and fantasy adventure and do a movie about a thirty-year-old guy who acts his age?" Leno's humor is conspicuously free of sexist remarks, and it is no surprise that he is one of the most popular performers in the country. Luckily, in other words, not all male comics are Benny Hills.

And although not all women's jokes are sexual jokes, the sexual jokes are perhaps the ones where a woman's particular perspective is etched most clearly. Women's sexual humor is centered on women's needs and desires, which is not surprising. And although the nature and depth of women's sexual desires sometimes seem to shock the men who overhear the stories, the same stories often serve to reassure the women who hear them— reassure us that we're no more alone in our fantasies than we are in our laughter.

When women can turn the lens of their humor on sexual matters, issues that are cloistered and closeted by years of inherited embarrassment and guilt can finally come into a clear, framed focus. When you can speak of something, name something, laugh at something, you show your control over it. The novelist Mary McCarthy once said that the essential difference between men and women is that women know that sex is basically comic—that it is something to laugh about and to laugh at. Sexual humor that celebrates women's bodies and desires is humor that can help to counteract all the years of thinking that a sexual joke must be told at a woman's expense.

7

How Many Feminists Does It Take to Change a Light Bulb?

....

Power, Politics, and Women's Humor

Learning the Hard Way
. . . .

When I started my first year as a student at Dartmouth College, there were four men for every woman. I thought I had it made. Dartmouth had only recently admitted women, and the administration thought it best to get the alumni accustomed to the idea by sneaking us in a few at a time. With such terrific odds in my favor socially, how could I lose? I'd dated in high school and although I wasn't exactly Miss Budweiser, I figured I'd have no problem getting a date every Saturday night. But I noticed an unnerving pattern. I'd meet a cute guy at a party and talk for a while. We would then be interrupted by some buddy of his who would drag him off to another room to watch a friend of theirs "power-boot" (the local vernacular for "projectile vomiting"), and I realized that the social situation was not what I had expected.

Then somebody explained to me that on the Dartmouth campus "They think you're a faggot if you like women more than beer." This statement indicated by its very vocabulary the advanced nature of the sentiment behind it. If a guy said he wanted to spend the weekend with his girlfriend, for example, he'd be taunted by his pals, who would yell in beery bass voices "Whatsa matter with you, Skip? We're gonna get plowed, absolutely blind this weekend, then we're *all* gonna power-boot. And you wanna see that broad again? Whaddayou, a faggot or something?"

It turned out that the male-female ratio did not prove to be the marvelous bonus I had anticipated. But still I figured that the school was good enough to justify spending the next few years getting down to studying and forgoing a wild social life. I thought it would all work out, that at least I would be accepted in my classes as a good student and get through the next couple of years without too much worry or trouble. Okay, I told myself, I could live with that and found in fact that dating guys from other schools was a healthy practice anyway.

But the real shock came in the classroom, where I was often one of two or three women. One professor, I remember, always prefaced calling on me or any other woman in the class by asking "Miss Barreca, *as a woman,* what is your reading of this text?" I was profoundly embarrassed to be asked my opinion as a woman, since it seemed somehow less authoritative than being asked my opinion as a student or as a "general" reader. At first, I jokingly replied that I would be happy to answer "as a person," but that it was hard for me to answer as a woman. When the professor didn't so much as smile, I knew that tactic wouldn't work. Every time I raised my hand to answer a question, I was asked my opinion *as a woman.* It frustrated and angered me, because I wanted to be treated as an individual and not as a representative of a group.

Just Like a Woman
. . . .

It took months to understand that, in the eyes of this teacher, I'd always be a "miss" rather than just another, ordinary student. When I realized that there was no alternative, I figured I'd go with it, exaggerate the situation enough so that I could at least enjoy myself. So I started prefacing every answer with the phrase "As I woman, I think Shakespeare means . . . ," "As a woman, it strikes me that Tennyson's point is . . ." But then I figured, why stop at this? I started to say "As a woman, I think the weather's rather cold for June." "As a woman, I think I'll have the meatloaf for dinner." "As a woman, I think I'll go to bed early tonight." It started out as a joke, but as it caught on (a number of my friends started to use the same strategy to make the professors and guys in general hear how their remarks sounded), we started to examine further. Maybe we really were always speaking as a woman. Maybe there was no such thing as speaking as "just" a person. Maybe we always spoke as women whenever we spoke. Maybe this joke wasn't such a joke.

So that even as I stopped saying "As I woman, I believe such-and-such," I started thinking it. It occurred to me that nothing was neuter or neutral. I saw that my responses were in part determined by the fact of my gender—as well as by other factors, like my class and ethnicity. I didn't read novels about war in the same way a man would, for example, since I hadn't been brought up to consider going to war as a soldier as a possible future for myself. I hadn't played war games as a kid, I didn't find the idea of war engaging. It did not have "universal appeal," since it didn't appeal to me, a narcissistic but nevertheless compelling argument. In the same way that the male students complained that Jane Austen was obviously a second-rate writer because all she was interested in was marriage (Mark Twain once said that it was "a pity they let her die a natural death"), so I decided to assert that Hemingway's concern for bullfighting was no concern for an intelligent, insightful woman. Of what interest is bullfighting to the contemporary female reader? Hemingway was therefore second-rate, by their definition, since his subject matter had limited appeal and seemed gender specific. I learned to answer "Of course" when asked whether I responded to things as a female. I learned to accept that and even enjoyed discovering the ways in which my viewpoint differed from the perspective offered by my male peers.

How Dare You Call Me a Feminist!

But even understanding that the world identified me first as a woman and only secondly as anything else didn't stop me from being horrified the first time somebody called me a "feminist." I thought being a feminist meant I couldn't wear lipstick or crave men with small behinds. I thought that "feminist" meant I couldn't send Peanuts cards to guys who I was afraid wouldn't call back, or buy stockings with seams. I thought "feminist" meant no more steamy flirtations or prolonged shopping trips. I thought it meant braided hair and short nails, maybe mandatory tofu. I certainly associated feminism with humorless, dour, and—worst of all—unblinkingly earnest women. That was because I was accepting the male version of things, which was sort of like believing the mouse's version of the cat, since it entailed being given access to a vision that could see nothing besides teeth and claws.

I was warned about so-called feminists. I was told by boyfriends, relatives, professors, and other disreputable sources that such women were ambitious, sharp-tongued, a little too smart for their own good. They told me that only women who couldn't get laid got political. They told me what was perhaps the biggest and most interesting lie of all: that independence and ambition were unattractive in a woman. They also suggested, subtly but seriously, that too much of a sense of humor in a woman made her unattractive (a comment to which the comedian Elayne

Boosler would reply "Comedy is very, very sexy when it's done right"). Luckily, during a moment that eclipsed all earlier illumination, I heard a female graduate student repeat a wonderful line from the writer Robin Morgan, "*We* are the women that men have warned us about." It was as if the little light bulb that appeared over Bugs Bunny's head when he got an idea suddenly appeared over mine. It seemed unnerving, actually, that I was gazing reprovingly at all those qualities that I myself possessed. I was certainly ambitious, ready to speak and eager to defend my position on a subject. I liked being a woman, was proud of my femininity, and believed myself to be equal to any task set before me by society—at least as well equipped to deal with it as any guy I sat next to in class (he could no more skin a bison than I could, and I could probably defend myself on Tenth Avenue more ably than he).

So, when I really thought about it, I was already a feminist no matter what I chose to call myself. When I looked around, I saw a lot of smart, funny women who also fit the bill. We were all feminists, whether or not we'd admitted it aloud before. It was sort of like admitting we were secretly Bad Girls, and for me the admission held the same sort of delightful relief. Oh, is *that* what I am? Is this what the word means, is this what the name names? Is this what a feminist is? Oh good!

This Is What a Feminist Looks Like

It's like when Gloria Steinem was told on her fortieth birthday "You don't look forty," to which she replied, "This is what forty looks like." When I was told after that moment of revelation, "You don't look/act/speak like a feminist," I answered, "*This* is what a feminist looks/acts/speaks like." These old narrow ideas of the feminist as a dour, sour-faced woman have got to go. Feminists are not a lonely tribe of women fenced off from the rest of society. Feminists read cookbooks and clip coupons from Sunday supplements. Feminists like to dance, flirt, and wear high heels, often doing all three at the same time. Feminists can like men—and enjoy the process of liking individual men for their own worth instead of valuing all men simply because they're male. Feminists enjoy the company of other women and value the company of other women. Feminists don't wish they were men; they celebrate their womanhood.

Nicole Hollander had Sylvia's daughter pose the eternal question "Ma, do you think I can be a feminist and still like men?" Sylvia replies, as she always does, in unequivocating terms: "Sure. Just like you can be a vegetarian and like fried chicken." While Hollander's example is wonderfully funny, it also indicates the way in which women struggle with the dos and don'ts of feminism. The point of feminism is not to alienate men, but for women to focus on our own concerns and needs, to establish our own values. These may or may not coincide with the already established values of our dominant culture, just as our concerns and needs may or may not fold neatly into a relationship. The point is to work on making decisions based on choices that are really choices instead of following a script—in other words, and in the terms of this book's central argument, it means learning to laugh at what we find funny instead of just following along with the laugh track.

I see, rather remarkably, my female students going through the same sorts of trials and self-examinations today in spite of the fifteen years of feminism that have passed. Some of these women students are planning to go to medical school. Some are engineering majors. They are track stars or nationally ranked basketball players. These young women certainly work hard, compete fiercely, and are not embarrassed about admitting that their goals are high. They work to put themselves through school. Most of them aren't considering getting married until they're several years into their chosen professions. Most of them leave home after graduation to make their way in cities across the country and to find interesting, challenging jobs.

Yet when I ask how many of them consider themselves feminists, only about a third in any one class will dare to raise their hands. These women may not be afraid of getting bad scores on the LSATs or GREs, but they're afraid of not getting a date. They can be independent, intelligent, and proud to be women. But a little word like "feminism" scares them. One girl, a student who'd taken two women-and-literature classes with me, said that she loved the material, that the books had changed how she thought about herself and her relationships with men. We were having coffee in my office, discussing the subversion of the marriage plot in the contemporary woman's novel, when I mentioned something about being pleased that her feminist perspective was being finely delineated by her careful work on the novel. "Oh, but I'm not a feminist," she said, surprising me. "I don't like that word." I gulped, and felt that, whatever work I'd done in class, I'd obviously left out a crucial discussion.

Why are so many women afraid to call themselves feminists?

The F Word

Catharine R. Stimpson wrote an article for *Ms.* in 1987 about how important it is for women to learn to say the "F Word" in public. Stimpson, who is the dean of the graduate school at Rutgers University, was of course referring to the word "feminism" when she used the term the "F Word." We know well enough that nobody's embarrassed to say the word "fuck" anymore, but a lot of women are still hesitant to say the word "feminism" in mixed company—as if saying "Yes, I'm a feminist" is much more unladylike than telling somebody, for example, to "fuck off."

The trouble is that, to a number of people, the two phrases are synonymous, which is a great pity. Stimpson suggests that if women continue to change in a positive way, then "people will be able to say 'feminist' as casually as they now say 'wife' or 'kid' or 'snack' "; she ends her article by calling for feminists to use "more audacity, more humor, when we speak of feminism." Stimpson once showed me how well and with what humor feminists deal with uncomfortable situations by having the good humor to joke me out of the horror I felt at having misspelled both her names—no easy trick when you think about it—in an article I'd published. She looked at me sternly, then laughed, and the laughter relieved me of the weight of my foolishness, because she obviously understood how bad I'd already made myself feel about it. It was a generous, welcoming gesture.

Most of feminism is made up of just such gestures. The last thing feminism is about is exclusion. Feminists can be defined as those women and men who recognize that the earth doesn't revolve around anybody's son—or around any one group. In a collection of essays on women's humor titled *Last Laughs: Perspectives on Women and Comedy*, Fay Weldon quotes this old joke: "Question: How many radical feminists does it take to change a light bulb? Answer: That's not funny!" Weldon then goes on to say that humor acts as a kind of shorthand; it "saves me from writing a long paragraph about how feminists get accused of not being able to make jokes, and a few of us certainly can't, which makes a few of us uneasy, which is why it's a joke in the first place."

When the radical feminist writer Andrea Dworkin writes "I'm a feminist. Not the fun kind," I always feel apologetic about replying "I'm a feminist too, but actually I am the fun kind," because we sometimes have to worry about seeming too frivolous to be good feminists. (Apparently Dworkin is actually a warm, funny woman, someone who does use humor to make her point when she appears in public.) The writer Kate Clinton has come up with a compact word for feminist humorists— "fumerists"—because it captures the idea of being funny and wanting to burn the house down all at once.

Feminist humor, according to Clinton, "is about making light in this land of reversals, where we are told as we are laughing, tears streaming down our faces, that we have no sense of humor." She goes on to say that "Men have used humor against women for so long—we know implicitly who is the butt of their jokes—that we do not trust humor. Masculine humor is deflective. It allows denial of responsibility, the oh-I-was-just-kidding disclaimer. It is escapist, something to gloss over and get through the hard times, without ever having to do any of the hard work of change. Masculine humor is essentially not about change."

The Difference Between Revolt and Revolution

The difference, in fact, between men's humor and women's humor seems to be the difference between revolt and revolution. Masculine humor has of course included digs at the conventions of the world, poked fun at the institutions and establishments, but without the truly anarchic edge that characterizes feminine humor. Women's humor calls into question the largest issues, questions the way the world is put together. Granted, some humor by male writers does the same—Woody Allen comes to mind—but whereas such humor is not a hallmark of male humor, it is characteristic of women's humor.

Agnes Repplier, an American essayist born in 1855, argues, "Humor distorts nothing, and only false gods are laughed off their earthly pedestals." In other words, an essentially sound target will not be damaged by humor; humor, as we've seen, depends on the perceived righting of an injustice. This is one reason women's humor does deal with the most fundamental concepts in our culture. Women's humor has a particular interest in challenging the most formidable structures, because they keep women from positions of power. Women's humor is about women speaking up. Women's humor takes subjects traditionally regarded as beyond joking for its subject matter. Repplier also said that "The worst in life, we are told, is compatible with the best in art. So, too, the worst in life is compatible with the best in humor." The poet Marianne Moore, born in 1887, wrote that "Humor saves a few steps; it saves years," and Katherine Mansfield, born in 1888, suggested in her journal that "To be wildly enthusiastic, or deadly serious— both are wrong. Both pass. One must keep ever present a sense of humor."

Professor Judy Little, whose scholarly book *Comedy and the Woman Writer* is one of the landmarks in the study of women and humor, suggests that a woman writer such as Virginia Woolf is, in fact, far more subversive than her male counterpart James Joyce, because Woolf calls into question not only the rules of religion but the need for religion at all. Little's argument suggests that, whereas a male writer might rave against the basic tenets of a system of beliefs, his female counterpart will be asking whether any belief system should be in power. Her question will be far more subversive than his because she's asking for the destruction of the system rather than for a change in it. Some male writers are, of course, subversive, and some women writers are conservative, but these examples do not render false the claim. Women's humor is irreverent, not only about one's self and about the details of life, but about the very "givens" of life itself. One could say, for example, that while some men do it— use humor that is truly subversive—some of the time, a great number of women do it most of the time. "The reason husbands and wives do not understand each other is because they belong to different sexes," said the early feminist Dorothy Dix. Putting the question of gender-specific perspectives into such simple terms makes the whole idea of a universal vision seem, well, funny.

Much male humor is aggressive and attempts to be control- ling, but, for all its yelling and punching, ultimately masculine comedy reinforces generally held belief systems, leaving general rules and regulations untouched except at the most superficial level. Male comedy is directed toward and assumes a predom- inantly male audience.

While this is not surprising, it is still a shock to those people who would like to continue to see comedy as "universal" instead of gender specific. But, interestingly, even the male comics see their work in gender-specific terms, at least insofar as they see their success linked to their "dicks," seeing even the microphone they work with as a "dick substitute." According to Betsy Borns's book *Comic Lives*, they see their comedy in terms of virility and impotence. They see some essentially male quality as the element that allows them to control the audience.

Robin Tyler, a feminist stand-up comic, responds to this idea of seeing success in comedy in male-defined terms. "The mind is much more powerful than the prick," suggests Tyler, adding "—and the mind doesn't go down in two minutes." Tyler's point seems to be that women's power is not derived from the same sources as men's, but that the female sources might in fact be richer and more effective, especially with a predominantly female audience.

The Split Between the Real and the Ideal
· ·

When Nicole Hollander's cartoon suggested that the hallmark of women's humor is its focus on the split between the real and the ideal, she touched on what is a central distinction between women's comedy and men's comedy. Whereas men occasionally challenge the idea of reality or the conventions of society, women do it regularly. Whereas men occasionally seem to subvert the standing order, women make subversion their business. When I think of the subversive nature of women's humor, I think of Jane Wagner and Lily Tomlin creating the character of Trudy in their play *The Search for Signs of Intelligent Life in the Universe*. A bag lady in an umbrella hat, Trudy knows that she'd "got the kind of madness Socrates talked about, 'A divine release of the soul from the yoke of custom and convention.' " Trudy is a wonderful link between the hysterically funny woman and the one who's simply labeled "hysterical." Trudy says "Maybe I didn't have a breakdown—maybe I had a breakthrough." This character knows that consensus doesn't create truth, that just because everybody believes something doesn't make it true—think of the world being flat, or of women being told they have no sense of humor.

Whether you choose to call it feminist humor or feminine humor, or "just" humor, if you're a woman, then you're making a woman's joke, laughing a woman's laugh. I would say that nearly all women's humor is in some way feminist humor (with the exception of those early, self-deprecating "I'm so ugly . . ." jokes associated with the very earliest comedians). I'd say that women's humor is almost by definition feminist because, in the same way that we can't help but speak as women, we can't help but be funny as women. We're inevitably informed by our gender. If you're using any of the strategies of humor we've discussed earlier, then I'd say that you're using feminist humor, because you're offering some sort of challenge to the system. You're taking on a new perspective, offering your statement or question when the system would encourage you to be silent. When you make a joke, when you laugh with your mouth open, or when you refuse to laugh at something you don't find funny even though you know you "should" laugh, then you're making a radical gesture. You're ignoring the script that tells you when to speak (almost never) and when to laugh (when someone else tells you to).

I'd say that anytime a woman breaks through a barrier set by society, she's making a feminist gesture of a sort, and every time a woman laughs, she's breaking through a barrier. Kate Clinton sees humor as a way into change. She writes, "Humor leads the way; it moves us past those inbred, ingrained resistances." Clinton goes on to describe her version of feminist humor as being like lichen, "secreting tiny amounts of acid, year after year, eating into the rock. Making places for water to gather, to freeze and crack the rocks a bit. Making soil, making way for grasses to grow. . . . It is the lichen which begins the splitting apart of the rocks, the changing of the shoreline, the shape of the earth. Feminist humor is serious, and it is about changing the world."

The comedian Joy Behar stated in an interview her belief that "It's important for a woman's point of view to be heard. People say to me, 'Do you speak as a woman?' No, I speak as a man. Of course I speak as a woman! What a stupid question that is. I'm a female. What? Am I supposed to speak as if I had a schlong? (That's Italian for 'facial hair')." Behar's point is that to ask someone if she "speaks as a woman" is as nonsensical as asking if someone speaks as "someone who lives in the twentieth century." There are certain assumptions that appear fairly basic. When women speak, we speak as women. We may not speak for all women, we're not necessarily representative of anyone besides ourselves, but when we speak it makes sense that we can't help but speak as who and what we are.

"It's So Hard to Be a Feminist If You Are a Woman"

Being a feminist raises complex issues even for those women who are committed to the cause of women's rights. Jane O'Reilly, in an essay reprinted in a collection of women's humor called *Pulling Our Own Strings*, writes, "I am often tired of being a feminist. I'm not even sure I am a feminist." O'Reilly wonders whether she can be a feminist and still be worried about her family, her appearance, her femininity, and with a sigh decides, "It's so hard to be a feminist if you are a woman."

But finally O'Reilly comes to the conclusion that it "helps to laugh. There is, after all, a certain inherent humor in being on the cutting edge of a social revolution. It is funny, actually, to be unsure of what you feel more offended by: the guests ignoring your opinions or not complimenting you on your soufflé." In this sentence, O'Reilly offers a wonderful example of the bind that so many of us find ourselves in: we want to be congratulated equally on our "traditionally feminine" skills or attributes (being a terrific cook, having terrific legs) and our newly acquired achievements (being made a partner in the firm or being elected mayor). Since women have been continually adding on to the list of what we have to do without taking anything off the list (you're still supposed to be a terrific cook even after you've been made a partner), we're unsure what we want to have praised first.

This became clear to me when a group of friends and I were watching the 1989 Miss America pageant. We were applauding and eating even more popcorn and making more sundaes than usual, because the revised format included rather challenging questions for the contestants—such as asking that they discuss the level of responsibility of the government in providing equal access to the disabled. It wasn't exactly the same as watching Geraldine Ferraro get nominated, but after twenty-five years of being glued to these pageants (against all principles, of course) it seemed as if the criteria were being adapted to indicate the changing values of contemporary society. All of the young women gave intelligently reasoned, even well-researched an- swers, whereas in the past their predecessors had been asked only whether they thought world peace would be a good idea (acceptable answer: "Yes, I think so, honestly"). Hooray, we thought, they're not treating these women as body parts, but instead asking them to use their heads. Imagine our surprise when, as soon as the contestant answered the question, she had to walk across the floor and present her little behind to the judges so that they could grade her ass as well as her answer. "Great," my friend Wendy wailed, "now you're supposed to have an amazing rear and a good mind. I really thought if you had one you couldn't be expected to have the other. I surrender. I'm putting a white flag on my ass so they can tell." We broke out another bottle of Kahlúa and opened another gallon of Breyer's in response. "If we were real feminists," said Bonnie through a mouthful of White Russian, "we wouldn't even be watching this, and we certainly wouldn't care what we looked like when we left the room because we'd be so sure that we made an overwhelmingly positive impression when we entered it." But then we were back to the funny, unnerving response "But this *is* what feminists act like—at least sometimes."

Toward a Funny Feminism?

Feminism, in fact, seems to be increasingly tied to humor. The leaders of the women's movement have historically harnessed humor for their purposes, as Professor Nancy Walker of Vanderbilt University has so carefully documented in her book *A Very Serious Thing*. Walker shows us that women's political and domestic humor has always been an effective challenge to long-held and oppressive ideas. Yet she is compelled to point out that, despite an underground tradition, women's humor "has been largely omitted from the official canon . . . been allowed to go out of print, to disappear from all but the dusty reaches of library shelves." Walker gives us insights not only into the history of women's humor but also into the reasons that our humor is not often read as being as subversive as it really is. She suggests that what appears to be submission to the stereotypes of mother, housewife, or bimbo is often a thinly veiled indictment of the society that trivializes a woman's life.

Women's humor is often directed at the bizarre value systems that have been regarded as "normal" for so long that it is difficult to see how ridiculous they really are. When Gabrielle Burton, addressing the Symposium on Women's Mental Health in 1976, said that "We'll all be better off when word gets around that cleaning a toilet produces no more and no less than a clean toilet; it does not produce strength of character, nor is it interesting work," she pointed out that what is considered valuable work for a woman is not always genuinely valuable. Burton wasn't making a joke per se, but by simply emphasizing the sorts of situations women find themselves in, she was uncovering and therefore making humorous an unreasonable arrangement. Sometimes just the very act of naming something, saying something out loud, admitting something about how we view our lives is enough to make us laugh. It's so absurd, we realize as soon as we see it clearly, that it's funny.

There seems to be a growing awareness among feminists that, if the women's movement is going to survive, it has to gather the courage to laugh at itself and the world that made half the human race the "other" half. Also there is an awareness that feminism must embrace women who have, for whatever reasons, adopted the traditional script as well as the ones who have chosen more radical departures. A shared territory of humor can be one place where various groups of women can meet. When women laugh together, we underscore the ways in which our experiences of the world connect us rather than divide us.

Women are beginning to complain that men don't get the joke, that they can't understand what's so funny. Elayne Boosler talks about the kind of humor that men can't get: "Men can say things in a department store that women can't say. When you're shopping with them and encourage them to try on a pair of trousers with some style, maybe a pair designed after 1978, men can say, 'But I already have a pair of black pants.' And men say things like, 'But you already own a pair of earrings just like the ones you're buying.' " Men, Boosler points out, will not understand about the need to save "nice" shopping bags from expensive stores and fold them neatly into exactly the right lines; the women in the audience laugh in recognition, whereas the men whisper "Why *do* you save those bags?" But, even concerning larger questions, women may laugh at issues men consider off limits—like the idea of men crying. Now, we know that men are "allowed" to cry, but it is like one of Jane Austen's truths universally ackowledged that women do not have contempt for men who cry but rather that women consider men who cry to be particularly dangerous, and so a fit subject for humor. Nora Ephron writes that we should ". . . beware of the man who cries. It's true that men who cry are sensitive to and in touch with feelings, but the only feelings they tend to be sensitive to and in touch with are their own." Women may laugh at these passages because they have experienced the dangerous, vulnerable man; men usually react very badly to crying jokes and cannot see any humor in them. Boosler can count on the laughter of the women in the audience even at the expense of their male companions. There's no need, as there was for Anne Beatts ten years ago, to leave off the references that only women will get. In fact, when Boosler discusses shopping, she doesn't deprecate it as some trivial activity. She places it into a political framework. "For a woman who's spent her day making sixty-five cents on a man's dollar in some demeaning, low-level job, it's an amazing experience to walk into a place and have someone say to her 'How can *I* help *you*?' "

When women laugh together—like the hooker, socialite, and bag lady at the end of *The Search for Signs of Intelligent Life in the Universe*—we recognize our similarities instead of focusing on our differences. The novelist and essayist Marilyn French in the afterword to *Intelligent Life* explains, "A major criticism leveled at feminist art by masculinists (male or female) is that it tends to belabor its points rather than simply assume them. But feminist art has to belabor its points—has to inform its audience that everything that exists is interconnected . . . that body and emotion are as important as mind, and that these three are more important than domination—because these ideas diverge from the mainstream. [*Intelligent Life*] is the first work I know of that simply takes it as a given that a mass audience will accept feminist attitudes."

When we laugh at one of the characters' description of her favorite vibrator as "a sort of Hamburger Helper for the boudoir" and her argument for its positive benefits—"Ladies, it simply takes the guesswork out of making love. 'But doesn't it kill romance?' you say. And I say, 'What doesn't?' "—we find a moment during which we share a witty denial that women are romantic, unworldly, and easily pleased.

When a radical, separatist feminist from San Francisco can laugh at the same material that amuses a born-again homemaker from Iowa, we've located a nexus point where the concerns of women converge. In other words, is it possible for Gloria Steinem and Jeane Kirkpatrick to laugh at the same material? It is possible that, being successful in their own right, both Steinem and Kirkpatrick would laugh at Miss Manners's (Judith Martin's) advice to a reader whose concern was this: "As a businessman, how do I allow a businesswoman to pay for my lunch?" Miss Manners's typically impeccable reply: "With credit card or cash, as she prefers." Or they might agree with Jill Ruckelshaus's observation: "It occurred to me when I was thirteen and wearing white gloves and Mary Janes and going to dancing school, that no one should have to move backwards all their lives."

Is it possible, finally, for the Bad Girl and the Good Girl to laugh at the same time and at the same thing without one worrying about appearing nerdy and the other worrying about appearing degenerate? It appears that humor offers the possibility for the more conservative and the more radical among us to come to some agreement. We seem to be moving closer together in what we consider appropriate material for women's laughter.

Television has changed so much that in an episode of the highly successful program *Murphy Brown,* Candice Bergen can say that she's going to start her own country and describe it in the following terms: "Women only. Two men to do the electrical and the plumbing. Maybe one guy to open jars." Mainstream television programs can now employ humor that is cunningly close to the more outrageous humor used by people like Nicole Hollander. Hollander's character Sylvia responds to a man's apparently rhetorical question "What would you do without us?" with the statement "What would the world be like without men? Free of crime and full of fat, happy women." None of this is very far from the writings of the radical feminist writer Mary Daly, a professor at Boston College, whose treatise on theological and academic systems, *Gyn/Ecology,* asks "Why has it seemed 'appropriate' in this culture that the plot of a popular book and film [*The Exorcist*] centers around a Jesuit who 'exorcises' a girl who is 'possessed'? Why is there no book or film about a woman who exorcises a Jesuit?"

At one point, Mary Daly addressed the question of women's humor directly. "For example," writes Daly, "the cliché 'She lacks a sense of humor'—applied by men to every threatening woman—is one basic 'electrode' embedded . . . deeply . . . into the fearful foreground of women's psyches. . . . The comment is urbane, insidious. It is . . . devastating if believed. It is [a device] used especially against the wittiest women, who are dismissed as 'sharp-tongued.' " Daly's fiercely militant book is also extremely witty, undermining on every page the possible assertion that a radical feminist is necessarily humorless.

One intriguing aspect of the heightening feminist awareness of the last few years is the way in which certain things that would have been perfectly acceptable a while back instantly become the subject not only of outrage but of humor—there are incidents that become comic just because they are no longer "naturally" acceptable. For example, Time Inc. ran a full-page ad on the back page of *The New York Times* that claimed "You don't build a company like this with lace on your underwear." Female executives, whether they sported lacy drawers or not, were at first horrified and then laughed hysterically over the mind-set that would produce such obviously outdated, inappropriate copy. The ad became an instant "inside" joke among the thousands of high-powered and ambitious women reading their copy of the *Times* before meeting their clients, workers, and colleagues. One highly placed executive told me that there were more conference calls made up of laughing women that morning than she imagined possible. Everybody was calling everybody else to share the moment that showed both how far we've come (at least it was clearly and obviously a bad, failed approach, so bad it was funny) and how far we have yet to go (enough people in a major corporation approved of that copy for it to go to press in the first place).

The same executive friend told me that the incident reminded her of the uproar that occurred when, several years ago, a copy of the Sears Roebuck catalogue mistakenly included a photograph of a male underwear model whose penis was clearly visible through the flap of his Y front. "Only in this case," she said, referring to the *Times* ad, "they were only waving their penis around metaphorically." Time Inc. subsequently apologized for any possible offense caused by the ad. Since the company does have an excellent track record when it comes to employing and promoting women, it seemed like a good idea to accept its apology and carry on.

The important aspect of this story, however, is the idea that women in positions of authority spontaneously and effectively manipulated into humor what would once have been an ordinary sexist remark. These women used the sexism of the ad against the perpetrators by laughing them out of their sanctimonious self-assurance. Surely the folks who placed the ad thought it was clubby and "only-boys-know-the-game" to make a remark that equates economic power with jockey shorts. It took, once again, a sort of emperor's-new-clothes mentality on the part of the women in the business community to say "Nope, this is not going to work, guys. It's actually *so* far off the mark that it's really funny." These women had arrived at the point where they knew that their position was unassailable, and they used humor to solidify their camaraderie while at the same time turning their antagonists' attempt at humor against them. "When you're in the head office, you can bet that you'll wear whatever panties you please," said my executive friend with a laugh.

How Far Can We Go?
. . . .

"How much fame, money, and power does a woman have to achieve on her own before you can punch her in the face?" writes P. J. O'Rourke, whose popular book *Modern Manners* was published in 1983. Is this funny? Are we still supposed to tolerate such a remark because it's—ha ha, get it?—delivered as a joke? It is still considered funny, we must remind ourselves when we're starting to feel complacent about our strides forward, to debase women's accomplishments and ambitions. The hidden anger of the supposedly sophisticated man can be more damaging than the overt degradation of comics like Clay and Kinison. The group that thinks it's okay to write advertising copy about lacy underwear also thinks it's healthy to vent a little anger in the manner of Ralph Kramden ("One of these days, right in the kisser") toward women in power.

O'Rourke's implied question is "When is a woman accomplished enough to be considered a man?" since fame, money, and power are all identified as male characteristics. Any woman who has these, in other words, should be prepared to step outside for a fistfight. Are women trying to be men? As one piece of popular graffiti has answered this question, "Women who aspire to be as good as men lack ambition." One appropriate response to such a question was the one given by Charlotte Whitten, a Canadian politician. Whitten, former mayor of Ottawa, coined the now widely quoted statement that posits "Whatever women do they must do twice as well as men to be thought half as good. Luckily, this is not difficult." Nicole Hollander has Sylvia listening to a television commentator explaining that "Man is the hunter and woman is the civilizing influence, and when women abandon that role, men become . . . ," and Sylvia supplies the ending to that sentence by chiming in, ". . . cranky, and start wars." But perhaps one of Hollander's most astute comments on the topic of the world's perceptions of women's roles is the one where a commentator says that "Women with names like Dawn and Cheryl have less of a chance for success in business than women with names like . . . ," and Sylvia fills in, ". . . Roger and Bill."

In such a cartoon, Hollander shows us through her humor that when women are refused power, it has more to do with the system than with the women. The political nature of so much women's humor supports Elayne Boosler's assertion that "the best who stand up, stand up for something." A generation earlier, Dorothy Parker made a distinction between wit and wisecracking: "Wit has truth in it; wisecracking is simply calisthenics with words."

8

She Who Laughs, Lasts

· · · · · · · · · · · · · · · · · ·

The Importance of
Defining and Using Our
Own Humor

Having Trouble vs. Making Trouble
· ·

Women are said to "have trouble" with endings—that is one of
the ways women's humor and women's talk in general differ
from men's. One of the clichés applied to women is that they
get halfway through a joke and then can't remember the punch
line. In several episodes of *I Love Lucy,* for example, Lucy tries
to tell a joke but cannot keep the story straight. She needs Ricky
to interrupt and help her out. The typical example of the feminine mis-telling of a joke usually relies on a woman's poor
memory. According to this stereotype, the Typical Woman will
begin the joke "How do you get to Carnegie Hall?" and instead
of giving the punch line "Practice, practice!" she'll say "Keep
trying" or use some other phrase that leaves out the funny part.
As with most clichés, we can immediately think of a thousand
women to whom such a remark does not apply, but there is
nevertheless something interesting about this piece of so-called
accepted wisdom.

While I've certainly found that most women can indeed remember jokes, I've also found it true that the "one-two punch line" format of most traditional jokes simply doesn't appeal to most women. It makes sense, then, that since such jokes don't appeal to women, women are less likely to remember them. It isn't that women can't remember a joke, but rather that most of the jokes women have been told haven't been *worth* remembering.

We consciously or unconsciously "lose" the information. The woman who says "Gee, honey, I just can't remember why the woman with no teeth is the perfect date. *You* tell the joke" at least doesn't have to participate in her own degradation. She disguises her own refusal in socially acceptable terms by appearing to be too "feminine" to take part in the "masculine" game of humor. She puts her escort on the spot by defaulting from the game. It's important to realize that she isn't "having trouble," but rather that she is "making trouble." She's making trouble because she's not playing the game, she's not reading the script, she's not supplying a punch line when it directs the punch at her—or others like her.

There's always been a big difference between having trouble, which means you can't do something, and making trouble, which means you're refusing to do something. Women would "have trouble" with comedy if we didn't have a comedy of our own. But as we've seen, women's humor has its own patterns, and while women's humor works differently from men's, there is no doubt that women's humor certainly works for women.

You can "have trouble" with something only if it pertains to you. I don't "have trouble" with walking a pit bull because I have nothing to do with pit bulls—it doesn't affect me, so I don't think of myself as "having trouble" with it.

I had a friend, in fact, who "had trouble" telling one sort of dog from another, despite the fact that she started dating a man who raised purebreds. "Arnold, which one is the spaniel?" she'd ask once a week, trying to indicate or manufacture an interest that she didn't really have. This woman was not exactly a slow learner; she was a well-respected surgeon who worked in a large teaching hospital. But she "had trouble" remembering which dog was which because, when it came down to it, she didn't care terribly much which dog was which. The relationship, as you'd imagine, was not destined for success. But when she stopped dating this one man, she no longer "had trouble" telling one dog from another, because she simply didn't bother with the issue. In the same way, most of us don't "have trouble" with getting the last line perfect, with reproducing exactly what we've been told, because it doesn't mean very much to us. We're seen as having trouble with it only because it bothers someone else, when others expect us to behave according to their rules.

I remember a dinner when a funny, smart man who obviously enjoyed the company of women and seemed a fairly good feminist himself admitted there was one thing about women that drove him crazy. We all turned to listen, surprised to hear him make such a categorical remark. "I know all these women who want to hear the endings of things first," he began, impassioned, in a voice laced with frustration and disbelief. "I mean, I go to the movies and I tell them a little bit about the story, but they interrupt me and want to know what happens at the end." At this point he put down his glass and laid both hands flat on the table before him, as if making a final and essential declaration on the differences between the sexes. "I refuse to tell them, but they insist on asking," he explained. "Then they tell me that they read the last few pages of the book first. I can't believe anybody would do that. They want to know the ending first. It drives me crazy." There was silence.

Then one woman asked him, after a moment, whether, when he gave a book report in the fourth grade, he'd always end the talk by saying the famous phrase "And if you want to find out what happens, you'll just have to read the book"? He admitted, rather defiantly, that he had. At that point I thought I'd add to the fray by saying that it wasn't a "deviant" or "bad" habit of women to want to hear the endings first, that it wasn't women "having trouble" with the endings, but that instead it was a Dick Thing to need to hear everything in one straight line, without any diversion and with a gradual buildup of suspense. It was a DT to have to get everything in the right order—it just didn't matter much to some women if we heard the end first or heard a story related "out of sequence," because we weren't as heavily invested in sequence as he seemed to be. Other women at the table added their stories and support to this position, explaining their inability to understand the masculine mind-set that argues there is only one right sequence to events. They had spent a great deal of time trying to train themselves to do such things "right," only to find out that doing it "right" meant doing it according to someone else's recipe. The initiator of the discussion, himself a novelist, could not accept such terrible, bizarre habits as normal, despite the fact that we reassured him that things could be worse than he even imagined—one woman admitted to going to movies before one showing of the film ended just so that she could see the ending first. He lifted his glass in despair and surrendered.

Coming Out of the Humor Closet

As we've seen, women tell jokes and stories in ways that make women laugh, and so indeed women generally have a good—sometimes terrific—sense of humor. We've seen the way that earlier experiences in our homes and families, schools and communities, taught us that when we laughed we should laugh behind closed doors. We were taught that what we laughed at had to stay among ourselves—it wasn't for public consumption. Our funny stories had to be kept as secret as our Kotex pads, stuffed away into pretty cases to disguise them and discussed only in all-female groups. But humor, like our periods, appeared distinctively female, routine, inevitable. Everybody had it, but few of us could admit this in front of a guy.

The television programs and movies we watched reinforced the idea that Good Girls didn't laugh out loud, and we learned that those girls who did laugh got to go out only on blind dates set up by their smiling but unlaughing friends. If you were going to laugh out loud, you were going to be played by Connie Francis or Eve Arden, not Kim Novak or Lauren Bacall, in the movie version of your life. The funny women were generally the supporting characters, not the leading ladies, and who wants to spend her life as a supporting character? We were instructed by screens, large and small, to smile rather than to laugh, to be docile and enigmatic instead of being saucy and honest. We were told that we'd be appreciated, sought after, and beloved if we played dumb, kept quiet, and didn't make a spectacle of ourselves. Then we started to learn that playing dumb, keeping quiet, and not calling attention to ourselves meant waiting around for the honor of some man's choosing us—rather than our choosing a man—in addition to losing us any chance of success in the business world. We learned that the traits supposedly reserved for guys—such as intelligence, ambition, economic acumen, and a sense of humor—were in fact all the factors that added up to winning in the workplace. We learned that the Bad Girls, the ones who spoke up and didn't hesitate to say what was on their minds, were the ones who embodied values that were in fact rewarded by the public world of commerce— an ability for quick thinking, a sense of timing, and a healthy disrespect for the system, which would eventually lead to the willingness to alter that system for the better.

What we learned, to speak plainly, is that we'd been duped, made to believe in a set of values that didn't do very much to help us toward happiness, self-esteem, or success. We started realizing that it's better to laugh out loud than to reproduce what one reporter from *The Wall Street Journal* called the "damaged-nerve endings" smile characterizing those women who are afraid to do anything but smile for fear of offending someone. This reporter said that such perpetual smiling was the smile of the "bunny in the headlights," a smile born of worry instead of pleasure. For too long the signs of our pleasure—smiling and laughing—have been used to make others feel better rather than used as a way to let others know how we feel.

"They Think We Want Everything and They're Right"

We've been told so often that women have no sense of humor, we have no trouble believing it—even when we're laughing. Why do men seem so invested in making sure women undervalue our sense of humor? "Men are frightened by women's humor," sums up Nicole Hollander, "because they think that when women are alone they're making fun of men." Hollander does not discount this fear. "This is perfectly true," she continues, "but they think we're making fun of their equipment when in fact there are so many more interesting things to make fun of—such as their value systems. Or the way they act when they're sick."

Men are worried that what has been considered a clearly defined male prerogative—having a sense of humor—will once again turn out to be available to women, not "naturally" male at all. "They think we want everything," says Hollander, adding, "And they're right." Women do want to be attractive and ambitious, intelligent and generous, funny themselves as well as appreciative of humor. The question is, why on earth shouldn't we want everything? Why has it taken so long to admit it? We have to stop worrying so much about enjoying ourselves—we're allowed to be happy, to take pleasure in the absurdities and comedies presented by our lives. None of the commandments says "Thou shalt not laugh." We've been conspirators in the women-have-no-sense-of-humor plot for too long.

A Radical Suggestion—Laugh Only at What's Funny

When women feel entitled to use our own humor, our appreciation of traditionally male humor might indeed slack off. We won't laugh at what we don't find funny because we'll have developed a clearer sense of what we *do* find funny. In other words, when we cultivate our appetites and develop our own palates for humor, what's been laid on the tables for years might not seem as appealing. We might push some of it away and ask for something different. But we'll also be responding more honestly, with more enthusiasm and energy, with less resentment and anger to what is before us.

When women stop laughing along with the laugh track, our laughter will mean a great deal more than it does at the moment, because it will reflect our own unmediated responses to a given situation. If somebody claps her hands only when the big neon applause sign lights up, the applause isn't worth very much, because it's scripted—we're just following orders. When someone applauds out of a spontaneous desire to render apparent her approval or delight, however, the gesture holds meaning and the receiver has earned his or her sense of accomplishment. Respect, like affection, is more valued and more valuable when it's freely given than when it's demanded or coerced.

Our mothers' generation had to face a world where women were far more unlikely to be able to support themselves and their families than we are today, so it is not surprising that they tried to teach us ways to conceal our humor because "the boss" might not like it—whether they meant the boss in the home or the boss at the job. They signaled to us that we should keep our humor in the kitchen, away from the eyes and ears of men. They were concerned for our welfare, but such advice was hard to overturn even by our own later experiences. We have in us a residual hesitation, an early response that often prevents us from using our wit to defend ourselves or enhance ourselves in public. We hear the echo of a well-meaning maternal voice telling us "Be careful, don't overdo it or you'll scare him away."

We've had to unlearn old information concerning our sense of humor in much the same way as we had to unlearn old information about women not having the intelligence to do research or the stamina to run marathons. We've had to lose the sense of false propriety that says we should censor our remarks, cutting out those that might seem too "sharp-tongued," because those that are "sharp-tongued" are often pointedly intelligent, smart, and timely.

Winning the Salt Wars

When we use our own humor to defend ourselves against jokes that we find offensive, we're employing our intelligence and awareness wisely. When a joke is made at our expense, there is no obligation on our part to have complicity in our degradation by laughing. Having a sense of humor no longer means laughing at his jokes even if they make us feel uneasy—having a sense of humor will mean defending ourselves by returning comment for comment, being prepared to confront the offense or withdraw from it.

In other words, the boy pouring the salt on our head deserves whatever reaction we can muster—short of setting fire to him or kicking his gerbil—he's set himself up as a target for our response. So that when one of our colleagues smiles leeringly and says "I just can't seem to picture you in a bathing suit," we have every right to reply "And God knows, Sam, I don't want to try picturing you in one. Frankly, I don't even like to think of you not wearing an overcoat and hat." The laughter he sought to gain at your expense will be turned back on him. Such a remark makes use of the sort of strategies women are taught in self-defense classes, where we've learned to turn the aggressor's energies back onto the aggressor.

Coming and Going

Having a sense of humor about sex is like having a sense of humor about death—both allow you to have perspective on an otherwise potentially overwhelming prospect. Humor allows you to elevate and explore rather than denigrate or hide your feelings. Humor doesn't dismiss a subject but rather often opens that subject up for discussion, especially when the subject is one that is not considered "fit" for public discussion. Humor breaks taboos by allowing us to talk about those issues closest to us.

We should see humor as a way of making our feelings and responses available to others without terrifying our listeners. When we can frame a difficult matter with humor, we can often reach someone who would otherwise withdraw. Humor is a show of both strength and vulnerability—you are willing to make the first move but you are trusting in the response of your listener. Making a generously funny comment, pointing to the absurdity of a situation, turning embarrassment or unease into something to be shared instead of repressed is risky, but it is also often exactly what is needed. An older woman I know was seriously ill for almost a year before her death. One of the things she minded most was what she called (intending the pun) the "deadly earnestness" of most of her visitors. "One of the unexpected side effects of my illness," she told me, "is that it seems to have made all of my friends incredibly boring. I need to rejoice in these last days of my life and everybody else is acting like they're already at the funeral." We took her comments seriously and one of the last things I remember about her was the way she laughed at a story being told about her daughter's reaction to the handsome male nurse attending her. A day during which we have laughed is a day that has not been wasted—to laugh is to affirm ourselves and our lives in a fundamental sense.

Beginnings
· · · · · · · · ·

Humor is a way to affirm ourselves, to rise to meet a challenge, channel fear into pleasure, translate pain into courage. "When in doubt," counsels Cynthia Heimel, "make a fool of yourself. There is a microscopically thin line between being brilliantly creative and acting like the most gigantic idiot on earth. So what the hell, leap." When we can really laugh, we've declared ourselves the winner, no matter what the situation, because our laughter is an indication of our perspective and control. Paradoxically, as we have seen, to be able to lose yourself in laughter is proof that you are confident enough to risk a moment of joyful abandon.

Women's humor may be undervalued, but it is priceless. It may have been hidden away, but it has been constant. It may have been ignored or challenged, but it has always been a secretly potent, delightfully dangerous, wonderfully seductive, and, most important, powerful way to make ourselves heard, to capture the attention, the heart, and the respect of our audience.

Throwing your head back and laughing out loud is always an experiment because you can never be sure how others will react. But it is also a manifestation of your willingness to give others the benefit of the doubt by assuming they will also rise to the occasion, by joining in and laughing with you.

When you tell a joke or a funny story or make a witty remark and not many others laugh with you, what you've made isn't a mistake. What you've made is a beginning.

Notes

∙∙∙∙∙∙∙∙∙∙∙∙∙∙∙∙∙∙∙∙∙

Chapter 1
∙∙∙∙∙∙∙∙∙

Page

5 "It is as important for a woman . . .": Interview with Mary Davis, vice president of Time-Warner Inc., and director of Magazine Manufacturing and Distribution, New York City, 1988.

6 "She didn't even laugh . . .": Anne Beatts, "Why More Women Aren't Funny," *New Woman* (March/April 1976): 22–28.

6–7 "In this culture . . .": Rose Laub Coser, "Laughter Among Colleagues: A Study of the Social Functions of Humor Among the Staff of a Mental Hospital," *Psychiatry* 23 (February 1960): 81–95.

7 "If you say that . . .": Anne Beatts, "Can a Woman Get a Laugh and a Man Too?" *Mademoiselle* (November 1975): 140ff.

Page

9   "Hm! How can you prove that?": Joanna Russ, "Dear Colleague: I Am Not an Honorary Male." Reprinted in *Pulling Our Own Strings: Feminist Humor and Satire*, Gloria Kaufman and Mary Kay Blakely, eds. (Bloomington: Indiana University Press, 1980): 182ff.

9–10 Professor Emily Toth . . . : Emily Toth, "Forbidden Jokes and Naughty Ladies," *Studies in American Humor* 4, nos. 1, 2 (1985): 8.

12   Women do not often laugh . . . : Interview with New York City–based psychoanalyst Dr. Natalie Becker, 1989.

13   "the humane humor rule": Emily Toth, "Female Wits," *Massachusetts Review* 22 (Winter 1981): 783–93.

14   Stand-up comedian Elayne Boosler, 1989.

16   "A girl with brains . . .": Anita Loos, *Gentlemen Prefer Blondes* (New York: Liveright, 1925): 11.

17   "Literary men . . .": Muriel Spark, *The Girls of Slender Means* (New York: Alfred A. Knopf, 1963): 61.

17   Loos could be "counted on . . .": Gary Carey, *Anita Loos* (New York: Alfred A. Knopf, 1988): 95–98.

19   "Comedy is itself an aggressive act . . .": Abbey Stein, quoted by Julia Klein, "The New Stand-up Comics," *Ms.* (October 1984): 116ff.

20   "I believed him . . .": Interview with stand-up comedian Susie Essman, New York City, 1989.

21   "Since we're all too scared . . .": Interview with writer Pamela West, New York City, 1989.

23   "Two strong women . . .": Joanna Russ, "What Can a Heroine Do? or Why Women Can't Write," *Images of Women in Fiction: Feminist Perspectives*, ed. Susan Koppelman Cornillon (Bowling Green, Ohio: Bowling Green University Popular Press: 1972): 3–20.

24   "Self-deprecation . . .": Nancy Walker, *A Very Serious*

Page

Thing: Women's Humor and American Culture (Minneapolis: University of Minnesota Press, 1988): 123.

25   "When male comics . . .": Paul E. McGhee, "The Role of Laughter and Humor in Growing Up Female," *Becoming Female: Perspectives on Development*, ed. Claire B. Kopp (New York: Plenum Press, 1979): 183–206.

25   In a landmark study . . . : Rose Laub Coser, "Laughter Among Colleagues: A Study of the Social Functions of Humor Among the Staff of a Mental Hospital," *Psychiatry* 23 (February 1960): 81–95.

27   "If somebody does something . . .": Gilda Radner, Interview in Denise Collier and Kathleen Beckett, *Spare Ribs: Women in the Humor Biz* (New York: St. Martin's, 1980): 133.

27   "if you're going to be made to look ridiculous . . .": Margaret Atwood, *Lady Oracle* (New York: Fawcett Press, 1976): 47–52.

28   "sense of humor got to be a joke . . .": Erma Bombeck, *Family—The Ties That Bind . . . and Gag!* (New York: Fawcett Crest, 1987): 223.

31   "Just below the surface . . .": Cynthia Heimel, *But Enough About You* (New York: Simon & Schuster, 1986): 148.

32   "Is she laughing at him?": Fay Weldon, *Female Friends* (London: Heinemann, 1975): 259–267.

35–36   "Have you ever heard of a father-in-law joke?": Interview with Dr. Bernice Sandler, director of the Project on the Status and Education of Women at the Association of American Colleges, Washington, D.C., 1989.

Chapter 2
· · · · · · · ·

Page

39   "*Cathy adores a minuet . . .*": Theme song to *The Patty Duke Show*, "The Cousins." Written by Sidney Ramin and Robert Wells. EMI U Catalogue Inc., 1963.

40   In their landmark book . . .: Sandra Gilbert and Susan Gubar, *The Madwoman in the Attic: The Woman Writer and the Nineteenth-Century Literary Imagination* (New Haven, Conn.: Yale University Press, 1979).

42   ". . . chutzpah . . .": Sarah Blacher Cohen. "The Jewish Literary Comediennes," *Comic Relief: Humor in Contemporary American Fiction* (Urbana: University of Illinois Press, 1978): 172–186.

43   Helen Taylor's study . . .: Helen Taylor, *Scarlett's Women: Gone With the Wind and Its Female Fans* (New Brunswick, N.J.: Rutgers University Press, 1989): 78.

49   ". . . except for women like Lucille Ball . . .": Penny Marshall, interview in Denise Collier and Kathleen Beckett, *Spare Ribs: Women in the Humor Biz* (New York: St. Martin's, 1980): 174.

50   . . ."fallen" knowledge to make a joke . . . : See Mahadev Apte's work in *Humor and Laughter: An Anthropological Approach* (Ithaca, N.Y.: Cornell University Press, 1985): 75–78.

51   "Rizzo's character . . .": Stockard Channing, interview in Denise Collier and Kathleen Beckett, *Spare Ribs: Women in the Humor Biz* (New York: St. Martin's, 1980): 57.

52   "Fear of Dating": Cynthia Heimel, *But Enough About You* (New York: Simon & Schuster, 1986): 158–159.

52   "I have this thing . . .": Abbey Stein, quoted in Julia Klein, "The New Stand-up Comics," *Ms.* (October 1984): 116ff.

53   "Please, I'll only put it in . . .": Beverly Mickins, quoted

Page

in Julia Klein, "The New Stand-up Comics," *Ms.* (October 1984): 116ff.

53 "Our heroine . . . ": Anita Loos, *Kiss Hollywood Good-By* (New York: Viking, 1974): 43.

54 "You can't make jokes . . .": Quoted in Gary Carey, *Anita Loos: A Biography* (New York: Alfred A. Knopf, 1988): 148.

56 "Women's humor, like that of minorities . . .": Nancy Walker, *A Very Serious Thing: Women's Humor and American Culture* (Minneapolis: University of Minnesota Press, 1988): 106.

56 "Comedy is an archetypal carrier of anger . . .": Judith Wilt, "The Laughter of Maidens, the Cackle of Matriarchs: Notes on the Collision between Comedy and Feminism," *Women and Literature*, ed. Janet Todd (New York, Holmes & Meier, 1980): 192.

57 "When women are funny . . .": Anne Beatts, interview in Denise Collier and Kathleen Beckett, *Spare Ribs: Women in the Humor Biz* (New York: St. Martin's, 1980): 25–27.

61 "There is a phrase . . .": Mary Russo, "Female Grotesques: Carnival and Theory." *Feminist Studies/Critical Studies*, ed. Theresa deLauretis (Bloomington: Indiana University Press, 1986): 213.

62 In a special issue . . . : *Gentleman's Quarterly* (August 1989): 217.

63 "A guy and a girl . . .": Carol Mitchell, "The Sexual Perspective in the Appreciation and Interpretation of Jokes," *Western Folklore* 36 (1977): 307–308.

64 In a 1975 study . . . : Frank J. Prerost, "The Indication of Sexual and Aggressive Similarities Through Humor Appreciation," *The Journal of Psychology* 91 (1975): 283–288.

Page

65   "Women are still less likely . . .": Carol Mitchell, "Hostility and Aggression Toward Males in Females Joke Telling," *Frontiers* 3, no. 3 (Fall 1978): 21.

65   "Men are going around . . .": Deanne Stillman, interview in Denise Collier and Kathleen Beckett, *Spare Ribs: Women in the Humor Biz* (New York: St. Martin's, 1980): 121ff.

66   In a recent interview . . . : Interview with Margaret Drabble by Ian Wojcik-Andrews, 1988. Forthcoming in *Daughter of Last Laughs*, ed. Regina Barreca (New York: Gordon & Breach).

66   "the same vocabulary . . .": Anne Beatts, interview in Denise Collier and Kathleen Beckett, *Spare Ribs: Women in the Humor Biz* (New York: St. Martin's, 1980): 24ff.

67   "women can laugh . . .": Nancy Walker, *A Very Serious Thing: Women's Humor and American Culture* (Minneapolis: University of Minnesota Press, 1988): 172.

67   "Oh, life . . ." and "By the time . . .": Dorothy Parker, *The Portable Dorothy Parker*, rev. ed. (New York: Viking, 1973): 96.

68   "something I think it was Kafka . . .": Jane Wagner, *The Search for Signs of Intelligent Life in the Universe* (New York: Harper & Row, 1986): 210.

68   "Our neighbor . . .": Fay Weldon, *Letters to Alice: On First Reading Jane Austen* (London: Coronet Books, 1984): 74.

Chapter 3
· · · · · · · ·

Page

71   "*I* find jokes about you funny . . .": Joanna Russ, "Dear Colleague: I Am Not an Honorary Male." Reprinted in *Pulling Our Own Strings: Feminist Humor and Satire,*

Page

Gloria Kaufman and Mary Kay Blakely, eds. (Bloomington: Indiana University Press, 1980): 182ff.

76 In a study done at the University of Southern California . . . : Jonathan Gutman and Robert E. Priest, "When Is Aggression Funny?" *Journal of Personality and Social Psychology* 12, no. 1 (1969): 60–65.

78 ". . . shockucomics . . .": Gerri Hirshey, "The Comedy of Hate," *Gentleman's Quarterly* (August 1989): 226ff.

81 "Smut is like . . .": Sigmund Freud, *Jokes and Their Relation to the Unconscious*, trans. James Strachey (New York: Norton, 1960): 98ff.

89 "Is the subject of jokes . . ." Ibid.: 51, 64ff.

94 "Being a good little Everygirl . . .": Cynthia Heimel, *Sex Tips for Girls* (New York: Simon & Schuster, 1983): 27–28.

96 "a way to have the last word": Interview with Susie Essman, 1989.

Chapter 4
. . . .

Page

102 "My grandmother . . .": Nicole Hollander, *The Whole Enchilada: A Spicy Collection of Sylvia* (New York: St. Martin's, 1986): Introduction.

102 "came from my mother . . .": Marilyn Sokel, interview in Denise Collier and Kathleen Beckett, *Spare Ribs: Women in the Humor Biz* (New York: St. Martin's, 1980): 107.

103 "I'll interview my mother": Gilda Radner, interview in ibid.: 131–140.

103 ". . . my family was very funny . . .": Wendy Wasserstein, interview by Esther Cohen in *Last Laughs: Perspectives on Women and Comedy*, ed. Regina Barreca (New York: Gordon & Breach, 1988): 257–270.

Page

103   According to the authors . . . : Ann Morrison et al., eds.,
       *Breaking the Glass Ceiling: Can Women Reach the Top
       of America's Largest Corporations?* (Reading: Addison-
       Wesley, 1987).

106   "It seems reasonable . . .": Childs and Pollo (1976), quoted
       in Paul E. McGhee, "The Role of Laughter and Humor
       in Growing up Female," *Becoming Female: Perspectives
       on Development*, ed. Claire B. Kopp (New York and Lon-
       don: Plenum Press, 1979): 184.

107   "Males should be the initiators . . .": Ibid.: 201–202.

109   "There's a line . . .": Wendy Wasserstein, interview by
       Esther Cohen in *Last Laughs: Perspectives on Women and
       Comedy*, ed. Regina Barreca (New York: Gordon &
       Breach, 1988): 258.

110   "Judy was a sweet . . .": Marcia Froelke Coburn, "The
       Prom Queen from Hell," *Gentleman's Quarterly* (August
       1989): 274.

111   "hardly appreciate the comic . . .": Henri Bergson,
       "Laughter: An Essay on the Meaning of the Comic." Re-
       printed in *The Philosophy of Laughter and Humor*, ed.
       John Morreall (Albany: SUNY Press, 1987): 119.

113   "The funny boys . . .": Interview with Mary Davis, vice
       president of Time-Warner, Inc., 1989.

118   "I always write . . .": Susan Silver, "Five Women Comedy
       Writers Talk About Being Funny for Money," *Mademoi-
       selle* (November 1975): 86.

118   "A feminist comic sensibility . . .": Lisa Merrill, "Feminist
       Humor: Rebellious and Self-affirming," *Last Laughs: Per-
       spectives on Women and Comedy*, ed. Regina Barreca
       (New York: Gordon & Breach, 1988): 271ff.

119   "Please, God . . .": Dorothy Parker, "The Telephone
       Call," *The Portable Dorothy Parker*, rev. ed. (New York:
       Viking, 1973): 119ff.

Chapter 5
· · · · · · · ·

123 "Not a single phrase . . .": Betty Lehan Harragan, *Games Mother Never Taught You: Corporate Gamesmanship for Women* (New York: Warner Books, 1977): 98.

124 "undermine a woman's . . .": Mary Jane Genova, "Wit Can Undermine a Woman's Career," *The New York Times*, Op-Ed section, November 2, 1988.

125 when women are placed in positions of power . . . : John B. Miner, "New Sources of Talent"; quoted in Donald O. Jewell, ed., *Women and Management: An Expanding Role* (Atlanta, Ga.: Georgia University Press, 1977).

125 "ability to interact": Marilyn Loden, *Feminine Leadership, or How to Succeed in Business Without Being One of the Boys* (New York: Times Books, 1985): 95.

126 "A person with humor": Jane Trahey, *Jane Trahey on Women and Power* (New York: Avon Books, 1977): 192.

126 "enjoys new ideas . . .": Michael Maccoby, *The Gamesman: Winning and Losing the Career Game* (New York: Bantam Books, 1978): 40–41; quoted in Marilyn Loden, *Feminine Leadership, or How to Succeed in Business Without Being One of the Boys* (New York: Times Books, 1985): 25.

127 "female style . . .": Lois Wyse, *The Six-Figure Woman (and How to Be One)* (New York: Simon & Schuster, 1975); quoted in Marilyn Loden, *Feminine Leadership, or How to Succeed in Business Without Being One of the Boys* (New York: Times Books, 1985): 73.

128 "a good rapport . . .": Ann Morrison et al., eds., *Breaking the Glass Ceiling: Can Women Reach the Top of America's Largest Corporations?* (Reading: Addison-Wesley, 1987): 40.

131 Dr. Harvey suggests . . . : Joan Harvey, *If I'm So Suc-*

Page

cessful, Why Do I Feel Like a Fake? The Impostor Phenomenon* (New York: Pocket Books, 1986).

133 "I have sort of . . .": Interview with financial executive
Lynette Lager, 1989.

134 "That would mean . . .": Betty Lehan Harrigan, *Games
Mother Never Taught You: Corporate Gamesmanship for
Women* (New York: Warner Books, 1977): 373.

134 "In all societies . . .": Tom Burns, "Friends, Enemies, and
the Polite Fiction," *American Sociological Review* 18, no.
6 (December 1953): 654–662.

135 "If one is caught . . .": William H. Martineau, "A Model
of the Social Function of Humor," *The Psychology of
Humor*, ed. Jeffrey Goldstein and Paul McGhee (New
York: Academic Press, 1972): 101ff.

136 "simultaneously a strong . . .": K. Lorenz (1963), "On
Aggression," quoted in ibid.

138 "The young men . . .": Interview with Carol DeSanti,
1989.

Chapter 6
· · · · · · · ·

Page

145 "Gender Differences in Humor": Nicole Hollander, reprinted in *Last Laughs: Perspectives on Women and Comedy*, ed. Regina Barreca (New York: Gordon & Breach,
1988).

149 "It used to be that . . .": Interview with comedian and
talk-show host, Joy Behar, New York City, 1989.

152 "It has been common knowledge . . .": Virginia Woolf,
A Room of One's Own (New York: Harcourt Brace Jovanovich, 1979): 77.

152 "It was all right . . .": Mary Gordon, quoted in Dale
Spender, *The Writing or the Sex? or Why You Don't Have*

Page

to *Read Women's Writing to Know It's No Good* (New York: Pergamon Press, 1989): 33.

153   "The quickest way . . .": Libby Reid, *You Don't Have to Pet to Be Popular: Cartoons by Libby Reid* (New York: Penguin, 1989).

153   "turn everything into a story . . .": Nora Ephron, *Heartburn* (New York: Pocket Books, 1983): 221.

154   "Maybe the ugly girls . . .": G. Legman, *No Laughing Matter: An Analysis of Sexual Humor* (New York: Grove Press, 1968): 258.

156   "Take it off . . .": Interview with stand-up comedian Lara Kightlinger, New York, 1989.

160   "group of girls . . .": Cynthia Heimel, *Sex Tips for Girls* (New York: Simon & Schuster, 1986): 188.

160   "Sure I want a man . . .": Interview with Joy Behar, 1989.

162   "Instead of prenuptual . . .": Deanne Stillman, *Girls in Suits at Lunch* (New York: Doubleday, 1988): 11.

162   "Treat him well": Cynthia Heimel, *Sex Tips for Girls* (New York: Simon & Schuster, 1986): 123.

167   "if suddenly, magically . . .": Gloria Steinem, "If Men Could Menstruate," *Ms.* (October 1978): 110.

Chapter 7
· · · · · · · ·

Page

177   "The 'F word' . . .": Catharine R. Stimpson, "The 'F' Word: Why Can't We Say It in Public?" *Ms.* (July/August 1987): 80ff.

178   ". . . is about making light . . .": Kate Clinton, "Making Light: Another Dimension, Notes on Feminist Humor." *Trivia: A Journal of Ideas* (Fall 1982): 39.

180   Professor Judy Little . . . : Judy Little, *Comedy and the Woman Writer: Woolf, Spark, and Feminism* (Lincoln:

Page

University of Nebraska Press, 1983), and "(En)Gendering Laughter: Woolf's *Orlando* as Contraband in the Age of Joyce," in *Last Laughs: Perspectives on Women and Comedy*, ed. Regina Barreca (New York: Gordon & Breach, 1988): 179ff.

181   ". . . dick substitute": Betsy Born, *Comic Lives: Inside the World of American Stand-up Comedy* (New York: Simon & Schuster, 1987).

181   "Maybe I didn't . . .": Jane Wagner, *The Search for Signs of Intelligent Life in the Universe* (New York: Harper & Row, 1986): 115.

182   "Humor leads the way . . .": Kate Clinton, "Making Light: Another Dimension, Notes on Feminist Humor." *Trivia: A Journal of Ideas* (Fall 1982): 39.

183   ". . . important for a woman's point of view . . ." Joy Behar. Interview by Kate Sullivan-Irwin in *Laugh Track: The Comedy Audience Magazine* (September 1989): 24.

183   "I am often tired . . .": Jane O'Reilly, "Clunks," *Pulling Our Own Strings: Feminist Humor and Satire*, Gloria Kaufman and Mary Kay Blakely, eds. (Bloomington: Indiana University Press, 1980): 72.

185   ". . . has been largely omitted . . .": Nancy Walker. *A Very Serious Thing: Women's Humor and American Culture* (Minneapolis: University of Minnesota Press, 1988): 120.

185   "We'll all be better off . . .": Gabrielle Burton, "No One Has a Corner on Depression, But Housewives Are Working on It." Address to the Symposium on Women's Mental Health, 1976. Reprinted in Gloria Kaufman and Mary Kay Blakely, eds., *Pulling Our Own Strings: Feminist Humor and Satire* (Bloomington: Indiana University Press, 1980): 138ff.

187   "A major criticism . . .": Marilyn French Afterwords. Jane

Page

Wagner, *The Search for Signs of Intelligent Life in the Universe*. (New York: Harper & Row, 1986): 219–223.

189 "Why has it seemed . . .": Mary Daly, *Gyn/Ecology: The Metaethics of Radical Feminism* (Boston: Beacon Press, 1978): 2.

Chapter 8
· · · · · · · ·

Page

198 "Men are frightened . . .": Interview with Nicole Hollander, creator of the *Sylvia* cartoon series, 1989.

201 "When in doubt . . .": Cynthia Heimel, "Lower Manhattan Survival Tactics," *Village Voice*, 1983; quoted in *The Penguin Dictionary of Modern Humourous Quotations*, comp. Fred Metcalf (London: Penguin, 1986): 62.

Bibliography

······················

Apte, Mahadev L. *Humor and Laughter: An Anthropological Approach*. Ithaca, N.Y.: Cornell University Press, 1985.

Atwood, Margaret. *Lady Oracle*. New York: Fawcett Press, 1976.

Baron, Robert A. "Aggression-Inhibiting Influence of Sexual Humor." *Journal of Personality and Social Psychology* 36, no. 2 (1978): 189–197.

Barreca, Regina, ed. *Last Laughs: Perspectives on Women and Comedy*. New York: Gordon & Breach, 1988.

Beatts, Anne. "Can a Woman Get a Laugh and a Man Too?" *Mademoiselle* (November 1975): 140ff.

———. "Why More Women Aren't Funny." *New Woman* (March/April 1976): 22–28.

Berger, Phil. "The New Comediennes." *The New York Times Magazine*, July 29, 1984: 27ff.

Berkowitz, Leonard. "Aggressive Humor as a Stimulus to Aggressive Responses." *Journal of Personality and Social Psychology* 16, no. 4 (1970): 710–717.

Billard, Mary. "Jawing with Jay Leno." *Gentleman's Quarterly* (August 1989): 221ff.

Bombeck, Erma. *Family—The Ties That Bind . . . and Gag!* New York: Fawcett Crest, 1987.

———. *Four of a Kind.* New York: McGraw Hill, 1985.

Brown, Michele, and Ann O'Connor, eds. *Hammer and Tongues: A Dictionary of Women's Wit and Humour.* London: Grafton Books, 1988.

Bunkers, Suzanne L. "Why Are These Women Laughing? The Power and Politics of Women's Humor." *Studies in American Humor* [New Series] 4, nos. 1, 2 (Spring/Summer 1985): 82–93.

Burns, Tom. "Friends, Enemies, and the Polite Fiction." *American Sociological Review* 18, no. 6 (December 1953): 654–662.

Cantor, Joanne R. "What Is Funny to Whom?" *Journal of Communication* 26 (Summer 1976): 164–72.

Carey, Gary. *Anita Loos: A Biography.* New York: Alfred A. Knopf, 1988.

Chapman, Antony J., and Nicholas J. Gadfield. "Is Sexist Humor Sexist?" *Journal of Communication* 26 (Summer 1976): 141–153.

Chast, Roz. *The Four Elements: Cartoons by Ros Chast.* New York: Harper & Row, 1988.

Cixous, Helene. "The Laugh of the Medusa." Translated by Keith and Paula Cohen. *Signs* 1, no. 4 (Summer 1976): 875–93.

Coburn, Marcia Froelke. "The Prom Queen from Hell." *Gentleman's Quarterly* (August 1989): 205ff.

Cohen, Sarah Blacher. "The Jewish Literary Comediennes." *Comic Relief: Humor in Contemporary American Fiction.* Urbana: University of Illinois Press, 1978: 172–186.

Collier, Denise, and Kathleen Beckett. *Spare Ribs: Women in the Humor Biz.* New York: St. Martin's, 1980.

Cooper, Cary L., and Marilyn J. Davidson, eds. *Women in Management: Career Development for Managerial Success.* London: Heinemann, 1984.

Coser, Rose Laub. "Laughter Among Colleagues: A Study of the Social Functions of Humor Among the Staff of a Mental Hospital." *Psychiatry* 23 (February 1960): 81–95.

Crawford, Mary. "Humor in Conversational Context: Beyond

Biases in the Study of Gender and Humor." *Representations: Social Constructions of Gender.* Edited by R. K. Unger. Forthcoming.

Daly, Mary. *Gyn/Ecology: The Metaethics of Radical Feminism.* Boston: Beacon Press, 1978.

Delaney, Janice, Mary Jane Lupton, and Emily Toth. *The Curse: A Cultural History of Menstruation.* Urbana and Chicago: University of Illinois Press, 1976.

Douglas, Mary. "Jokes." *Implicit Meanings: Essays in Anthropology.* London: Routledge & Kegan Paul, 1975: 90–114.

———. "The Social Control of Cognition: Some Factors in Joke Perception." *Man* 3 (1968): 361–376.

Dowling, Colette. *The Cinderella Complex: Women's Hidden Fear of Independence.* (New York: Summit, 1981.

Drabble, Margaret. *The Radiant Way.* New York: Ivy Books, 1987.

Eco, Umberto. "Frames of Comic 'Freedom.' " *Carnival!* Edited by Thomas A. Sebeok. Berlin: Mouton, 1984: 1–9.

Eimerl, Sarel. "Can Women Be Funny? Humor Has Nothing to Do with Sex . . . Or Does It?" *Mademoiselle* (November 1962): 151ff.

Ephron, Nora. *Heartburn.* New York: Pocket Books, 1983.

Farb, Peter. "Speaking Seriously About Humor." *Massachusetts Review* 22, no. 4 (Winter 1981): 760–776.

Farrell, Warren. *Why Men Are the Way They Are: The Male-Female Dynamic.* New York: McGraw-Hill, 1986.

Freud, Sigmund. *Jokes and Their Relation to the Unconscious.* Translated by James Strachey. New York: Norton, 1960.

Genova, Mary Jane. "Wit Can Undermine a Woman's Career." *The New York Times*, Op-Ed., November 2, 1988.

Gilbert, Sandra, and Susan Gubar. *The Madwoman in the Attic: The Woman Writer and the Nineteenth-Century Literary Imagination.* New Haven, Conn.: Yale University Press, 1979.

Gross, Amy. "Lily Tomlin on Lily Tomlin." *Mademoiselle* (November 1975): 141ff.

Grotjahn, Martin. *Beyond Laughter.* New York: McGraw-Hill, 1957.

Gutman, Jonathan, and Robert F. Priest. "When Is Aggression Funny?" *Journal of Personality and Social Psychology* 12, no. 1 (1969): 60–65.

Harragan, Betty Lehan. *Games Mother Never Taught You: Corporate Gamesmanship for Women.* New York: Warner Books, 1977.

Heimel, Cynthia. *But Enough About You.* New York: Simon & Schuster, 1986.

———. *Sex Tips for Girls.* New York: Simon & Schuster, 1983.

Hirshey, Gerri. "The Comedy of Hate." *Gentleman's Quarterly* (August 1989): 226ff.

Jong, Erica. *Fear of Flying.* New York: Holt, Rinehart & Winston, 1973.

Kahn-Hut, Rachel, Arlene Kaplan Daniels, and Richard Colvard, eds. *Women and Work: Problems and Perspectives.* New York: Oxford University Press, 1982.

Kaufman, Gloria, and Mary Kay Blakely, eds. *Pulling Our Own Strings: Feminist Humor and Satire.* Bloomington: Indiana University Press, 1980.

Klein, Julia. "The New Stand-up Comics." *Ms.* (October 1984): 116ff.

Legman, G. *No Laughing Matter: An Analysis of Sexual Humor.* vol. 1. Bloomington: Indiana University Press, 1968.

Little, Judy. *Comedy and the Woman Writer: Woolf, Spark, and Feminism.* Lincoln: University of Nebraska Press, 1983.

Loden, Marilyn. *Feminine Leadership, or How to Succeed in Business Without Being One of the Boys.* New York: Times Books, 1985.

Loos, Anita. *Gentlemen Prefer Blondes.* New York: Liveright, 1925.

———. *Kiss Hollywood Good-By.* New York: Viking, 1974.

Loring, Rosalind, and Theodora Wells. *Breakthrough: Women into Management.* New York: Van Nostrand Reinhold, 1972.

Losco, Jean, and Seymour Epstein. "Humor Preference as a Subtle Measure of Attitudes Toward the Same and the Opposite Sex." *Journal of Personality* 43, no. 2 (1975): 321–334.

McGhee, Paul E. "The Role of Laughter and Humor in Growing Up Female." *Becoming Female: Perspectives on Development.* Edited by Claire B. Kopp. New York: Plenum Press, 1979: 183–206.

McLane, Helen J. *Selecting, Developing and Retaining Women Executives.* New York: Van Nostrand Reinhold, 1980.

Metcalf, Fred, comp. *The Penguin Dictionary of Modern Humourous Quotations.* London: Penguin, 1986.

Millman, Marcia, and Rosabeth Moss Kanter, eds. *Another Voice: Feminist Perspectives on Social Life and Social Science.* New York: Anchor Press, 1975.

Mitchell, Carol. "Hostility and Aggression Toward Males in Female Joke Telling." *Frontiers* 3, no. 3 (Fall 1978): 19–23.

———. "Some Differences in Male and Female Joke-Telling." *Women's Folklore, Women's Culture.* Edited by Rosan A. Jordan and Susan J. Kalcik. Philadelphia: University of Pennsylvania Press, 1985.

———. "The Sexual Perspective in the Appreciation and Interpretation of Jokes." *Western Folklore* 36 (1977): 303–329.

O'Connell, Walter E. "Resignation, Humor and Wit." *Psychoanalytic Review* 51 (1964–65): 49–56.

Parker, Dorothy. *The Penguin Dorothy Parker.* London: Penguin, 1977.

———. *The Portable Dorothy Parker.* rev. ed. New York: Viking, 1973.

Partnow, Elaine, ed. *The Quotable Woman.* New York: Anchor Books, 1978.

Pogrebin, Letty Cottin. *How to Make It in a Man's World.* New York: Doubleday, 1970.

Polhemus, Robert M. *Comic Faith: The Great Tradition from Austen to Joyce.* Chicago: University of Chicago Press, 1980.

Prerost, Frank J. "The Indication of Sexual and Aggressive Similarities Through Humor Appreciation." *The Journal of Psychology* 91 (1975): 283–288.

Rainer, Peter. "Interview: 5 Women Comedy Writers Talk About Being Funny for Money." *Mademoiselle* (November 1975): 86.

Reid, Libby. *You Don't Have to Pet to Be Popular: Cartoons by Libby Reid*. New York: Penguin, 1989.

Russ, Joanna. *How to Suppress Women's Writing*. Austin: University of Texas Press, 1983.

———. "What Can a Heroine Do? or Why Women Can't Write." *Images of Women in Fiction: Feminist Perspectives*. Edited by Susan Koppelman Cornillon. Bowling Green, Ohio: Bowling Green University Popular Press: 1972: 3–20.

Russo, Mary. "Female Grotesques: Carnival and Theory." *Feminist Studies/Critical Studies*. Edited by Theresa deLauretis. Bloomington: Indiana University Press, 1986.

Rychlak, Joseph F. *Personality and Life-Style of Young Male Managers: A Logical Learning Theory Analysis*. New York: Academic Press, 1982.

Sarris, Andrew. "Funny Ladies in the Movies and Why They're an Endangered Species." *Mademoiselle* (November 1975): 138ff.

Spanckeren, Kathryn Van. "A Funny Thing Happened on the Way to the Apocalypse: Laurie Anderson and Humor in Women's Performance Art." *Studies in American Humor* [New Series] 4, nos. 1, 2 (Spring/Summer 1985): 94–104.

Spender, Dale. *The Writing or the Sex, or Why You Don't Have to Read Women's Writing to Know It's No Good*. New York: Pergamon Press, 1989.

Steinem, Gloria. "If Men Could Menstruate." *Ms.* (October 1978): 110.

Stillion, Judith M., and Hedy White. "Feminist Humor: Who Appreciates It and Why?" *Psychology of Women Quarterly* II (1987): 219–232.

Stimpson, Catharine R. "The 'F' Word: Why Can't We Say It in Public?" *Ms* (July/August 1987): 80ff.

Sullivan-Irwin, Kate. "Joy Behar: Joy Shtick." *Laugh Track* (September 1989): 24–25.

Taylor, Helen. *Scarlett's Women: Gone With the Wind and Its Female Fans*. New Brunswick, N.J.: Rutgers University Press, 1989.

Toth, Emily. "Female Wits." *Massachusetts Review* 22, no. 4 (Winter 1981): 783–793.

———. "Forbidden Jokes and Naughty Ladies." *Studies in American Humor* [New Series] 4, nos. 1, 2 (Spring/Summer 1985): 7–17.

Trahey, Jane. *Jane Trahey on Women and Power.* New York: Avon Books, 1977.

Wagner, Jane. *The Search for Signs of Intelligent Life in the Universe.* New York: Harper & Row, 1986.

Walker, Nancy. *A Very Serious Thing: Women's Humor and American Culture.* Minneapolis: University of Minnesota Press, 1988.

———. "Do Feminists Ever Laugh? Women's Humor and Women's Rights." *International Journal of Women's Studies* 4, no. 1 (January/February 1981): 1–9.

———, and Zita Dresner, eds. *Redressing the Balance: American Women's Literary Humor from Colonial Times to the 1980's.* Jackson and London: University Press of Mississippi, 1988.

Weisstein, Naomi. "Why We Aren't Laughing . . . Any More." *Ms* (November 1973): 43–51ff.

Weldon, Fay. *Down Among the Women.* Chicago: Academy Chicago Publishers, 1984.

———. *Female Friends.* London: Heinemann, 1975.

———. *The Life and Loves of a She-Devil.* New York: Pantheon, 1983.

Wilt, Judith. "The Laughter of Maidens, the Cackle of Matriarchs: Notes on the Collision Between Comedy and Feminism." *Women and Literature.* Edited by Janet Todd. New York: Holmes & Meier, 1980.

Woolf, Virginia. *Women and Writing.* New York: Harcourt Brace Jovanovich, 1979.